PICKETING

PICKETING

Industrial Disputes, Tactics and the Law

Peggy Kahn, Norman Lewis, Rowland Livock
and Paul Wiles with the assistance of John Mesher

ROUTLEDGE & KEGAN PAUL
London, Boston, Melbourne and Henley

First published in 1983
by Routledge & Kegan Paul plc
39 Store Street, London WC1E 7DD,
9 Park Street, Boston, Mass. 02108, USA,
296 Beaconsfield Parade, Middle Park,
Melbourne, 3206, Australia, and
Broadway House, Newtown Road,
Henley-on-Thames, Oxon RG9 1EN
Set in Plantin by
Input Typesetting Ltd, London
and printed in Great Britain by
T.J. Press (Padstow) Ltd
Padstow, Cornwall

Library of Congress Cataloging in Publication Data
Main entry under title:

Picketing: industrial disputes, tactics, and the law.

Bibliography: p.
Includes index.
1. Picketing – Great Britain. 2. Labor disputes – Great Britain. 3. Labor
laws and legislation – Great Britain.
I. Kahn, Peggy, 1953–   .
KD3077.P52 1983   344.41'018927   82–24087

ISBN 0–7100–9534–1 (pbk)   344.10418927

Contents

Preface

This book draws on research commissioned by the Monitoring of Labour Legislation Panel of the Social Sciences Research Council (SSRC) in 1980. Our brief was to monitor the effects of the 1980 Employment Act on industrial relations in so far as they dealt with picketing and secondary action. The timing of the award meant that although we should ideally have wished to have conducted a 'before and after study' this proved impossible in the event. By the time our fieldwork began much of industry's thinking was already clearly affected by the climate which the Act's passage had produced. This is one of the constraints, though only one, which impinged upon the particular research strategy employed. The others should be outlined.

First, the resources. We have been able to employ two full-time research officers, who although very experienced and knowledgeable, could not hope to cover the whole of Britain's diverse industrial economy assisted as they were, in fieldwork terms, by three others engaged in a range of full-time academic commitments.

The second major constraint was perhaps more serious. We were one of two teams supported by the SSRC to examine the 'picketing' provisions, the other being a team recruited by the University of Oxford, comprised of Mr Paul Davies, and Dr Mark Freedland. The Oxford team's remit was to conduct a national survey of attitudes and behaviour affected by the legislation though we understand that this was to be reinforced by more detailed work conducted in the West Midlands. This clearly necessitated some measure of demarcation and in the end we decided to concentrate our efforts on two regions in close proximity to the University of Sheffield. Our regions became South Yorkshire and Humberside. South Yorkshire is of course the crucible of British industry traditionally, and the home of steel, engineering and coal. Humberside is in many ways a more isolated community but houses a good deal of light engineering, a large food processing industry and a wide range of service industries. It attracted us also because of its maritime traditions, fishing, the merchant marine and, not least, the docks.

Our strategy became then one of detailed case studies and broad sectoral analysis whether or not in the industries concerned industrial action was taking place. We tried to understand the anatomies of these industries by reference to detailed interviews of the various interests – management (line and boardroom) and labour (local, regional and, occasionally, national). We returned to many of these industries for repeat interviews, for progress reports, for attitudes towards the legislation, the economic climate, and so on. We attempted in a number of diverse circumstances to chart the annual pay reviews and other negotiating and bargaining processes. Occasionally they resulted in breakdown, occasionally in industrial action and in these cases we attempted to understand the reasons for the breakdown and crucially to examine the tactics available to both sides of industry. A tactical appreciation of the constraints of different employment sectors became a major plank of our work and one which we examine closely in Chapter 5 though it runs through all the Chapters comprising Part 2 of the book. Given our brief of course we paid special attention to picketing and to secondary industrial action and to the effect, if any, of the salient provisions of the 1980 Act.

Several other points concerning our research approach should be made. First, although our fieldwork has been heavily concentrated around case studies we have followed all the major instances of industrial action in our regions, whether or not the Employment Act was infringed. Thus we have covered, primary picketing, secondary picketing, demonstrations, sit-ins and the like. Some of this action has been lawful, some unlawful and some problematic. Some unlawful behaviour related to the 1980 Act, some did not. Only in very limited sets of circumstances have legal infractions been prosecuted or the subject of civil action.

Second, although we stuck resolutely to our regions for most of our work, we have occasionally been compelled to go beyond them. Clear examples relate to multi-plant companies where some plants were situated within our regions and some were not. The relations of production, the nature of trade-union organisation and other factors have all conspired to suggest that explanation may have required a broader geographical examination. In this respect we found ourselves in Greater Manchester on a number of occasions. In like vein we found that in multi-plant companies and those which were subject to a degree of vertical organisation the locus of decision-making moved from our regions or became interdependent with our regional decision-making structures. This was sometimes true in relation to multi-national companies and also in relation to the public sector.

So far we have not mentioned the police. From the outset they were expected to play a major role in our research given the conflation of the civil and criminal law produced by the 1980 Employment Act. In consequence we sought the co-operation of the Chief Constables of South Yorkshire and Humberside for our work, especially in relation to picketing and public order incidents. Their unstinting co-operation has helped our endeavours to a very considerable degree. However, given that the Oxford team had the responsibility for conducting a national survey we have not been able to examine the policing of the Act in as broad a setting as we would have liked. Given the somewhat differing organisational structures of British police forces this is an impediment but we have nevertheless tried to locate our discussion of the police in Chapter 4 within a set of larger national concerns.

We have compressed our research for the purposes of this book very greatly indeed. From time to time we have highlighted particular, though anonymous, instances of industrial behaviour, examples of which appear in the following pages. More broadly we have tried to develop explanatory frameworks which, of course, are more than mere empirical generalisations. Nevertheless our ability to theorise in this way is in part dependent upon the range of our research, and in order to produce a sense of proportion we should perhaps make some attempt at this juncture to quantify our activities.

Across our regions we have engaged in almost 400 interviews, attendances at meetings or attendances at picket lines. This, as we must repeat, has involved management, workers, union officials and police officers. We have observed five sit-ins, around a dozen instances of secondary picketing both in the public and private sectors, and ranging from passing incidents to continuous secondary picketing lasting more than a month. We have observed several examples of industrial action clearly taking place outside the confines of the 'trade dispute' golden formula (for which see Chapter 3) including 'days of action' organised by *inter alia*, the Trades Union Congress. Our research has then been fairly extensive. Hopefully, therefore, the originality of our work lies in the relationship between our detailed fieldwork and a broader description of the articulation between political economy, industrial relations and the law.

Acknowledgments

We are most grateful to the Monitoring of Labour Legislation Panel of the Social Science Research Council who commissioned us to examine the impact of sections of the 1980 Employment Act. We must stress, however, that the views expressed in this book are those of the authors and not necessarily those of the Social Science Research Council or its Monitoring of Labour Legislation Panel who funded this research.

Many of our colleagues and associates helped in our research and production of this manuscript. We hope that by mentioning some by name we will not offend those who are omitted.

John Mesher participated in the fieldwork research, was always ready with legal expertise and helped in some of the final drafting. Professor Sir John Wood was unstinting with his advice. More generally our colleagues tolerated our obsessive interest in 'picketing' and were a great source of encouragement.

Les Hargreaves helped by discussing the research as it progressed whilst he pursued his own, parallel work on the mass-media coverage of industrial disputes. Jill Gascoigne, a sandwich student from Bath University, joined the research team for a while and helped with interviewing.

Carole Gillespie was secretary to the project throughout, and Vera Marsh and Annie Lutwama also typed much of our material. Our debt to them is very real.

Our greatest debt is to those people in South Yorkshire and Humberside, and occasionally elsewhere, who gave of their time to talk to us. The list would fill pages of this book and yet because of our undertaking of confidentiality none of them is named in these pages. The Chief Constables of South Yorkshire and Humberside granted us access to their officers, and all of them were most helpful and patient. Management, employers' associations, lawyers, trade-union officials, trades councils, politicians and political workers, and countless men and women involved in industrial disputes helped with our research. It is to all of these that this book is dedicated.

Centre for Criminological
and Socio-Legal Studies

Abbreviations

ACAS	Advisory, Conciliation and Arbitration Service
ACC	Association of County Councils
ACPO	Association of Chief Police Officers
AHA	Area Health Authorities
AMA	Association of Metropolitan Authorities
ASLEF	Associated Society of Locomotive Engineers and Firemen
AUEW	Amalgamated Union of Engineering Workers
BISPA	British Independent Steel Producers' Association
BSC	British Steel Corporation
CBI	Confederation of British Industry
CCSU	Council of Civil Service Unions
CEGB	Central Electricity Generating Board
ConFed	Confederation of Shipbuilding and Engineering Unions
COSLA	Convention (Committee) of Scottish Local Authorities
CPSA	Civil and Public Servants' Association
DC	District Committee (AUEW)
DE	Department of Employment
DHSS	Department of Health and Social Security
EEF	Engineering Employers' Federation
EFMEW	Enginemen, Firemen, Mechanics and Electrical Workers' Union (now merged with the T & G q.v.)
EPU	Electronic Processing Unit
FBU	Fire Brigades Union
FDA	First Division Association
GFMA	Grimsby Fish Merchants' Association

GLC	Greater London Council
GM(WU)	General and Municipal Workers' Union
IRSF	Inland Revenue Staff Federation
ISTC	Iron and Steel Trades Confederation
ITWF	International Transport Workers' Federation
NAFO	National Association Fire Officers
NALGO	National Association of Local Government Officers
NAPE	National Association of Port Employers
NASDU	National Association of Stevedores and Dockers Union
NATO	North Atlantic Treaty Organisation
NBPI	National Board for Prices and Incomes
NCB	National Coal Board
NDLB	National Dock Labour Board
NHS	National Health Service
NIRC	National Industrial Relations Court
NJC	National Joint Council
NJIC	National Joint Industrial Council
NUAAW	National Union of Agricultural and Allied Workers
NUB	National Union of Boilermakers
NUM	National Union of Mineworkers
NUPE	National Union of Public Employees
NUR	National Union of Railwaymen
NUS	National Union of Seamen
PRU	Pay Research Unit
PSBR	Public Sector Borrowing Requirement
PSU	Police Support Unit
RFU	Retained Firemen's Union
RHA	Road Haulage Association
RHAs	Regional Health Authorities
SCPS	Society of Civil and Public Servants
SDP	Social Democratic Party
SOGAT	Society of Graphical and Allied Trades
SSRC	Social Science Research Council
SWP	Socialist Workers' Party
T & G (TGWU)	Transport and General Workers' Union
TUC	Trades Union Congress
TULRA	Trade Union and Labour Relations Act

TUR	Temporary Unattached Register
UCW	Union of Communication Workers
UIP	Unfair Industrial Practice
URTU	United Road Transport Union

Part 1

I
Introduction

A central feature of industrial relations in any relatively free society is a set of processes which seek to institutionalise conflict between labour and capital. That is what almost all forms of labour law are directed to and is the *raison d'être* of bargaining and dispute resolution in all their manifestations. The Conservative government which came to power in 1979 was committed to using legislation to modify these processes and did so, initially at any rate, with the 1980 Employment Act. This sought to tilt the balance of power in the legal framework for industrial disputes since, it was argued, previous legislation had favoured too strongly the trade unions. In particular the Act attempted to curb the use of picketing and secondary action. This book, and the research upon which it is based, seeks to examine the impact of this legislation on industrial relations and particularly on the use of those dispute tactics it was most specifically aimed at. We will discuss the two years immediately following the passing of the Act when it was still fresh in people's minds, and before its impact became conflated with the passage of yet more industrial legislation.

The apparently obvious way to have examined the impact of the 1980 Employment Act would have been to study all the arrests made in conformity with it and its Code of Picketing Practice, and all writs issued under sections 16 and 17 (the picketing and secondary action provisions). If we had done so we would have found ourselves staring into an abyss since the use made of the Act during its first two years has been slight in these terms. Assessing the Act in this way might lead one to the conclusion that it has had virtually no impact and was a political failure. Such a judgment would be quite wrong as the rest of this book will demonstrate. The criteria suggested above for judging the efficacy of the Act may appear obvious but if used in isolation ignore the even more obvious fact that law operates within a social, political and economic context. It is this fact which dictates the criteria for deciding the impact of legislation. For those of us engaged on researching that impact the need to examine law within its context also determines the framework of study and the methods which will be necessary. When we say that law exists within a context we do not simply mean that the context has to be painted as a kind of backdrop. Rather, a law and the uses made of it only exist within their context. Ideas of law may have life as abstractions but specific laws only have meaning within the historical particulars in which they were created. Treating a piece of legislation as if it could be examined in isolation may be an amusing, if self-indulgent, game for scholastic exercise but it is no way to study the practical import of law.

For our purposes there were four main areas which provided the context of the 1980 Act. First, there was the relation of the Act to other government strategies affecting industry and more broadly to the development of post-war British political economy. Second, since law also has its own history, there was the question of how the new legislation related to the particular logic of British labour law. Third, as the Act was aimed at affecting the use of particular tactics we had to understand the determinants of tactics during industrial disputes so as to define how the boundaries of legal impact were proscribed. Finally, we had to explore how the police as the main state agency charged with controlling events such as picketing respond to this behaviour. Each of these areas will be discussed in later chapters and together constitute Part 1 of the book. Part 2 shows what impact the 1980 Act has had in different kinds of industries and, as the Preface explains, is based upon our research into industrial disputes occurring over the last two years mainly in South Yorkshire and Humberside. Part 1, therefore, essentially defines the nature of the questions to be asked in Part 2 : if we are not going to assess the impact of the Act in the ways initially suggested then how are we to do so?

Industrial politics, industrial disputes and the law

The way in which we have chosen to gauge the effect of the 1980 law is to set it in the context of conflict institutionalisation. That institutionalisation we argue must be observed against two major sets of constraints; domestic and national. The domestic level is the nature and structure of the industry concerned and its industrial relations history; the national relates to the totality of government intervention in industrial politics through a series of devices perhaps the most significant of which is its general attitude to the management of the economy. Before, however, turning to these broader concerns we ought to say something about the economic climate existing during our two-year research period and also about the national industrial-relations climate.

The period in question has been one of increasing unemployment and declining industrial production. This has been accompanied by a very marked reduction in the number of industrial disputes recorded and the number of days at work lost through industrial action. Thus, in 1981 the Department of Employment record of stoppages of work caused by industrial disputes documented a decrease of two-thirds in the total number of days lost compared to the average over the previous ten years and at 4.2 million was the lowest annual total recorded since 1969. It is important to note that within that total 1.1 million were accounted for by the civil service pay dispute between March and August of that year (Department of Employment, 1982, pp. 289-95). The trend during 1982 has been for public sector disputes in the National Health Service and the railways to increase the monthly average figures for numbers of days lost while the number of stoppages recorded continued to fall. Perhaps it should also be added that the figures for 1981 exclude disputes falling outside the DE's definition of an industrial dispute. Thus:

> The figures therefore exclude, for example, stoppages by an estimated 10,000 fishermen mainly from Scotland and the North of England who laid up their vessels for various periods between February 3 and 20 in protest against lack of government control over the import of cheap fish; absences from work on June 30 by an estimated 20,000 Lothian Council employees in protest against the government's proposal to cut the Council's rate support grant; a stoppage on July 13 by about 90,000 British Gas Corporation employees in protest against the government's proposal to sell gas showrooms; and absences from work on October 21 by about 11,000 car industry workers in protest against the high numbers of vehicles being imported (Department of Employment, 1982, p. 289.)

What emerges from this is that the impact of law must be examined against a deepening recession which would itself have been certain to dampen down a good deal of conflict. In addition the figures for days lost due to industrial disputes are only as high as they are mainly due to conflict which is a direct result of government policy and initiatives. We need to be able to take these influences into account in assessing the legal impact.

We have naturally examined the public sector in some detail and we devote two chapters in the second part of the book to it. This is necessary either because the government is itself the employer or because of its influence over the behaviour of the formal employer. This is important from the point of view of tactical choices made during disputes since the government as employer or paymaster will sometimes have available to it powers, responsibilities and influences which are not paralleled in the private sector. Special considerations too may apply to the way in which organised labour in the public sector can or is prepared to respond to issues with which it finds itself wrestling. Furthermore, the public sector enjoys a special, though not necessarily privileged place in British industrial politics. This has conventionally been noted in times of bursts of enthusiasm for incomes policies, wage restraint and the like. However, this is too narrow a focus for its special position since pricing policies and other matters of a seemingly commercial nature have periodically intruded, for example, into the nationalised industries. Here then industrial politics and industrial relations began to intermingle. The post-1979 period is a very special phase of public sector industrial politics and one in which the influence of industrial relations law as such has to be very carefully located. Although, as we discuss in Chapter 2, the interrelationship between industrial politics and industrial relations has always been close in modern times, the fact that the present government approach to political economy represents a sharp break in the post-war understandings means that special attention must be paid to its economic strategy and its implications for workplace relations.

This of itself would justify our interest in industrial politics in the public sector but would say little about the rest of the industrial economy. In fact successive British governments have been keenly concerned with aspects of industrial politics since at least the closing decades of the nineteenth century, though to varying degrees and subject to periodic fluctuations (Middlemas, 1979).

British labour law and government strategies

In Chapter 3 we briefly review collective British labour law and show that from at least 1891 our governments have been concerned in varying degrees to encourage responsible trade unionism and to seek to institutionalise conflict through arrangements made to advance collective bargaining at the expense of overt conflict. Such conflict could have undermined public order if sufficiently serious and at an even more heightened level could have threatened parliamentary institutions themselves. After all this was what happened in much of Western Europe throughout the 1920s and 1930s. That it did not in Britain says much for the stability of its political and cultural traditions and institutions. It means that, the 1926 strike apart, Britain managed its industrial politics both consciously and successfully, if success is to be judged by the avoidance of serious crises. This can be said not only of the inter-war years but of the war years themselves.

Since the Second World War all governments have been concerned to manage the mixed economy after one fashion or another. All have been concerned either to court labour and capital throughout this period or at the very least to associate them with responsibilities for the health and temper of the larger economy. We describe these developments in Chapter 2, and, to a lesser extent, in the following chapter. What we are concerned to do here is to explain the relationship of what can best be called political economy to industrial politics, to the methods of institutionalising conflict between capital and labour and between either or both and the state's economic choices. Explaining methods of institutionalising conflict involves to a greater or lesser degree the formal legal system, though as we shall argue, that formal system is less influential in Britain than in most industrialised Western societies. In short what we here wish to do is to explicate the context within which we have placed our fieldwork.

All governments this century, then, have been concerned with industrial relations either in terms of simple crisis avoidance or in terms of managing the economy or both. All have been involved in fashioning or encouraging machinery or institutions designed to serve these ends and all have used law and/or other weapons at the disposal of the state to advance these ends. By other state weapons we mean monetary and fiscal measures, the discretion to award grants, concessions, to hold out contracts or to withold them, to incorporate groups or to isolate them and so on. It has been called, in a slightly different context, governing by other means (Hood, 1982).

Much recent scholarship has shown that Britain is less of a Rechtstaat (a legally ordered polity), less concerned with the 'legal-rational', and much more inclined to govern according to bureaucratic/administrative means than almost any other Western democracy, in spite of our constant rhetoric concerning the rule of law (see e.g. Kamenka and Tay, 1975; Poggi, 1978; Barker, 1982; Dyson, 1980). This is what we mean when we say that Britain has a much less developed system of public law than most countries of Continental Europe, or even the United States which in other respects does not enjoy a strong state tradition. To take but one example: by the early twentieth century German and French administrative law had been developed into a sophisticated body of knowledge which comprised a systematic set of general principles and related them to such specific topics as finance and the police. There was for instance strong emphasis on public finance in both public life at large and the legal academies in particular (see e.g. Dyson, 1980 pp.94-7, 181-3). This has been almost entirely absent in Britain where legal scholarship has only very recently begun to concern itself with state economic policy (see e.g. Daintith, 1974, 1979 and Ganz, 1977). The result of this fragmentation has been both less clear-headedness about public purposes than might be thought appropriate, less direct and overt state planning, and most particularly less openness and less public debate than many would regard as appropriate given our democratic expectations.

The fact that fragmentation has occurred and that the formal legal system has been less directly employed than other devices should not, however, be allowed to obscure the fact that the state has been as involved in the country's social and industrial life in Britain as has been the case elsewhere. It is simply that different mechanisms have been at work. Thus to restrict our current analysis to the formal legal order would be to delude ourselves and our readers and in particular to fail to locate the Employment Act in its active context. When the doyen of British labour law, Professor Otto Kahn-Freund said that he regarded law as a secondary force in human affairs, and especially in labour relations (Kahn-Freund, 1977), we believe he meant the formal legal system.

Nevertheless state initiatives in a wider sense can and do play a significant part, while still not occupying the centre of the industrial relations stage. The centre of that stage is still the domain of the power relationships existing between capital and labour, albeit as mediated by the state through a number of mechanisms, including the formal legal system. If the boundary between legislation and collective bargaining largely results from the facts of political and economic history (Kahn-Freund, 1977) then *a fortiori* that is true of the mechanisms of mediation *in toto*. In Britain especially then the panoply of instrumentalities for effecting policy must be examined as a whole, the isolation of the formal legal order being the surest way to obfuscate the relationship between the state and the system of industrial relations. That is why we have adopted our particular research strategy, but before returning to that one further issue should not be allowed to escape attention.

One of the central ironies of contemporary industrial politics emerges from the preceding argument when set on the stage of post-1979 industrial relations. We argue later that although the 1980 Act itself was the product of contending forces within the Conservative Party and the government, a developing harmony between economic policy and industrial relations attitudes began increasingly to characterise the stance of the government thereafter. In consequence the economic policies being pursued have become a key issue in industrial relations post-1980, and especially after Mr Prior's departure from the Department of Employment. Yet, as we shall see, the political philosophy of the present government relies heavily upon the ideas of Professor Hayek and his views concerning the 'minimalist' state and the role and functions of trade unions therein. In perhaps his best known work Professor Hayek extols 'the rule of law' and the Rechtstaat, the disappearance of which is heralded by broad formulae lacking in the specificity of clear rules of the legal-rational variety (Hayek, 1976, ch.6). The irony, though Mrs Thatcher's government is no different from say the Callaghan administration in this respect, is that the Employment Act is not only immeasurably difficult to understand in advance but is clearly far less significant an influence on industrial relations than is the use of administrative/bureaucratic measures applied across the public sector in particular, or the use of non-'legal' monetarist mechanisms across British industry in general.

Industrial disputes and tactics

It seemed to us obvious that if we were to attempt to evaluate the impact of legislation then not only should we examine industrial behaviour where that legislation was *not* infringed (behaviour for which the legislation may or may not have been responsible) but that we should also delve deeper and examine industrial structures, organisations and histories to see whether the behaviour outlawed by the 1980 Act was tactically ever relevant to those industries. What we found, which we chart elsewhere, was that picketing for instance made little sense in some industrial situations, that secondary picketing or blacking was irrelevant to many others. Certain tactics, not prohibited by the Act but which could produce the effects which the Act wished to deter, had been developed, which were peculiar to the needs of yet other industries. Sometimes we found that a range of tactics did make sense in a particular situation, some of which the Act took cognisance of and some which it did not. It was in these conjunctures that it became particularly interesting to attempt to draw out any possible effects which the legislation was having.

As we shall indicate in Chapter 4 an analysis of the tactical choices available to industrial parties has been an important focus of our research. We have come to understand that the tactics available depended upon the nature of the industry concerned, the product which emerges, its destination, the organisational nature of management and union, the degree of worker organisation and so on. These determinants are clearly infinitely more important than most influences which could be brought to bear by outsiders, whether in the form of law or not. Indeed, once we began to examine the organisational and technical imperatives affecting tactics it became abundantly clear that, to take something like secondary picketing for example, the law in seeking to outlaw certain behaviour was bound to operate differentially and was bound to be more or less relevant according to the nature of the productive process being observed. If secondary picketing, let us say, made no operational sense in an industry then any law seeking to control it would be superfluous in that industry at least and of problematic utility in many others. If one wished it would be possible to construct a typology of tactics appropriate to particular sectors and see how far law such as is contained in the Employment Act 1980 could have any chance of affecting industrial behaviour. We discuss such distinctions, and our choice of industrial sectors for examination in Part 2 derives from them.

Having located the impact of law in this way we can then ask what manner of intervention *might* affect the decision as to the tactics to be adopted by either management or workers in the course of handling conflict. Further, what might in any particular sector affect or contribute to the emergence or submerging of conflict as such. The answers which emerge are complex as we shall hopefully later be able to show. What is of the essence, however, is that far from being able to describe a straightforward causal connection between the existence of law and industrial behaviour, the relationship is in fact subtle, contingent and often very, very oblique. Over and above this fact it is important to be aware that sometimes the relationship between law and action or conduct is not intended to be direct even by those responsible for introducing legislation.

Law is sometimes formulated without any very great expectation that it will have a direct impact on behaviour. It may be concerned to effect a whole spectrum of purposes relating to cultural, political or psychological expectations. Law may, for example, help create a changed will or set of general beliefs which serve to buttress some other government policy. To the extent that they are its primary purposes it may have succeeded widely without any directly discernible impact on the behaviour it addresses. Law which is suffused with strong emotive overtones is especially susceptible to such motivation and within that tradition trade-union law is strongly represented.

For all these reasons we have sought to examine tactical choices made by the two sides of industry both within and outside of industrial disputes. We have attempted this through detailed empirical research which links these choices (including the ones impelled by law in general and the 1980 Act in particular) to a more general anatomy of the political economy of industrial disputes. That political economy rests upon the articulation between the power relations in industry and the face of industrial politics. In examining that articulation we have made the long decline of the British economy a lynch pin of our analysis. It is the linkage between Part 1 and Part 2 of the book which is the core of our work. Part 1 explains the set of theoretical concerns which have caused us to order our fieldwork in the way we have chosen. It attempts to locate our labour laws, in general, and the current generation of them, in particular, within the historical pattern of political economy in Britain, taking particular note of the articulation between the interests of the state and the system of industrial relations, public and private.

What we have attempted to do is to find an explanatory framework for the relationship between domestic industrial relations and industrial politics. That framework depends on the shifting interests of the British state as mediated by a system of formal laws, informal understandings based on civility and expedience and the workings of the state apparatus. This apparatus includes, of course, the civil service, the military and the police. The former have traditionally engaged the leaders of industry in fashions periodically direct and indirect while the police, especially, have enjoyed a tradition of autonomy and neutrality within the public operation of industrial relations, threatened only by celebrated moments of national crisis.

Although the interests of the British state have been subject to shifts and changes of direction we have focused on the broad-based and uninterrupted concern with the issue of economic decline. This issue more than most others has influenced the way in which successive governments have concerned themselves with industrial relations. In spite of marked changes in emphasis it is clear that most post-war British governments have set out to sell co-operation and incorporation to management and labour in order to arrest this process of decline. It is equally clear that the very recent past has borne witness to a dramatic change in this political and industrial landscape. Some other elements in the state, most notably the police, have also been forced into uncovenanted changes in direction by the force of contemporary events, national and international.

The period of our research has been one radically different from those of recent history. The economic orthodoxies have been replaced by the new, a belief in the automatic improvement of living standards has been arrested and socio-political expectations have been transformed. The pebble that is the Employment Act has been dropped almost casually into this political pool. In attempting to account for the ripples we have tried to examine the whole environment. The living reality of industrial life in various sectors of the economy we have sought to interpret in the light of these overall concerns.

2
The political economy of post-war Britain and the rise of the new Conservatism

The political economy of post-war Britain has been dominated by the underlying structural decline of the British economy. Britain's industrial economy has in fact been in decline since the late nineteenth century, but imperial trade and two World Wars temporarily disguised this longer-term trend. Moreover, the post-war commitment to Keynesianism tended to focus political attention more on short-term problems of demand than on longer term and deeper difficulties of industrial production itself.

The Labour government elected in 1945 created a mixed economy of private and public enterprises and considerably extended welfare provisions. They thereby increased the relative size of the public sector. Full employment and economic growth, it was felt, could be achieved by demand management strategies. Such an explicit commitment to Keynesian social and economic goals quickly drew representatives of both labour and capital into close co-operation with the government, though such tripartite co-operation was in many ways a continuation of existing trends (see Middlemas, 1979).

The policies of the post-war Labour government therefore depended to a large extent upon the co-operation of both sides of industry in economic management. Although specific policies, such as nationalisation, were perceived and indeed presented as radical socialist strategies, the overall policy was aimed at successful management of a capitalist economy. Social goals were to be achieved by creating economic growth rather than radically restructuring society. The co-operation of capital with the post-war government was therefore possible. Similarly the Conservative government which came to power in 1951 was able to accept the general framework it inherited and indeed much of the general policy, whilst rejecting specific acts such as steel and road haulage nationalisation.

Until the 1960s governments continued to operate on the basis of this post-war settlement, bolstered by the post-war economic boom. However, the long-term decline of the British economy continued, as other advanced capitalist countries engaged in modernisation of their industries and as Empire was abandoned. The post-war settlement was therefore always fragile and inevitably came under strain as decline continued. Nevertheless, the central idea of the post-war settlement – that the economy could be successfully managed by some version of tripartite co-operation – continued as the basic belief of British government.

Relative bipartisanship on economic matters, known during the period as 'Butskellism', had clear implications for labour law. Legal abstentionism, although historically something of a myth (R. Lewis, 1976), characterised the period. The implicit economic concordat also seemed well understood by the judiciary, as witness the refusal to develop the tortious liability of union officials in the leading case of Thompson v. Deakin in 1952.

Many factors made it difficult for the British economy to adapt to its changing environment, and certain contradictions between the interests of industry and a large finance capital sector meant that even priorities were not easy to agree upon. Gradually, however, both parties did begin to see the necessity of some kind of longer-term planning of the economy, which addressed problems of supply and production, as well as demand. However, planning initiatives remained weak. In 1962, for example, the Conservative Party set up the National Economic Development Council as a tripartite forum and developed various policies aimed at modernising the economy, and the Labour government elected in 1964 subsequently created new ministries to oversee economic planning: the Department of Economic Affairs and the Ministry of Technology. However, although the Department of Economic Affairs drew up a National Plan, it was abandoned in the sterling crisis of 1966. The conflict between the needs of indicative planning and the international role of sterling was a constant theme of this period. Successive British governments chose the path of deflation rather than devaluation when faced with sterling crises, and the result was that even weak attempts at economic planning were never carried through.

Deflation in response to a sterling crisis was just one factor which helped create the so-called 'stop-go' cycles in the British economy. These created a longer-term impression that the economy was out of control and led to frequent policy switches. In this period the trade unions began to be seen as contributing both to the underlying longer-term problem of the British economy and to the difficulties of short-term economic management. Jessop has argued that the historical nature of British industrialisation created a defensive trade-union structure resistant to workplace reorganisation (1979). In that sense the trade unions did make a contribution to inhibiting the modernisation of British industry. On the other hand, as 'stop' succeeded 'go', deflationary measures were directed against wage increases. Governments veered between trying to incorporate the trade unions into a national structure of economic management, and controlling union activity directly through incomes policy or trade union legislation. Throughout the 1960s these conflicting and confused attitudes towards the unions were reflected in British labour law. As we shall see in Chapter 3, the relatively limited amount of legislation, the Prices and Incomes Act 1966 aside, introduced was either pro-union or union-incorporating, while the judiciary was forging formidable tortious liabilities for trade-union officials.

In the 1960s and after, all governments tried to solve the problems of the British economy through more interventionist strategies embracing various degrees of neo-corporatist structures. A besetting problem for this kind of industrial politics, however, was that British trade-union power developed out of plant and local level strength and not from general national unionism, in much the same way as the power of industrial capital had not been historically centralised. From the early 1960s onwards, therefore, governments encouraged the strengthening of national-level representation as a basis for tripartite economic management. For industry this meant the encouragement of trade associations and the second Wilson government acted, for example, as midwife to the Confederation of British Industry. For the trade unions it has meant support of the Trades Union Congress by incorporation of its representatives into many national bodies, and various attempts to strengthen national union leadership against local levels; sometimes through legislation.

The result of such pressures, as regards trade unions, was that from the 1950s onwards British governments proclaimed that there was a trade-union problem, and from the 1960s onwards attempted to solve it by various forms of intervention. The problem which was identified as needing reform changed, however: at one time it was restrictive practices and demarcation disputes: then unofficial strikes and union discipline; next the use of particular tactics by public sector workers. The attempted solutions also varied.

In the 1950s the Conservative Party pamphlet *A Giant's Strength* advocated trade-union registration to cause unions to exert greater control over their officers and members. Academic writers such as Flanders and Clegg (1954), on the other hand, advocated a general reform of the procedures and institutions for collective bargaining. At the same time there was a growing concern with the impact of trade unions on individual rights. Inferences about the need for 'moderate' workforce control over leaders coexisted uneasily with the assumption that union officials with more control over membership would result in more 'responsible' industrial relations. It was a dilemma which would continue until the second stage of the industrial relations strategy under Margaret Thatcher's government: with the abandonment of corporatism, strong union leadership became less important.

The result of these debates in the 1960s was the Donovan Commission: a Royal Commission to examine labour relations in general but actually concentrating on the trade-union problem. The investigation was suggested by the Conservatives but carried out under a Labour administration. From Donovan onwards, industrial relations policy occupied a central place in party politics.

The Donovan Report was a lengthy and complex document, but it was in many ways the classic public text of a neo-corporatist nature. It was directed centrally to the 'problem' of unofficial strikes associated with fragmented bargaining and the attendant obsession with 'wage drift'. Its major recommendations reflected those concerns in arguing for a formal structuring of workplace procedures. This formalisation of the 'unofficial industrial relations system' would, it was hoped, help to reduce unofficial strikes, create greater harmony, and thereby help to identify methods whereby wage drift could be resisted.

The Commission's majority was not persuaded that legal regulation was necessary to effect the desired changes, at least in the short run. Instead, belief in the voluntary tradition of British industrial relations was re-emphasised, though buttressed by a number of institutional changes. Not the least important of these was the establishment of a new Commission charged with assisting in the restructuring of bargaining procedures and thereby with imposing greater order. The belief that legislation directed at trade-union practices was undesirable was perhaps reinforced by the reception given to the Prices and Incomes Act 1966. This Act dignified incomes policy by accompanying it, *inter alia*, with the criminal law for infractions of the new neo-Keynesian orthodoxy, and interestingly enough the Wilson-Callaghan administration was to use a bureaucratic/ administrative system for enforcing its incomes concordat a decade later. This experiment with the formal legal order was later to be seen as epitomising and justifying the belief that law and industrial relations mingled like oil and water, and that such uses of law threatened to undermine the rule of law itself. In reality the bureaucratic/administrative, the informal or discretionary legal system, had simply been transferred from other areas of state activity into the sphere of industrial relations.

This, however, is to anticipate. In 1969 the Wilson government had introduced a White Paper, the celebrated *In Place of Strife* which, while broadly accepting Donovan, included the so-called penal clauses to regulate strike action in a fairly limited set of circumstances. These clauses, introduced by the then darling of the left, Barbara Castle, were clearly a concession to a public opinion increasingly convinced that something had to be done about the union problem. In lampooning the White Paper as 'In Place of Sanity', the leading labour lawyer, Professor Wedderburn, writing in *The Times*, seemed, *inter alia*, to be identifying the deviance of proposals which seemed likely to damage the institutional frameworks conceived to develop consensus economic policies.

In abandoning these clauses in the face of impassioned union hostility, the government accepted the TUC's 'solemn and binding undertaking' to deal with unofficial strikes. Labour politicians, for the foreseeable future, had abandoned the formal legal system as a means of persuading organised labour to jump into the corporatist bed. From now on consensus economic policies, in so far as they were not to be diluted with monetarist notions, were to be achieved by a mixture of persuasion and the 'informal Whitehall legal system'.

The Conservative Government of 1970-1

Just before Donovan had reported in 1968 the Conservative Party had produced its own analysis of our system of labour relations and the need for legal regulation. Entitled *Fair Deal at Work* it opted for large scale legal reform without ever totally abandoning the economic policies of post-war Conservative liberals. The ensuing Industrial Relations Act of course made union co-operation in the post-war settlement effectively impossible, though in the Selsdon period 1970-2 the Heath government did not seem to care much. None the less, the Act, for all its inconsistencies and contradictions (laws to curb unofficial elements, laws to render a militant leadership accountable to the grass roots) had, at its core, a body of labour law which sought to ensure an ordered system of vertical accountability. Although its main provisions were almost certainly directed to procuring official union policing of disputes through means which we describe in Chapter 3, they would, if successful, also have created vital institutional reforms which would have rendered effective service to tripartism or neo-corporatism in the longer term.

However, that was not to be. The confrontations and legal *causes célèbres* of the following years meant that the famous U-turn of 1972 reintroduced incomes policy without corporatist co-operation. Resort to compulsion, including law in the form of the Price Commission and the Pay Board, became the order of the day. The fall of the Heath government, the direct result of a confrontation with the unions, meant that law directed 'against' trade unions and their officials seemed to be off the political agenda for a generation. It was difficult to conceive of that kind of labour law succeeding if the consensus policies of the post-war period were to be pursued. What was not clear at the time was the possible dominance of a new kind of economic strategy, which might increase the chances of survival of law directed against the trade unions.

The Labour Government, 1974-9

In the event, the Labour government of 1974 needed to repeal the 1971 Act in order to rebuild union co-operation in state planning. The Trades Union and Labour Relations Act (TULRA) of 1974 therefore returned to the trade unions many of the immunities previously enjoyed. The restoration of these immunities was the price of trade-union co-operation in the economic and industrial strategies contained in the election manifesto. The Labour government reaffirmed its commitment to the post-war settlement, including the welfare state and the corporatist regulation of the economy. The TUC and CBI were to varying degrees wooed in relation to the employment and industrial policies of the Government, though the 'social contract' seemed to ensure that the unions would be the more advantaged party. The distinctly industrial relations legislation aside, the new tripartite structures were embedded in much of the legislation of the period, such as the health and safety legislation and the Industry Act.

However, like so many post-war governments, the Labour government was to fall foul of a central contradiction in managing long-term decline. The balance of payments crisis which overtook the Labour government in 1976 was once again solved by domestic deflation. The terms which the International Monetary Fund demanded of Britain involved some commitment to monetarist economic strategies, although the failure of Keynesian economic management to control increasing inflation was already moving the Treasury in this direction. The deflationary measures which the Callaghan government introduced involved turning away from neo-Keynesian economic strategies, yet those strategies were central to the post-war settlement and the whole corporatist drift. The Labour government was therefore left with an industrial relations policy and legal framework still committed to corporatist management, but with a financial strategy based increasingly on monetarist assumptions. The conflict between these two produced the inevitable industrial relations explosion. When the government tried to impose a tough incomes policy without union agreement the result was a wave of strikes and the 'winter of discontent'. The legislative framework the government had created with TULRA was, of course, unable to control this outburst, not least because it was never designed to control the unions.

What did occur was a revival of the national debate concerning the control of trade unions, and especially certain tactics such as picketing and secondary action. This was an opportunity which the Conservative Party, under its new leader, Mrs Thatcher, was easily able to exploit in the 1979 election. Labour policies continued to lack credibility because they still contained the central contradiction of a monetarist economic strategy presented within a corporatist framework. The Conservative policy was burdened by no such contradiction. Furthermore, the TUC was left still wedded to the ideas and actions of some version of corporatism but facing a government which was committed to its abandonment.

The new Conservatism

The Conservative government which came to power in 1979 was radically different from any post-war government: or at least that is what it claimed for itself, and its rhetoric did seem to signal quite new departures. During the election campaign the Conservatives had made the trade unions a central focus. On the one hand, they gave the trade unions a significant role in their analysis of the reasons for industrial decline, and, on the other, the 'winter of discontent' provided the means for linking trade unions to the emotive issue of law and order. Without necessarily specifying precisely what was proposed the Conservatives created the impression that they would do something about the trade unions, and this would be linked to a very firm stand on law and order. The rhetoric was very different from the predominantly tripartite approach of most of the post-war period, and even from the Heath government's attempt to use law to reform the unions.

Rhetoric, of course, can be empty and later we will examine how far the rhetoric fitted the actions and proposals. There is, after all, a commonly held belief in Britain that governments come and governments go but the civil service goes on developing a gradual policy: we need to explore therefore how far the industrial background for conflict was in any significant sense changed by the new government's policies. Rhetoric in and of itself of course can have some power to shape events, so let us examine first the intellectual basis for this rhetoric and how it emerged as the dominant ideology of the Conservative Party. It is necessary to understand such matters if we are to gain a clear picture of the government's world-view on industrial relations and to see how far this necessitates the use of traditional legal techniques and how far economic, fiscal and industrial strategies, which are largely non law-dependent. Examining the impact of legislation is always fraught with difficulties but if we are to seek to measure the impact of the 1980 Employment Act we can only do so by locating it within the unique contemporary form of political economy. We can then examine the industrial relations strategy, including legal reforms, in the light of industrial structures, histories and contexts. This is the framework within which our research fieldwork must be seen.

Monetarism

Mrs Thatcher's government has increasingly been identified with the set of economic theories known as 'monetarism'. There is no single monetarist theory, although the work of Professor Milton Friedman comes close to this, but rather a number of economists whose ideas are generally grouped together under this heading.

In simplified form, monetarism rests upon several main propositions. The prime of these is that excessive expansion of the money supply is both a necessary and sufficient cause of inflation. Inflation reduces the economic certainty necessary for investment and growth and renders goods uncompetitive in world markets. Ultimately inflation reduces the political stability upon which economic order depends. Whilst all monetarists agree that a stable money supply is the ideal, they do not always agree on how rampant inflation is to be cured. In Britain some economists, notably those associated with Manchester University in the 1970s, argued that this could only be achieved safely by a gradual reduction in the money supply. Anything else, they suggested, might have destabilising effects in other parts of the economy or social structure. Others, however, argued that only the shock tactics of a rapid reduction in the money supply would discourage inflationary expectations sufficiently (see Congdon, 1978).

The Conservative government, with its sharp spending reductions, exhortations toward 'realistic expectations' among the workforce, insistence upon the unavoidability of social suffering if the economy is to recover, and public display of refusing to U-turn, tends towards this shock-tactic variant of monetarism. In this view, firmness and single-minded economic discipline are necessary for the transition period from inflation and recession to a vigorous self-regulating market.

Central to monetarism is the belief that the market is capable of self-regulation. Most economic problems – inflation, recession, excessive rates of unemployment are thought only to continue because market mechanisms which would restore a natural balance have been blocked or interfered with. Monetarism therefore holds in general that government attempts to regulate the economy are undesirable, either because limited economic knowledge and time-lags produce market distortions, or because the unpredictability of government action destroys the certainty and predictability upon which the market rests. The only essential role for government in the economy is the provision of a stable money supply: upon that basis natural market mechanisms will provide a self-regulated economy. The remaining functions of government are the maintenance of order and a possible minimal, and strictly temporary, economic role where for special reasons the market fails to provide an essential good or service. The government, at least in theory, follows this doctrine. As their chief theorist, Sir Keith Joseph, put it: 'Governments can help hold the ring, provide infrastructure, maintain a stable currency, a framework of laws, implementation of law and order, provision of a safety net, defence of property rights and all other rights involved in the economic process' (1978). How far such a doctrine can be implemented in a society where governments have traditionally been regarded as responsible for a range of related economic and social goals and with large public and dependent sectors, is not always clear.

Monetarists have certain technical objections to public expenditure. Their disapproval is based upon government's ability to print or borrow money without constraint and so evade market disciplines; what ought to be market decisions become administrative ones. Controlling the money supply, without controlling public expenditure, would devastate private industry but not necessarily affect the public sector. The monetarist solution to this problem is to make the public sector subject to 'market discipline'. The technical instrument for achieving this in Britain has been the Public Expenditure Survey Committee and the use of 'cash limits' in the public sector, originally introduced by the Labour Chancellor Denis Healey. The present government has continued to use this mechanism in circumstances where the public sector is looked upon with an obvious disfavour. This seems in part to be based on the acceptance of the argument that public sector investment displaces, or 'crowds out' private sector investment. Some members of the government even seem to accept an historical version of this thesis, in which the growth of the public sector has been responsible for the increasing ills of private industry (see Eltis and Bacon, 1976). For whatever reason, the government has produced opposition to public expenditure beyond that which some monetarist economists feel is justified. This has major implications for industrial relations in the public sector which we seek to draw out in Chapters 6 and 7. Given the background we are describing it would be reasonable to assume that law would have a differentiated effect in the public and private sector. We examine the details of this assumption in later chapters.

Trade unions are regarded as a problem by monetarists because, it is claimed, as monopolists, they interfere with the free workings of the market. Furthermore, because they have used their power to raise wages beyond the level justified by marginal productivity in an industry, they push unemployment beyond the level which would otherwise occur. This, it is argued, has been combined in Britain in many cases with a deeply conservative attitude which has resisted technological change. These monetarist arguments have frequently been deployed by government economic ministers, although the factual accuracy of the monopolist premise is, to say the least, debatable.

Neo-liberalism

The other main plank of the present government's rhetoric has been a neo-liberal political philosophy. If Professor Friedman is seen as the architect of their economic doctrine, then Professor F.A. Hayek is the primary source of their political philosophy. Neo-liberalism essentially believes in reducing the state and the business of government to the minimum. A free economic market is the mechanism by which individual wants or desires can be satisfied without being incompatible with social interaction. The only valid function of government is to protect this mechanism from interference. Whilst even Professor Hayek recognises that a truly minimalist state is impractical in an advanced economy, any extension beyond it must be hedged with rigid conditions (Hayek, 1979, Ch. 14). Government provision of some goods or services is a necessary evil, but if possible the necessity should be removed. The growth of the state's activities are seen as 'collectivism' which necessarily threatens the 'freedom' of the market. When government tries to plan the economy, or enter in a coercive way into the market, then government itself threatens freedom.

According to this philosophy trade unions not only distort the market, but also infringe the political liberty that a free market offers. By bringing pressure to bear on government to regulate the market in their interest they distort the market and cause growing government intervention in the economy and expansionist monetary policy. The basis of this power is seen as private coercion, resting, as Mr Enoch Powell argued as early as 1968, on legal privileges: the freedom to intimidate through picketing, threats of exclusion from the closed shop, etc., the freedom to raise the cost of goods and services, and the immunity of trade unions from actions in tort (Powell, 1969). The policy prescriptions which follow tend to include the removal of traditional rights and immunities and the disengagement of trade unions from channels of political influence and power. Some of those prescriptions are to be found in the 1980 Employment Act, while others are on the horizon at the time of writing in the shape of the Employment Bill 1982.

History of ideas

This has been the rhetoric and all the points mentioned above were repeatedly made by senior ministers of Mrs Thatcher's government during its first three years. But where do such ideas originate, and how did they become the guiding philosophy of the government?

Monetarist economic ideas began to re-emerge in Britain in the late 1960s, but were scorned by most of the governing establishment. However, the Conservative government which came to power in 1970 under Edward Heath did attempt to implement neo-liberal ideas about reducing state intervention in the economy. It reversed many of the interventionist strategies in the previous Labour government, privatised various state-owned enterprises, and passed the 1971 Industrial Relations Act to curb the influence of the trade unions, and to make them more 'responsible.' By 1972 Edward Heath had performed his famous policy U-turn, returned to neo-Keynesian economic strategies and to a large degree abandoned the trade-union strategy implied in the Industrial Relations Act. The new policies pushed the government into a pragmatic management of the economy designed to achieve broad social objectives via a growing set of corporatist institutions, legally supported by the 1972 Industry Act (see Blackaby, 1978). Mr Heath's neo-liberal experiment from 1970-2 was an interregnum in post-war government: the historical trend had more generally been for the gradual development of a corporatist framework for the state. Such a strategy crucially depended upon the government's ability to develop constructive tripartite relations with capital and labour. However, the final ignominious collapse of the Heath government and the role played by the unions, raised the spectre that the Tory Party was incapable of fostering such relations, and that the Labour Party was the 'natural party of government'. The Labour Party certainly drew this conclusion and, on its return to office, proceeded to build tripartite frameworks and passed the Trades Union and Labour Relations Act in 1974 to remove the attempts made in 1971 to reduce the trade unions' influence.

Within the Conservative Party, however, there were two different reactions to the experience of the Heath government (see Grant, 1982, pp. 77-8). On the one hand, there were those who saw the 1970-2 period as a sort of minor experiment which somehow got out of hand, and regarded the later period as the correct course. In this view the defeat in 1974 was the result of a tactical error and misunderstandings derived from the earlier period. This faction within the Conservative Party saw the way forward as developing closer relations with the trade unions, so that the Party could demonstrate its ability to run a corporatist state. Mr Prior, the employment shadow spokesman, spent the years of opposition pursuing this strategy most assiduously. Another faction within the Conservative Party felt humiliated by the 1974 defeat, and believed it demonstrated the need to stick to neo-liberal policies in spite of short-term opposition. Furthermore, the failures of the policies of Heath's Chancellor, Mr Anthony Barber, were perceived as a demonstration of the inadequacies of neo-Keynesian demand management strategies, and the resulting inflation as evidence for monetarist arguments concerning the importance of the money supply.

Monetarists in the 1970s had to fight the scorn of much of industry, the Treasury, most of the civil service, most of the Press, and the traditional intellectual establishment. The developing monetarist group within the Tory Party therefore formed early alliances outside the usual establishment and, whilst they later received support from such powerful sources as the City and *The Times*, their anti-corporatism estranged them from many of the governing institutions of post-war Britain. They have remained almost as suspicious of the Confederation of British Industry as of the Trades Union Congress, and have continued to harbour doubts about the loyalty of the civil service. On the other hand, they have regarded some newer groupings, such as the Institute of Directors, as their natural allies.

When Mrs Thatcher defeated Mr Heath for the leadership of the Conservative Party she did so as representative of this group, and her leadership fused monetarism and neo-liberalism. More importantly she located these as doctrine for the aspiring working class and commercial middle class. This new conservatism had a broad popularist style quite different from the patrician toryism and liberal conservatism of the past. Until the arrival of this new force the British state seemed irrevocably set on a corporatist trend, and only the broad power base provided by popularist politics could have changed this. The new conservatives were committed ideologues not constrained by loyalty to the traditional establishment, and legitimated their policies by direct reference to the people's wishes. They were the most radical group ever to gain power in post-war Britain.

It is important in the context of the 1980 Employment Act to realise that while Mrs Thatcher had won the leadership battle, an alternative trend within the Party was still powerful. Indeed, the alternative was still regarded by many as true Toryism and Mrs Thatcher's election victory as an error which had occurred by accident. Although it was Mrs Thatcher's style and her politics which won the 1979 election, she was still not totally dominant within the Party. Her first Cabinet therefore had to pay attention to alternative ideas in the Party, and her policies were similarly constrained in some areas. As all readers of the popular press know, the result was a continuing battle between what became known as the 'wets' and the 'drys' in the cabinet, out of which Mrs Thatcher gradually asserted her leadership over the government. Not only was the form of the employment legislation the result of these countervailing notions within the government but the legislative impact as such could only be registered in the context of the new government's developing economic strategies, especially perhaps in the public sector.

Pressures for industrial legislation

The philosophies of the new conservatism pointed to legislation to curb the powers of the trade unions. However, the failure of the 1971 Industrial Relations Act meant that the Party as a whole was extremely cautious about the form such legislation should take.

Within the British state significant elements were opposed to implementing 'restrictive' legislation on trade unions. The police and the Home Office feared that any criminal legislation would be perceived as sectional, and might therefore undermine their claim to impartial authority, a matter which we develop at greater length in Chapter 5. The Civil Service generally, but especially the Department of Employment with its traditions rooted in the old Ministry of Labour, were still largely committed to corporatist institutions and endeavours. Finally, when Mrs Thatcher came to power, the state had incorporated 'peak' institutions of capital and labour whose power and even *raison d'être* would be threatened by anti-corporatist ideas. While the government had increasingly disengaged from these organisations, they were nevertheless still powerful forces within the state itself at the time the 1980 Employment Act was framed.

Not only were elements within the state opposed to rigorous trade union legislation, but elements in the Conservative Party were equally opposed. Mr Prior's patient work with the trade unions while in opposition, and his powerful position as representative of other interests in the Party meant that he had to be appointed as Secretary for Employment. His experience of the 1970-4 government had also persuaded him of the need for dialogue with the unions. He not only managed to modify the original proposals for trade-union legislation, but, until his departure to Northern Ireland, seemed prepared to set his face against legislation of a radical nature.

Outside the state apparatus some of the most powerful representatives of organised capital were also opposed to certain forms of trade union legislation. The Confederation of British Industry by virtue of its own history still preferred tripartite solutions, and the Engineering Employers Federation for example had pragmatic objections to a real assault on the closed shop. Industrial capital, and especially large companies, craved predictability and certainty more than anything else. They feared radical legislation which might later be overthrown, and brought concerted pressure for a bi-partisan or non-party approach to industrial relations. British industrial capital had come to terms with trade unions, and to some extent valued the discipline and simplification they provided in industrial relations, although the position of finance capital in the City never fitted comfortably into that mould.

The 1980 Employment Act

We shall discuss the legal details of the 1980 Employment Act in the next chapter. The important point to note in the present context is that the Act emerged out of conflicting forces within the government and the Conservative Party. Even whilst it was passing through parliament there was pressure for firmer legislation. Mr Prior resisted this pressure, but bowed to it indirectly by producing two 'Codes of Practice' on picketing and the closed shop. These codes suggested as good practice many things (such as limiting the number of pickets) which sections of the Party would like to have seen the subject of legislation.

It should perhaps be added that pressure to strengthen the 1980 Bill was increased as a result of the mass picketing at Hadfield's in South Yorkshire resulting in the House of Lords lamenting, in the case of *Duport* v. *Sirs*, the unsatisfactory state of a law which allowed the unions to embroil 'neutral' parties with impunity. We discuss this aspect of the 1980 Act in Chapter 3 and the effect of the steel strike on policing in Chapter 5.

The pressure on Mr Prior continued even after the Act was passed. He tried to fend this off by talking of the Act as a first stage, and issued a Green Paper on possible further legislation. The response to that Paper was inexorably pushing him to legislate further when Mrs Thatcher solved the conflicting pressures by removing Mr Prior to Northern Ireland. His replacement as Minister of Employment, Mr Norman Tebbit, was one of Mrs Thatcher's original 'gang of four', and a clear supporter of the new conservatism.

Was there a radical change?

The 1979 election campaign was dominated by the themes put forward by the new conservatism. Other conservatives suggested less radical actions and many commentators pointed to their speeches as evidence that the radicalism of Mrs Thatcher and her supporters was mere election rhetoric. The Labour Party, as we have already discussed, was so trapped by the contradictions between its industrial and economic policies that it was no match for Mrs Thatcher's clarity and had already fatally lost public support. What was new about the Conservative rhetoric was that the economic policy of monetarism fitted together with a non-interventionist industrial strategy, and a general neo-liberal philosophy. It was a coherent ideology of simple interlocking policies. Furthermore, its popularist style freed it from being constrained by any of the old shibboleths of the establishment. Ironically even previous Labour Governments had been constrained in this way: especially by the international role of sterling and the balance of payments.

What the government actually did when it initially gained office was not necessarily as radical or new as the rhetoric. Indeed, Dr Wyn Grant in his study of the political economy of industrial policy points out that even some of the key instruments of interventionist planning were maintained (Grant, 1982). However, there are two points to bear in mind. First, as we have already examined in the case of industrial relations legislation, the government as a whole did not necessarily share the coherent ideology of the election campaign. Gradually, however, the government has collectively begun to think in this way, and Mr Tebbit's arrival at the Department of Employment signals the shift in that area. Second, dismantling the instruments of corporatist planning developed over a long period simply cannot be achieved overnight. Furthermore, no matter how much one believes in the efficacy of the market, one cannot create market disciplines simply by destroying corporatist structures. Mrs Thatcher understood this problem from the beginning and talked constantly of the need to change attitudes and create a 'new sense of realism'. In other words the market is a cultural as well as an economic phenomenon.

The rhetoric of the new government, then, far from being merely a facade for its policies and the institutional changes they created, was a critical part of its attempt to transform radically British society and its institutions. Not only must we examine how far the Employment Act 1980 related to other areas of policy, such as changes in social-security legislation and general economic policy, but also how it resonated at the ideological level with other areas of government endeavour, and whether it helped create a new market culture. The problem with Mr Prior was that independently of the content of the Act, he constantly deployed a rhetoric which did not serve these needs. The Bill currently passing through Parliament – vehemently denounced by the Labour movement as 'Tebbit's Law' – must have been largely drafted under Mr Prior. Indeed, most of it was in response to the pressures created by Mr Prior's Green Paper. Mr Tebbit, however, brought a quite different rhetoric to the legislation. Mr Tebbit quite clearly wants to change the behaviour of trade unions in so far as he believes they interfere with the market. Mr Prior wished to control wild excesses so that government and unions could work together. The need for a clear ideological fit between employment policy and industrial policy for a government with such radical intentions is clear once one remembers that responsibility for major industrial areas is split between a number of different government departments and ministers. The Department of Employment is responsible for creating a legal framework for industrial conflicts, but other departments make discursions which constrain the tactical choices available during such conflicts.

This then was the political economy which led to the 1980 Employment Act. Law, however, has its own history to some extent independent of such events. We must therefore now turn to a brief examination of the recent history of labour law to explain how that also crucially affected the content and form of the 1980 Act.

3
British labour law and the emergence of the 1980 Act

We have just discussed in outline the recent history of British political economy and its relation to law but now it is necessary for us to locate the specifically British pattern of labour law within that debate. Only then will we be able to look at the specifics of the Employment Act 1980 with which we are centrally concerned.

It has been commonplace to regard the law as largely abstentionist within recent British labour relations history. In fact in a literal sense this has never been strictly true. It is generally understood that until the Trade Union Act 1871 organised labour had been beset with legal constraints and impediments which rendered it impossible for ordinary working men to contest their conditions on anything resembling equal terms with their employers. (See generally the admirable Kahn-Freund, 1977.) Even then the interpretation of the 1871 legislation by the judiciary was unfavourable to the trade unions, so that not until 1875 with the passage of the Conspiracy and Protection of Property Act could the emancipation of the unions from traditional legal chains be said to be established. The Sheffield 'outrages' had been the immediate cause of the appointment in 1867 of a Royal Commission to investigate the causes of industrial conflict and from that body (or at least its minority) emerged the proposition that responsible trade unionism and the promotion of collective bargaining would best serve the interests of industrial peace. That intellectual breakthrough made possible the legislation of the 1870s, including the Employers and Workmen Act 1875 which effectively removed the sectional excesses of the criminal law which had, during the course of the century, seen 'literally thousands of trade unionists . . . imprisoned' (R. Lewis, 1976).

That historical moment explains a great deal about the development of British labour law and industrial relations. We shall return briefly to an overview of the law shortly but the accepted notions of the 1870s were to become vitally influential for another century. Let us dwell on this theme for a moment. The legalisation of trade unions as entities, and their ability to bargain with employers in such a way that their agreements became part of their members individual contracts of employment, gave historical support to the English legal practice of pragmatic, 'unprincipled' law-making. This conjuncture needs also to be set in the context of early developing, decentralised trade unions, fragmented capital and what we would now perhaps call a 'weak state' within the wider 'state' traditions. (See Dyson, 1980.) Trade unionists were also and understandably opposed to the legal system and judges who seemed unable by their training and inclinations to understand notions concerning collective life. All their common-law training concentrated their minds upon the rights and liabilities of individuals and not upon larger notions of group conflict and state concerns. The response of the judges in the thirty or so years following the 1871 Act was to reinforce organised labour in its hostility to law and legal regulation.

A number of important repercussions of this analysis can now be seen. First, the development of the law relating to industrial conflict became a cat-and-mouse, partly dialectical development of liabilities, privileges and immunities unravelled and re-packed by judiciary and legislature in turn, but nearly always in the context of the law of tort which created rights and duties for individuals at large without taking cognizance of group dynamics. Or at least that is the interpretation most favourable to the judiciary. In any event what was foreclosed was a general code of labour law ceding positive rights and obligations in relation to strikes, security of a job or financial nature, a direct impetus to bargaining and so on. Second, and relatedly, the absence of a developed and principled labour law was accompanied by an acceptance that wages, hours and other conditions of employment fell to be established by collective bargaining and not by statutory regulation. There were of course exceptions but the general drift was to regulate the whole of the employment relationship through an informal legal order in the shape of agreements negotiated by the trade unions and the employer. They, between them, became the law-makers though in such a way that as far as the traditional formal legal system was concerned their bargains operated in law, in so far as they did at all, through the curiously British concept of the contract of employment. The law and industrial life have thus been in a state of tension between these facets of the employment relationship with collective arrangements sometimes incorporated into the contract and sometimes not. The singular nature of the contract of employment, and its pretence of having no direct association with the phenomenon of organised labour, also had important repercussions for the legal vicissitudes surrounding the law of tort and the liabilities imposed upon trade unionists in connection with industrial action. Let us examine the implications of this statement a little further.

Voluntary collective bargaining was given official impetus by a series of legal and administrative devices. Perhaps beginning with the Fair Wages Resolution of 1891 (the successor to which is, almost incredibly, under attack at the time of writing), passing through the Conciliation Act 1896, the Industrial Courts Act 1919, the establishment of the Whitley Councils and so on, we find a legal/ administrative framework, little more, directed to encouraging collectively bargained outcomes to 'manage' industrial conflict. Since the law was not concerned to regulate in any more direct sense and certainly not prepared to give support to substantive rights of a collective nature, labour law in its relationship to industrial conflict took the form increasingly of providing immunities to individuals engaged in industrial action. As we have already indicated such 'immunities' were constantly being circumscribed in such a way that trade-union hostility threatened harmonious bargained outcomes not only in ordinary labour-management relations, but also in relation to attempts at producing co-operation in overall economic management and particularly tripartism.

In short, while the law has sought in limited sets of circumstances to encourage voluntary collective bargaining, it has not been directly interventionist in the sense of producing considered principles for labour law which would coincide with the state's own view of the place of labour relations within the larger framework of industrial politics. A clear philosophy of political economy, such as that earlier described for the radical conservatism of post-1979, would of course make possible a 'principled' set of labour laws. However, the 1980 Act, as we shall see, was based firmly on this early pragmatic tradition.

While the law may not have been directly interventionist in the sense just described it does not follow of course that it has been inactive. It certainly does not follow either that it has been abstentionist. What is clearly the case is that, apart from a period of some thirteen years following 1951, there have occurred a whole series of legal interventions directed at limiting the freedom of action of trade unionists to take industrial action. Those thirteen years largely co-incided with the boom, never-had-it-so-good, period of post-war British life when the upsurge in world trade and the favourable terms of that trade in relation to the 'developed' economies meant that the problem of long-term decline could be temporarily over-looked in the face of an uncovenanted cornucopia. This statement may deserve a mild digression since it helps to account for much traditional trade-union antagonism to the law.

After the Trade Disputes Act 1906, the effect of which we shall turn to shortly, many commentators believe that a post-nineteenth-century settlement with the unions, a *modus vivendi*, was achieved in circumstances where trade unions and their members were afforded immunities denied to all other citizens. This is, in fact, an extremely partial view of the matter.

Hot upon the passage of the 1906 Act came of course the cel-ebrated Osbourne case (1910 A.C. 87) which sought to invalidate financial support for the Labour Party which had been instrumental in persuading the Liberal government of Campbell-Bannerman to introduce the 1906 measures. Although the force of this decision was abated by the Trade Union Act of 1913 the outbreak of war in 1914 was the signal for fresh legislation. The Munitions of War Act 1915 prohibited strikes and lockouts and provided for compulsory arbitration in order to sustain the war effort. While it is true that this legislation was introduced with the consent of the 'official' trade-union movement the nascent shop stewards movement had begun to express the view that labour was being asked to make unequal sacrifices to promote war ends which were not popular in every quarter. (See Middlemas, 1979, ch.3.)

In the event the measure was repealed in 1919 with the outbreak of peace. As is now well known (see Middlemas, 1979), though it has not always been the conventional wisdom, Lloyd George made a vigorous attempt to institutionalise tripartism and to bind the trade-union movement into a new constitutional settlement. Despite early successes the General Strike represented the collapse of these attempts with the result that the Trade Disputes and Trade Union Act of 1927 was introduced and remained on the statute book for nearly twenty years. Its provisions look remarkably similar to the combination of legal and bureaucratic measures which characterise the post-1979 Conservative Administration, a matter which may well be thought to relate to a common epochal attitude to 'co-operative industrial politics' whether directed to crisis-avoidance, as was probably the case during the Lloyd-George era, or more activist economic considerations at a later time. Its main provisions related to isolating civil servants from the main body of organised labour structures, the prohibition of the closed shop for public authorities, criminal liabilities for strikes calculated to coerce the government and the restriction of the lawful ambit of picketing. The consequence of recession, declining trade-union membership and power meant that the Act was little used in the event. At the time of writing that has largely been the fate of the 1980 Employment Act.

The Second World War saw the introduction of the Conditions of Employment and National Arbitration Order, 1940, no. 1305 which sought to reproduce the essential nature of the 1915 Act. Prohibitions on industrial action within the context of compulsory arbitration were its identifying characteristics. Interestingly enough it survived until 1951 when it was replaced by Order 1376 which removed the constraints on strike action but retained, for the short-term, until 1959, an element of compulsory arbitration. Although legal compulsion characterises this period it has to be noted that in reality the measures were as effective as they were only because they enjoyed a wide measure of support. This is an important argument because attempts at actually enforcing these laws were so conspicuously unsuccessful. The famous Betteshanger Colliery prosecution, so graphically described in an appendix to the Donovan Report in 1966, allied to the political embarrassment engendered by the attempts to prosecute gas workers in 1950 and dockers in 1951, became central components of labour folklore: a lore which carried at its heart the message that anti-union legislation would simply be without significant effect. The years that have followed have seen numerous attempts to test the validity of this important cultural belief.

Labour law post-1906

The Trade Disputes Act 1906 was passed to neutralise the dangers exposed first by the development of a number of common law torts which laid trade unionists open to civil actions by those damaged, and second and most immediately the Taff Vale decision of 1901. This decision created civil liability for trade unions *per se*, thereby vulnerably exposing their funds. The receding dangers of the criminal law had been overtaken by a series of new torts which were capable of being used against those taking industrial action. Most important of these were inducing breaches of contract (whether contracts of employment or those of a commercial nature), and civil conspiracy, both of which had particular relevance for the organisation of strikes and other industrial action.

The 1906 Act exempted trade unions from any liability in tort and protected individuals when acting 'in contemplation or furtherance of a trade dispute'. This latter phrase, sometimes referred to as the 'golden formula' seemed straightforward enough at the time but was to turn out to be both vitally important and exceedingly troublesome. The individual protection then was afforded by granting immunity against these emergent torts provided that the golden formula applied. The union movement, deeply suspicious of law of any kind, simply wished to remove these contemporary threats. For the most part it did not seek to use the law as a positive instrument towards achieving those larger goals which were to be primarily achieved through the extension of collective bargaining, backed by threats of industrial action, undertaken with legal impunity.

In consequence the Act made it 'not actionable' to induce a breach of contract of employment, or to conspire to act to harm another unless the act would have been independently actionable if undertaken by one person acting alone. It also provided that an act was not to be actionable on the ground only that it constituted an interference with the trade or business of another person.

The 1906 Act stood as the cornerstone of trade dispute law until 1971. Although there were developments in the torts protected against, they did not substantially affect the scope of the protection until the decision of the House of Lords in 1964 in *Rookes* v. *Barnard* ([1964] A.C. 1129). There the ancient tort of intimidation was disinterred. The essence of this action is that if C threatens B with an unlawful act unless he acts to the detriment of A, and B does so, then C has committed a tort against A. The crucial step of *Rookes* v. *Barnard* was to expand the range of unlawful acts from the previous requirements of physical violence to breach of contract, so that the defendant's threat that contracts of employment with the employer in question would be broken unless that employer dismissed the plaintiff now constituted the tort. The incoming Labour government of 1964 acted quickly to protect against this new tort, in circumstances where the golden formula applied, in the shape of the Trade Disputes Act 1965. It is not clear that the Act was adequately drafted to suit its purposes.

Two things should perhaps be added to describe the law of industrial conflict at this time. First, from 1964 onwards the judiciary was in an active and creative frame of mind in terms of finding new means to create liabilities for those organising industrial action. These means were essentially to develop liability for inducing or procuring breaches of commercial contract, where for example blacking or secondary action occurred, and to narrow the scope of the golden formula. This was an ongoing feature of the mid and late 1960s (see Davies and Freedland, 1979).

The second point worth making relates to the interlocutory injunction. Since we are describing liabilities against named individuals, and since most such labour activists will not be men of means, it may be thought that the civil law constituted an empty threat. This, however, would be to reckon without the effect of the interlocutory labour injunction. The primary purpose of an employer or customer taking legal action against a union activist would be to have the offending action lifted. This can be done by showing a 'prima facie' infraction of the civil law which allows a temporary or interlocutory order to be issued. The offending action would be enjoined until such time as the substantive legal issue came to trial at a much later date. This of course rarely happens since the immediate tactical advantage is gained provided the order is complied with (see Anderman and Davies, 1973). So far as we are aware, in the period under review, such orders issued by the High Court were ordinarily respected. To this extent the conventional labour folklore was undermined though a reassessment was to take place after 1971.

This brief summary of the post-1906 period is important for two reasons. The Heath legislation apart, all industrial disputes legislation, including the 1980 Act is drawn in terms of the common law torts, their development, the immunities provided against their entrapping trade unionists and consequent redevelopment. Thus, although phenomenologically contentious, 'secondary' action (perhaps the 1971 Act apart) has not usually represented a legal phenomenon in British labour law. It has attracted voluminous case-law and comment in the United States but *legally* it is not of itself a no-go area here. Any incidental illegalities occurring during the course of secondary action will relate to the more or less random impact of gaps in the 'immunities'. Even the 1980 Act, as we shall see, does not cleanly disconnect legal primary action from illegal secondary action. The field is a technical maze which even experienced lawyers find difficult to navigate. This can have important consequences for political rhetoric, for ideology and for the state of perceptions of the actors in the workplace drama. These consequences are historically almost certainly accidental, as we have tried to illustrate. They can, nevertheless, be usefully traded upon in terms of the political messages which are from time to time passed to the electorate.

Finally, although as we have stressed the criminal law has been found for much of this century to be largely ineffective in preventing or aborting industrial action, the civil law was thought until 1971 to be likely to be respected. This was a constant theme during the debates on labour law which accompanied the run-up to the 1970 general election. The fact that a breach of an interlocutory injunction would constitute a contempt of court, itself an affair of the criminal law, seemed not to register or at least not to affect the issue. If, however, the 'customary' respect for the civil law was called into question then the repercussions for attempts at legislating for the 'problem' of industrial action could be crucial. This is one of the main features of interest for the next historical phase of British labour law.

The Industrial Relations Act 1971

The 1971 Act provides a curious interlude in this history. In view of its generally agreed failure, the details of its provisions can be ignored but the broad principles are still of interest (see N. Lewis, 1976; and Weeks et al., 1975). Three kinds of 'unfair industrial practice' (UIP) were introduced, committed only in contemplation or furtherance of a trade dispute (renamed industrial dispute and redefined). Outside this area the common law prevailed, with the traditional immunities, but within it there was only to be liability for a UIP, to be determined by the National Industrial Relations Court. It was a UIP to induce or threaten to induce a breach of contract except for registered trade unions or persons acting on their behalf. It was itself a UIP to take industrial action in support of a

UIP, and also to take industrial action against parties extraneous to the dispute. There were also provisions for the Secretary of State to impose a cooling-off period or a strike ballot in some disputes.

To some extent these provisions were a reaction against the technicality of the common law and an attempt to specify what kind of industrial action was legitimate. However, it will be seen that the main provisions used the common law concepts of inducing breach of contract, and, since unions themselves could be liable for UIPs, raised the fearsome question of when a union would be vicariously liable for action taken by its officials/stewards/members (see Heaton's Transport [1973] A.C.15; Howitt Transport [1973] I.C.R.1; G.A.S. [1976] I.R.L.R.225). The main thrust though was against the 'problem' of unofficial strikes. Although the Donovan Commission had identified unofficial strikes as merely a symptom of unstructured bargaining practices and had in general rejected legal controls, a narrow majority had recommended restricting the benefit of the Trade Disputes Act protection against liability for inducing breach of contract to registered trade unions. But registration under the 1971 Act entailed much more control over union rules than had been envisaged by Donovan and, as is well known, the great majority of unions refused to register. The result was that virtually all industrial action, official or unofficial, became an UIP, since some breach of contract would almost always be induced or threatened.

The remedies thus theoretically available to employers were not widely used. The uproar and national strike action over the possible imprisonment of three dockers in the *Churchman* case ([1972] I.C.R.222), and the actual imprisonment of the 'Pentonville Five' in the *Midland Cold Storage* case ([1972] I.C.R.230), showed the consequences of 'martyring' individuals. The individuals concerned were freed following the intervention of the Official Solicitor and the decision of the House of Lords in the *Heaton's* case that the primary means of enforcement should be against the funds of organisations, not individuals, made matters no better. This kind of enforcement could be equally disastrous, as shown by the *Con-Mech* case ([1973] I.C.R.620) in which the sequestration of the financial assets of the AUEW by the National Industrial Relations Court provoked a national strike, only ended by the payment of the AUEW's £47,000 liability by a group of anonymous donors.

The overall effect was to strengthen the fundamental opposition of the union movement to the 1971 Act and anything associated with it. For employers it demonstrated once again the secondary force of legal sanctions. For government it indicated institutions which would best be avoided in future. It seemed to presage the end of law directed against individual action for the foreseeable future.

The Labour government 1974-9

One of the first acts of the incoming Labour administration was to repeal the 1971 Act, though reenacting the unfair dismissal provisions, and to restore the traditional immunities. Though at first the government's narrow majority precluded their passing the legislation which they desired we shall treat the Trade Union and Labour Relations Act 1974 (TULRA) and the Amendment Act 1976 together for present purposes. In fact not only were the terms of the 1906 and 1965 Acts reproduced but the immunities were extended. First, by reversing the *Rookes* v. *Barnard* possibilities of extended tortuous immunity through the treatment of a breach of contract as itself unlawful means. Second (and vitally), by extending the immunities to inducing breaches of commercial contract. Finally, by immunising against the tort which had been developing throughout the 1960s; viz. interference with the performance of a contract short of actual breach. Lord Scarman summarised the position in 1979 in the leading case of *NWL* v. *Woods* ([1979] I.C.R.867), when he declared that the law was 'back to what Parliament had intended when it enacted the 1906 Act, but stronger and clearer than it was'.

A trade union's general immunity to action in tort was restored, the 'golden formula' was reinstated and developments extending the entrapment by interlocutory injunctions were also abbreviated where a trade dispute existed. The old pattern had then re-emerged. It is interesting that the trade-union response after 1974 had been to remove all law whatsoever from the field of industrial conflict. When confronted with the realisation that a simple removal of the 1971 Act would place trade unionists back where they were in the 1870s, they were prepared to settle for a reinstatement and extension of the traditional 'immunities' rather than opting for a set of larger statements more positively expressed concerning the right to strike, picket etc., though such arguments were beginning to be heard. The main thrust of new legal development in the field of labour law was in fact to be found in the Employment Protection Act 1975 which not only greatly extended individual employment rights, but also gave support to certain collective trade-union endeavours, most prominently in relation to statutory rights of recognition. This, it will be recalled, was all a part of the so-called social contract. In return for trade-union moderation in relation to wage claims, and promises of general co-operation, considerable legal concessions were made. However, this was done in circumstances where the seeming one-sidedness of the bargain caused many to feel that the trade unions were now well and truly an independent estate quite outside traditional assumptions about the rule of law. These feelings began to be reflected in a number of ways by the judiciary.

The major strike by the judiciary was made against the recognition provisions of the 1975 Act in the celebrated Grunwick case in 1977 ([1978] I.C.R.231). The House of Lords contemporaneously emasculated the recognition procedure and incidentally expressed some of the general distaste which the public had felt over the mass picketing and violent incidents accompanying the Grunwick 'siege' which had become one of the greatest post-war *causes célèbres*. Almost everyone in the broader labour movement had identified with the cause of the Asian workers previously employed by Grunwick, and yet the picketing helped formulate the new public mood of distaste at what was felt to be the lawlessness of the trade-union movement.

Elsewhere the judges were working within the interstices of the TULRA legislation. The Court of Appeal for instance in *Associated Newspapers* v. *Wade* in 1979 ([1979] I.C.R.664) had sought to extend the liabilities of trade unionists through an unfolding and ever developing law of tort. In particular there were attempts to redefine the protection afforded by the golden formula in a number of leading cases before the House of Lords such as the *MacShane and Duport* litigation (1980) ([1980] I.C.R.42), and the *Woods* case ([1980] I.C.R.181) already referred to.

The Court of Appeal, under Lord Denning, did little to hide its dislike of some aspects of TULRA. Although the House of Lords were prepared to put down what they saw as unconstitutional attempts at judicial legislation by the Court of Appeal, often in strong terms, they were also prepared to express strong views about the merits of TULRA. This seemed to come to a head in the *Duport Steels* case where Lord Diplock referred to his conclusion on the meaning of the golden formula as 'intrinsically repugnant to anyone who has spent his life in the practice of the law or the administration of justice'; and Lord Keith described trade unionists as privileged persons able to bring about disastrous consequences with legal impunity. It is rather hard to contain this recent battle between the Court of Appeal and the House of Lords within an explanation in terms of the individualistic traditions and concepts of the common law. The Court of Appeal appears to have taken an overtly antagonistic stand to the legislation itself. The House of Lords has upheld the letter of the protecting statutes while emphasising the differences from tradition, and reinforcing the notion that unions and their members are 'above the law'. The government had already reacted to the *MacShane* decision by producing a Consultative Document on Secondary Industrial Action which suggested endorsing the 'Denning view' but as will be seen this was not the solution ultimately adopted in the 1980 Employment Act. Be that as it may, public opinion was seemingly becoming increasingly anti-trade union through the convergence of a number of different factors. Not the least of these was the 1979 'winter of discontent', accompanied as it was by apparent union indifference to the needs of the sick, and even to the burying of the dead, when public sector workers sought to rebel against the logic of the government's developing economic policies, increasingly influenced by monetarist notions. If tripartism was at an end then so also would be support for the immunities enjoyed by the labour movement. How though could an incoming government legislate on the trade-union problem without repeating the mistakes of the Heath years? We shall see the response in the shape of the 1980 Act in a moment, but first we must make an excursus to describe the law and its traditional relationship to the phenomenon of picketing.

Picketing

Picketing as such is not a legal concept. It is a social phenomenon which may or may not involve either a breach of the criminal law, or the civil law. Unlike the position in say the USA the legality of a picket line does not depend very greatly on the purposes of the picket, but rather upon the methods adopted. For the most part, the ordinary criminal law applies to picketing while on the civil side liability will depend upon the enormous complexity of British collective labour law already outlined. Let us look briefly at the position as it obtained before the 1980 Employment Act.

First, the criminal law. Any crime committed on a picket line is no less a crime because it occurs in contemplation or furtherance of a trade dispute. We shall not here catalogue all the crimes which can be committed in such circumstances but crimes of violence or behaviour likely to cause a breach of the peace are the obvious examples. A police officer may intervene to prevent behaviour which might lead to a breach of the peace and courts have placed great reliance on the opinion of the officer on the spot. Failure to comply with instructions in such circumstances amounts to the offence of obstructing a police officer in the execution of his duty. The case of *Piddington* v. *Bates* ([1961] 1 W.L.R.62) in 1960 clearly exemplifies this state of affairs: there the defendant ignored the police officer's instruction that only two pickets at each door would be allowed and was convicted for obstruction even though no violence or disorder was identified. Similarly, obstruction of the highway will suffice. In *Tynan* v. *Balmer* ([1967] Q.B.91) sending 40 pickets round in circles to block the entrance of a factory was a criminal offence as is the attempt to stop vehicles even for the purpose of communicating information if it is against the express wishes of the drivers. Section 15 TULRA, following the 1906 formula, states that it is lawful in contemplation or furtherance of a trade dispute to attend merely for the purpose of communicating information or for peacefully persuading any person to work or abstain from working. The relationship of this provision to the Conspiracy and Protection of Property Act 1875 which makes watching and besetting a criminal offence, and to obstruction and public nuisance are still not entirely clear. However, for all practical purposes, one can say that most picketing, whether peaceful or not, would be in breach of some aspect of the criminal law. The vital questions to ask then revolve around police presence on a picket line and the manner in which police discretion is exercised. We address ourselves to these questions in some detail in Chapter 5.

So far as civil liability is concerned section 15 of TULRA only protects against torts which might be constituted by mere attendance. This is a complex area of the law but suffice it to say that the only tort unequivocally protected in this way is the obscure tort of trespass to the highway. On the other hand, if a picket induces a breach of contract (employment or commercial), interferes with business etc., then section 15 offers no protection. Any protection afforded will be by way of section 13 TULRA – the 'traditional immunities' already described. Our belief is that the limits of section 13 had never been fully explored and were almost certainly narrower than commonly assumed. Be that as it may, the law relating to picketing, as opposed to causing commercial damage, needed no strengthening on almost any view of the law. What was happening, however, was that the civil and criminal law features of picketing were beginning to be conflated in the public mind. Whether or not the civil law needed to be altered is not for us to say. What is interesting is the form the 1980 Act took in relation to the picketing issue and the nature of the accompanying debate.

The 1979 Conservative government

The Conservative manifesto for the 1979 election said that Labour had 'by heaping privilege without responsibility on the trade unions . . . given a minority of extremists the power to abuse individual liberties and to thwart Britain's chances of success'. Between 1974 and 1976 'Labour enacted a "militants charter" of trade union legislation. It tilted the balance of power in bargaining throughout industry away from responsible management and towards unions.' In the particular context of trade dispute law the manifesto said

> We shall ensure that the protection of the law is available to those not concerned in the dispute but who at present can suffer severely from secondary action (picketing, blacking and blockading). This means an immediate review of the existing law on immunities in the light of recent decisions, followed by such amendment as may be appropriate of the 1976 legislation in this field. We shall also make any further changes that are necessary so that a citizen's right to work and go about his or her lawful business free from intimidation or obstruction is guaranteed.

The right to picket would be limited to a person's own place of work.

The emphasis was thus on the argument that the protection given in trade disputes amounted to unjustifiable privileges ('trade unions are put above the law'), and on the argument that the 1974-6 legislation significantly extended that protection. As has already been noted, Lord Scarman in *NWL* v. *Woods* took the view that legislation put the law back to what was intended in 1906, but stronger and clearer. The main point of difference seemed to be the extension of section 13 protection to interference with all contracts, rather than merely contracts of employment. The Conservative opposition in 1974-76 argued that this extension licensed industrial action even if directed against those far removed from the original dispute. The Labour argument was that if interference with contracts of employment was protected then most interference with commercial contracts would not be unlawful for the means of interference would no longer be unlawful. Thus the extended section 13 was clarifying the law – setting it out expressly rather than by implication – and thereby strengthening it. Much depended on perceptions of what the law had been before 1971, as came to the fore in the battle between Court of Appeal and House of Lords over the golden formula.

The government made few amendments to employment legislation immediately but issued a number of working papers for consultation. The working paper on 'Picketing' was in the first batch of three on proposed industrial relations legislation issued in July 1979. The general issue of secondary action was said there to be under consideration as part of a general review of the law on immunities, and the suggestions made were fairly general. The working paper asserted that there was widespread public concern at recent developments in the use of picketing, particularly to put pressure on companies not directly involved in disputes. Easier communication and transport enabled pickets to travel longer distances and picketing was more organised, sometimes by unofficial groups. The growth of the closed shop had also increased the effectiveness of picketing. There were indications of an increasing use of intimidation, either physical or through threats of loss of union membership. Finally there was an express reference back to the disputes of the winter of 1978-9 as showing the need for early action. The specific proposals were to restrict picketing to parties to a dispute at their own place of work, and to amend section 13 in consequence. No new criminal offence would be created and voluntary guidance would remain important.

When the Employment Bill was introduced it included a clause on picketing, but not one on secondary action in general. Then the

House of Lords handed down its judgments in the *MacShane* case in December 1979, rejecting the Court of Appeal's view on the golden formula which had attempted to limit protection to circumstances objectively defined rather than those in the minds of trade unionists themselves. The House of Lords then restored the law to what the majority of labour lawyers had always assumed it to be, a subjective test, but there was a good deal of argument on the basis that the House of Lords had introduced a dangerous new concept. Since the House of Lords had destroyed the possibility that the Court of Appeal's doctrine could limit the protection given to secondary action, the Employment Bill proposed two additions to the golden formula. These were that the action had to be reasonably capable of furthering the trade dispute and for the predominant purpose of furthering the dispute. In the event, it was decided not to alter the golden formula in this way, because 'it left the judges so much in the driving seat.' (Mr J. Prior, House of Commons Debates, 17 April 1980.)

The Employment Act 1980

The 1980 Act is something of a mishmash, dealing as it does with closed shop issues, the abolition of the statutory recognition procedure, removal of the provisions maintaining the level of terms and conditions of employment bargained or generally obtaining in an industry, as well as the central matters with which we shall be concerned. The impression presented was that the Act was simply tidying up a series of minor unsatisfactory states of affairs, remedying anomalies and the like. No clear purpose seemed to inform it but there was little doubt that it was essentially intended to limit trade-union power. It did so, however, in such a way as to avoid the collective anger of the trade-union movement and it clearly managed to avoid uniting the movement against its provisions in the way which had occurred in 1971. The restrictions on legal liability are the ones with which we have been concerned and in particular with sections 16 and 17 dealing respectively with picketing and secondary action. Let us examine these briefly.

Section 16 and picketing

By section 16 parliament has substituted a new section 15 TULRA which now confines the protection of that section to those who, with limited exceptions, picket at their own place of work. The essence of the new rules, however, lies in the provisions of section 16 of the new Act which states that those who picket outside the scope of the new section 15 TULRA will lose not only whatever protection section 15 itself afforded but also that of section 13. Thus a link is forged between the two sections. It must be made abundantly clear, in spite of much public opinion to the contrary, that the effect of the section is to place the responsibility for enforcing the new picketing provisions upon employers using the civil law, and especially, one would suppose, injunctive relief.

The main purpose of this provision is, in some senses at least – though the criminal law has *not* been directly changed – to outlaw secondary picketing. In fact the section defines lawful picketing by reference to the place of work so that some primary picketing is thereby caught. For example, workers from one plant picketing another plant in a multi-plant firm. In particular, with the exception of a limited class of trade-union official, 'outsiders' fall without the protection of TULRA though there are formidable legal difficulties in their being sued by a party affected. There are also limited sets of circumstances where other employees, not directly party to the primary dispute might picket at their own (secondary) place of work. Thus the primary/secondary divide is an over-simplification under the 1980 Act.

We shall make no attempt here to exhaust the technicalities of section 16 but we should develop one or two points, if only to show how very complex the new law is and how the public debate and rhetoric is not matched by the reality of the legislation itself. For instance, someone acting outside section 15 TULRA would most obviously be seen to lose protection for inducing breaches of contract. However, it must be said that he or she would lose the whole of the protection of section 13 TULRA in such an event, including for instance conspiracy to injure. This becomes more significant when it is considered that even someone picketing at his or her own primary place of work could lose the statutory protection if acting together with others who were not so lawfully present.

We have stressed that the section refers to the civil law. We have also argued earlier that section 15 TULRA may or may not affect the existing criminal law. Much was made of the changes to both criminal and civil law during the course of debates in the House though how far such a position can be defended is very problematic.

What is clear is that the terms of such debates, allied to the curious status of the attendant Codes of Practice, have confounded the public, and we shall argue in Chapter 5 to some extent the police, about the essential nature of the new law. We discuss in Chapter 5 the police response to the provisions and although that response was differentiated it can be said with some confidence that the general police view is that the criminal laws relating to picketing are and were perfectly adequate as they stood. Let us, however, look very briefly at the Code of Practice accompanying section 16.

Section 3 of the 1980 Act empowers the Secretary of State for Employment to issue Codes of Practice containing practical guidance for the purpose of promoting the improvement of industrial relations. These are to be taken into account in any court proceedings to which they are relevant. Hopes of a voluntary code agreed with the TUC having failed, draft codes on picketing and the closed shop were issued on 5 August 1980. The Picketing Code, after some amendments, came into effect on 17 December 1980. The Code might be expected to have more impact than the amendments made by the 1980 Act for it attempts to explain all the law on picketing and give guidance on good practice in the conduct of picketing. Several instances where the explanation of the law is dubious could be given but can be exemplified by reference to the narrow interpretation of 'place of work', and an over-wide statement of the effect of an injunction on individuals. The Code does say that it is for the courts to interpret the law in particular cases but especially beyond sections B and C, the line between explanation and guidance becomes blurred. For instance, the famous reference to six pickets per entrance occurs in para.31 in section E, which is apparently giving guidance on good practice. Para.31 says that large numbers on picket lines are likely to give rise to fear and resentment amongst those seeking to cross the line even where no criminal offence is committed, and to exacerbate disputes. 'Accordingly, pickets and their organisers should ensure that in general the number of pickets does not exceed six at any entrance to a workplace, though frequently a smaller number will be appropriate.' The status of this guidance is far from clear. Similarly in sections F and G quite detailed rules are set out for picket organisers and for the maintenance of essential supplies and services, although there is no legal basis for any of their requirements.

We would repeat then that the combination of the Code and

section 17 produces at least in the minds of large sections of the public, the labour movement and the police a conflation of the civil and the criminal law. Although it is for the employer or customer to initiate proceedings under the section there exists the irresistible temptation to speculate that an attempt has been made to create the impression that something other than that which has been done has in fact been done. We return to this during our examination of the impact of the Act.

Secondary action

The *McShane and Duport Steel* cases raised again in the public mind (having been dealt with in sections 97-8 of the 1971 Act), through the question of subjective and objective intent of those taking industrial action, the issue of whether forms of secondary action that were regarded as too remote from the primary dispute should be rendered illegal. Section 17 of the 1980 Act, introduced substantially as a result of the effect of these two cases in the public mind, deals centrally with this issue. Such matters were likely to receive much public support after the publicity given, for example, to the picketing of Hadfields in Sheffield by the steel unions in circumstances where they were not directly in dispute with the private steel sector. The *McShane* case simply reinforced public feeling on this issue.

We are here concerned only to give a very superficial account of the impact and intent of a section whose technical complexity would almost certainly overwhelm the general reader. Some over-generalisation is therefore inevitable but we can nevertheless describe the thrust of the provision in reasonably clear terms. First, the section removes the protection of section 13 TULRA (inducing breach of contract etc.) where the contract concerned is, in ordinary parlance, a commercial contract and the breach is induced by secondary action which is not justifiable by reference to the rest of section 17. There is then a partial repeal of those provisions of the 1976 Amendment Act which relate to contracts which are not contracts of employment. The extent of the repeal is couched in terms of those secondary acts which the section regards as justifiable and those which it does not.

Very roughly secondary action is regarded as action which induces breaches of contracts of employment between a secondary employer and his employees so that a commercial contract between the primary and secondary employers is adversely affected. However, such secondary action under the section is justifiable if its aim is to disrupt the supply of goods or services during the course of the dispute between the party to the dispute and the secondary employer – i.e. the one against whom threats of breach of the contract of employment is made. It is also necessary for the secondary action to be likely to achieve its declared purpose. There are also other justifiable and non-justifiable forms of secondary action laid down in the section with which we shall not burden the reader.

What is the main impact of the narrowed immunity relating to secondary action? In order for secondary action to be justifiable it has to be targeted inwards towards the employer in dispute and not outwards to other suppliers or businesses, even with the intention of hurting the employer in dispute indirectly. So presumably if the primary employer has closed because of the dispute, supplies are not needed and there is in effect no supply during the dispute which could be lawfully disrupted. There are severe difficulties in interpreting the section where the contracts concerned involve hauliers or other middlemen, while major problems exist in relation to companies 'associated' with the primary employer and the timing of the entering into of a contract for the supply of goods or services which are the subject of the secondary action. We shall pass over them lest this brief summary turns into a treatise on the technicalities of labour law. We must, however, add that the section insists that the secondary action was likely to achieve the purposes made allowable by its earlier provisions so making an objective test of the 'contemplation or furtherance of a trade dispute' formulation which the Court of Appeal had attempted to construe earlier in the cases already adverted to.

Two general points should be made. First, the section does not, if one wishes to be purist, introduce new forms of liability but simply reduces the scope of the statutory immunity to common law liability. This as we have seen is in the best traditions of British labour law with the exception of the 1971 Act. The government was at pains not to repeat the error of introducing a new *code* into labour law, thereby laying itself open to the charge that it was changing the rules of the game. This was of course entirely consonant with the 'softly-softly' claims which were so much part of the political rhetoric of the period. Second, constructing the narrowed immunities in this way rendered the law exceedingly complex and technical so that it was both very difficult to explain in simple terms what was being effected, and also almost impossible to plan industrial tactics, at least from the trade-union side, in such a way as to maximise the impact desired whilst taking the new law into account. In the interests of completeness it ought perhaps to be added that section 18 of the Act places restrictions on secondary action in the form of blacking where the purpose of the action is to compel workers employed by the primary employer to join a trade union. We shall not dwell on this provision.

Conclusion

British labour law has never been truly coherent; it has, with the curious exception of the 1970-4 period which itself was only a partial deflection from the norm, never been rigorously codified in such a way that it related itself to overall state policy. As we saw in the Introduction, this is true for most aspects of law and public or semi-public life in this country; no doubt to a substantial degree because Britain has been traditionally a 'weak' state in that a compenetration has occurred between civil society and governmental concerns. (See Poggi, 1978, ch.6).

Nevertheless public purposes have existed in Britain which go beyond the mandates of particular governments whether we are speaking of crisis management (of which waging war is a very special sort) or the management of the economy in terms of relatively uncomplicated Keynesian aggregates, more sophisticated forms of indicative planning, three-cornered arrangements or whatever. Our labour laws have impinged on these changing objectives from time to time with unfortunate time-lags often creating a lack of fit between law and particular policies. Because of the absence of a coherent and purposive public law it has become difficult for ordinary citizens to see precisely how successive governments have sought to implement public goals. Law has not been much used for the regulation of economic affairs for instance so that it has been extraordinarily difficult to look for 'fit', 'kilter', 'mesh' or whatever between law and other institutional means for moving towards desired objectives. A narrowed concept of law has meant that the effects of the traditional legal form, apparently enjoying its own autonomy and being usually directed to immediate evils, have been extraordinarily difficult to trace. This is clearly and especially true of labour law. It would be a mistake, however, not to look for legal efficacy in terms of the whole apparatus of state institutions and forms. This has not ordinarily been done and our work is an attempt to lay some of that groundwork.

The 1980 Act has emerged out of the traditions we have been describing but to an extent is within and without them if the whole state machine is being examined. In form the Act is clearly part of the seamless web of British labour law, but already by 1971 this was beginning to relate to a clear governmental view of political economy and industrial politics. That view was to become increasingly more clearly seen in the years immediately after 1979. To that extent it became necessary for us to examine different industrial sectors with different historical and structural backgrounds within a framework of those aggregate state institutions of which the formal legal system was but a part.

In the next chapter we turn to industrial disputes and industrial tactics. We shall attempt to examine how the structure of the work situation constrains or affects the tactics deployed by parties to an industrial dispute. Law, as but one method of institutionalising such conflict, will be examined within that framework. The 1980 Employment Act is a minor factor within the context of industrial structures at large, and especially within the whole conspectus of industrial politics. The book explores that wider world as it emerged during the industrial disputes we studied. Even the professed purposes of the 1980 Act would not have been effective to contain many of the forms of industrial action which we go on to describe, and which the logic of industrial organisations often seem to impel. None the less we might expect the Act to be directly influential at the margins and perhaps indirectly effective in terms of attitudes and expectations. What follows seeks to examine the detail of its impact at the time of writing.

4
Industrial disputes and tactics

In this chapter we will discuss the importance of industrial settings and economic policy for disputes and dispute tactics, including picketing and secondary action. Such discussion will put into context state legal interventions and perhaps illustrate the recalcitrance of industrial disputes to legal control.

Conflict, disputes and industrial tactics

Let us begin with the obvious, but frequently ignored, fact that industrial conflict is very common. Any developed system of production, which depends on organising the labour of large bodies of people, is bound to involve contentious decisions. If such a system is also organised so as to extract profit, then there will be structurally antagonistic interests which will from time to time result in overt conflict. In other words, conflict between labour and capital is inherent in a capitalist economy. As a matter of fact, conflict over the organisation of work is common although it does not always reveal itself as visible disputes: it may alternatively be registered by high absenteeism or even sabotage. If the general processes of production are to continue then such conflict must be successfully managed, and if capitalism as a particular form of production is to exist then the immanent conflict between capital and labour must be avoided. This means that some successful mechanisms for dispute settlement, whether institutions which routinise conflict, or court-like decision-making must be maintained. Additionally, beliefs which mask or transcend the conflict between labour and capital, such as identification of a 'national interest' or acceptance of managerial authority, must be promoted to reduce the possibility of disputes and help contain the political consequences of those which do occur.

In post-war Britain most disputes have been regularly and routinely dealt with, and very few disputes have been successfully politicised into broad class terms. Nevertheless, the danger of failure at either of these levels remains, and such failure would necessarily create difficulties in the processes of production. Such a danger will always be a concern to the state, but in a country where government had become centrally involved with managing the economy then such possible causes of disruption had to be dealt with by the political institutions of the state. Political attention has therefore continuously focused on the problem of unresolved disputes and strikes, as their major manifestation, became known as the 'British disease'. Academic attempts to question whether Britain was more strike prone were almost beside the point: the central historical problem of industrial decline had been transmogrified into the political question of how the government could control industrial relations. As alternative economic strategies were adopted to halt decline so different kinds of industrial disputes were defined as problems needing state intervention.

For example, in the late 1950s and 1960s government policy was aimed at the reorganisation of industry which, it was claimed, often still bore the hallmarks of early industrialisation. Certain dispute tactics which had emerged out of the old structures were defined as part of the problem. Disputes over job demarcation, and the tactics used to pursue them, were presented as epitomizing the old structure and the attitudes they engendered. Demarcation disputes soon became the visible symbol of outmoded industrial attitudes which had supposedly prevented reorganisation in the past. The highly complex problems of reorganising decaying industrial sectors was transformed into the more manageable political problem of removing demarcation disputes.

Later, the political focus shifted to the problem of how unofficial strikes undermined the state's ability, in co-operation with union leaderships, to manage the economy through tripartite decision-making, including incomes policy. The number of unofficial disputes had increased in relation to official ones in such key sectors as coal mining, docks, shipbuilding and motor-vehicle production, and the new form of policy-making focused particular attention on such disputes.

By the 1970s tripartite relations, involving discussion and compromise among government, industry and the unions, had developed into a possible, if fragile, basis for state policy-making. Some dispute tactics, however, and especially secondary and mass picketing, threatened this framework. Although these tactics were rare they were a key means of building oppositional action, sometimes by-passing official union channels. A few important incidents occurred during the 1970-4 Tory government in which mass picketing, such as that at Saltley, threatened not only the development of corporatist planning but also parliamentarism as opposed to mobilisational class politics. These tactics took on a political meaning which the fall of the Heath government burned indelibly into the Tory Party consciousness. As we have seen the potential political meaning of these same tactics was to play an important role in the new ideology associated with Mrs Thatcher's government.

Whilst, therefore, the 'union problem' may have been almost constantly on the political agenda of post-war Britain, the three above examples illustrate how the precise nature of the 'problem' has shifted. Successive governments have tried to create new frameworks for industrial relations which have been designed to routinise the solution to those kinds of industrial disputes identified as critically disruptive to their economic strategies. In this sense there have not been a number of attempts to find a solution to the trade-union problem, but various attempts to solve different problems about industrial conflict and disputes.

Conflict then is an ever present potential in industry, and therefore disputes are common. In post-war Britain the attempts to arrest economic decline, in part by governmental industrial policy, have necessarily meant that those disputes which challenged the policy of the day have been seen as an especial problem. Structural conflict, however, only becomes an actual dispute both when the conflict is focused on a particular issue, and when tactical choices are made by the protagonists as to how the conflict is to be pursued. What becomes visible to those outside a dispute is often determined by the tactics used. All industrial disputes involve tactical decisions about how the resources available to the parties are to be manipulated. Tactical choices, however, are more than simply technical choices about the efficacy of different means. Tactics themselves carry political messages within the context of their use. On the one hand, tactical choices can be made by the parties on the basis of formally or informally understood procedures for pursuing disputes. Most strikes and much picketing take place within such a framework and because so routinised is not usually seen as politically problematic. On the other hand, tactics may be chosen which deliberately break such understandings. Routine management of dispute settlement is broken and those beliefs and understandings which normally mask the conflict between labour and capital are abandoned. What these beliefs and understandings consist of are, of course, historically and contextually specific. At one time or place management lay-offs of non-involved workers during a strike, or strikers picketing of customers, may be seen as breaches of such understandings. At a different time or place the same behaviour may be regarded as a routinised part of the process of dispute settlement.

This normalisation of certain tactical choices does not occur just at the level of the firm, or even of the industry. As has been stated, different industrial policies in Britain have made certain kinds of disputes especially problematic, but each new government policy for industrial relations logically generates its tactical antithesis: the tactic which is capable of challenging not just the existing accommodation between labour and capital within an industry but of calling into question the government's ability to control industrial conflict and the state's right to arbitrate in such affairs.

The industrial history of post-war Britain is littered with battles which in their time played, or attempted to play, such a role – the 1966 Seaman's strike, the Pentonville Five, Saltley, Grunwick, Hadfields etc. – where one protagonist used a tactic which politically questioned the existing industrial concords and reawakened class conflict.

Tactics are the form of expression given to a conflict which always lies nascent. A decision by management not to pursue what has been the traditional means of negotiating the annual wage settlement is a tactical choice which may raise the ever present conflict over wage levels into a dispute. All parties in industry have the capacity to deploy tactics which will mask or reveal dispute possibilities. As we shall see later, not all parties have the same power to make crucial tactical choices: fringe political groups, for example, constantly urge tactical choices which would breach normal dispute settlement procedures and politicise a dispute into overt class conflict, but generally speaking their urging is ignored. Nor is it the case that the consequences of tactical choices are foreseen, nor necessarily intended by those making them. However, the choice of tactics in creating disputes which then challenge a government's industrial strategy is inevitably seen as a rational political choice. If 'secondary picketing' is presented as an especial threat to a particular economic strategy, then workers who choose such a tactic will be portrayed as challenging the government. If their choice is seen as rational and political then it follows that it is open to be affected by legal deterrence. Various attempts have therefore been made, together with particular economic strategies, to deter those tactics which would be most threatening either by legal prohibition or by legal support for normalising methods of dispute settlement which exclude them.

Such faith in the deterrent power of law, however, ignores two crucial factors. First, as already noted, those making choices do not necessarily possess the information, knowledge, or accurate foresight of consequences which such a legal strategy assumes. Second, the extent of the choices available in deciding tactics are a direct product of the context and form of each particular industrial dispute.

Tactics and the nature of production and distribution

The tactics available to workforces vary considerably, from all-out strikes with secondary support to overtime bans and work-to-rules. The employment of tactics is not necessarily exclusive. Certain less intensive tactics may be used to try to win at lower costs or to prepare the ground for sharper stages of conflict. For example, overtime bans are a method of warning employers, of laying bare the levels of basic wage rates and so stoking wage militancy, and of running down stocks which might buffer employers in periods of labour withdrawal. All-out strikes and selective strikes are often accompanied by picketing and forms of secondary action. However, all-out action attracts secondary action more readily than selective action. Secondary workers are certainly reluctant to strike when some members involved in the primary dispute are still working, and the target of selective action is often narrow and restricted enough for secondary action to be unnecessary.

In addition tactics such as picketing, which may appear uniform, actually have a variety of purposes. Picketing may for instance be directed against workforces, where union or non-union labour is attempting to maintain production despite strike calls. Picketing may be directed against supplies, especially when production con-

tinues despite strike calls. Picketing may be employed to stop removal of goods, either when production is continuing or when there
are stocks. When ASLEF pickets the railways though members are
solidly out and traffic is halted, the picket is a symbolic demonstration with little impact on production. When health workers picket
and leaflet heavily, with uniformed professionals clearly visible, the
picket is an active attempt to communicate specific information to
the public. Similarly, when civil servants picket benefit offices they
not only inform the public of their grievances but also instruct
clients about alternative arrangements.

Tactics and countertactics represent strategic choices by actors in
given economic and industrial situations. The choice of tactics is
structured by objective factors, such as the nature of production
and distribution, mediated through the understandings and beliefs
of those making them. Much of the rest of this book is concerned
with how in fact such choices are made, and how this relates to any
attempt to use law to affect particular choices. Each industry, and
every dispute within each industry, has its historically unique set of
objective constraints on the tactical choices available. However, the
constraints are structured around certain general aspects of the work
situation which provide a framework for locating and describing the
unique historical event. These may be characterised as the nature
of production (technical imperatives); the organisation of labour in
production (social organisation) and the nature of work; the organisation of capital; the representational forms of workers and management; and the organisation of supply and distribution. Each of
these can take a variety of forms in different work situations, and
it is the way in which these different forms are combined in a
particular empirical case which provides the constraining framework
for tactical choices. We will examine briefly how the aspects can
vary and illustrate how such variation creates or denies tactical
possibilities. Later in the book we will examine how such variations
actually affected the choices made during the disputes we observed,
and how far the law may have had any impact on this process.

The nature of production

Different forms of production have certain technically determined
aspects which, independently of their social organisation, structure
workplace organisation to some degree. These technical determi-

nants are by no means the only cause of different forms of production. However, it does mean that, for example, steel production or coalmining look remarkably similar, and have certain common features, wherever they are found and within whatever political or social framework. This nature of production also structures the availability of tactical choices during an industrial dispute.

Most basically, whether the output of production is a commodity or service bears upon possible choices. Where a stockable commodity is produced, unions and management are at once faced with two separate processes that can be manipulated: production, on the one hand, and distribution on the other. Where a service is offered, the moment of production is also that of distribution and consumption; both unions and management have only one process to interrupt or continue. For example, in both mining and engineering which are industrial processes which produce (stockable) commodities, picketing is frequently necessary to halt both distribution and consumption. Management may continue to distribute stocks while production is halted. And where, as often occurs, some stocks are held away from the production site, 'secondary' picketing may be useful. The use of picketing and secondary action has been important in the recent history of disputes in these industries. This is not some accidental consequence of, say, particularly bloody-minded union leaderships, but rather follows from the nature of production once a serious dispute occurs. On the other hand, in service industries, such as railways, and public services, such as fire and health, interrupting production also interrupts consumption. Secondary picketing may be necessary to halt production at certain sites or to strengthen service workers' pickets, but not to halt a separate process of distribution.

The timing and continuity of production is also crucial. In continuous process industries such as petrochemicals and steel where shutdowns threaten the instruments of production themselves safe shut-downs may require a lengthy period. In both industries, therefore, short, all-out actions are rare, and action may instead be concentrated among ancillary workers or upon the use of tactics such as overtime bans and non-coverage. There are other industries in which the time cycles of production determine tactics. In the vegetable processing industry the harvest is a crucial time, and in the newspaper industry product deadlines are short and the saleability of the product time-bound. In construction and other industries there are often penalty clauses for late completion of the contract and many energy-producing industries, such as coal, are in peak demand in winter. In all of these instances, strategically timed industrial action can have a disproportionate effect, and therefore timing will be a paramount tactical consideration. On the other hand, interruptions to emergency services – which are unpredictably but nearly constantly in demand when withdrawn – are immediately effective and serious. Strikes and primary picketing against production at key times are obviously powerful tactics in industries where the nature of production is related to a particular time cycle.

Whether industries are capital- or labour-intensive affects the possibilities of management or others deploying substitute labour for striking workers. Where management to worker ratios are high, some substitution by management may be possible at least in the short-term. Such substitution occurred in both light engineering and computer companies during our research although output levels were reduced. Labour-intensive parts of any production process are especially susceptible to the use of substitute labour and the importance of picketing is, in these circumstances, to prevent blackleg labour.

Tactics are also critically affected by the concentration and location of control over production. The technical organisation of production can make certain workers so strategic that they are the key to effective action. This in turn can decrease the need for secondary action. For example, the railways cannot operate without the signal system, and as signalling has become more centralised and automated, the withdrawal of a few key signalmen can disrupt large parts of the railway system. Equally, the centralisation and computerisation of public revenue collection and disbursement has created a strategic group of workers in a few key civil-service computer centres. Finally, in much of manufacturing industry, certain maintenance craftsmen are critical to the whole process.

The technical nature of production, then, can create or deny certain tactics. This is not to say that such tactics will necessarily be chosen, but simply that a particular technical production process holds out certain possibilities. Sometimes the possibility created is so devastating that all parties will hold back from its use. Frequently, in such cases special arrangements are made so that the social business of disputes and conflict between capital and labour can continue without catastrophic damage to the instruments of production: steel workers will allow a blast-furnace to be gradually cooled and miners will allow safety maintenance during a strike. Sometimes highly complex arrangements are made to guard against such accords breaking down: old aero engines have been deployed at power stations to allow a gradual shut-down. Occasionally a tactic is so hugely dangerous that the state simply threatens naked force against its use: Britain's nuclear power stations, for example, have armed guards and the military have passed through attempted picket lines. Tactical choices, however, are never determined by simply the form of production but also by its social organisation.

The organisation of work

Even within the same technical production work may be socially organised in different ways. Particular economic systems, such as capitalism, need do little to affect the technical processes of production but can do much to alter the social arrangements. Tactical choices may also be constrained by this social division of labour.

Particularly interesting is the degree of specialisation and interdependence of the production process and the distribution of skills. An interdependent, co-ordinated production process such as vehicle manufacture means that a stoppage at one point affects production at other points on the line. On the other hand, if vehicle production is instead organised by unit production then the tactical implications of withdrawing labour from units is different, since the work process may continue unhindered on other units. Generally where a form of labour is integral to a co-ordinated production process its withdrawal or manipulation will have a direct impact without recourse to additional tactics such as picketing.

Where manufacture is organised so as to depend upon skilled craftsmen for production or maintenance, the importance of their labour to production means that even the most limited industrial action will have some impact. Strike action by welders, for example, in the manufacture of central-heating systems in Hull resulted in other departments being affected by lay-offs. The threatened national strike over pay of maintenance fitters in flour-making in 1980 had the potential to bring all flour-milling in the country to a halt.

Labour substitution is clearly an option in areas where organisation has made skill requirements either low, easy to transfer, or other skilled workers easily available. However, not all work traditionally classified as unskilled or semi-skilled is amenable to direct labour substitution. In the water or coal industries, the production process requires skill and knowledge for reasons of safety and the protection of the production process. In those industries, as well, detailed local knowledge – of a face, of a set of taps and switches – may also be irreplaceable. The knowledge is acquired from experience and will not be mechanically transferable. In other areas, such as data processing, manual dexterity may not be easily substituted, and certain work situations may require detailed, caring knowledge of particular clients. Even assuming that direct labour substitution is plausible in terms of formal skill requirements, there is no guarantee that the social integration of production will be satisfactory. For example, there is no guarantee that the use of blacklegs in a light engineering factory can maintain quality or levels of output, nor that troops can effectively substitute in a major waste disposal or collection strike. Furthermore, the ability of the military to act as substitute labour has declined considerably in the post-war period as more jobs have become technically specialised.

The spatial organisation of labour may also be of critical importance to tactics, especially to the degree of worker solidarity. In certain industries, such as coal mining and dockwork where the degree of labour mobility into and out of other employment is low, these ties of solidarity are especially strong. In coal mining organisation into face teams further enhances solidarity. Similarly, the growth of 'factory offices' and large computer centres in the civil service has increased solidarity among some groups of civil servants. On the other hand, lorry drivers and certain service workers are geographically isolated, and tactics must therefore attempt to co-ordinate widely dispersed workers.

Finally, the time-organisation of work is important. The degree to which shiftworkers or those working large amounts of overtime can participate in union organisation or certain types of industrial action may be problematic, and seasonal and part-time working affect available tactics. For example, on some occasions part-time workers have been loath to participate in action, especially selective actions falling during their limited work periods.

Representation

The selection of tactics by management and workers may also depend upon the relative weight of different representational forms among workers and, perhaps to a lesser extent, management. Management, of course, is not normally as dependent as labour upon an immediately available organisation to defend its interests if only because these interests are protected by the structural dynamics of a capitalist economy. On the other hand, it is only workplace organisation which confers upon workers a degree of power resembling that of capital and its managers. At a national level the organisation of the collective interests of either capital or labour into representational forms has been equally problematic from the point of view of influencing government tactics in disputes. We have also already mentioned how the historically fragmented nature of capital in Britain has presented political problems for the pursuit of state economic planning, thereby presenting national political problems over the tactics of industrial conflict.

A few key organisational characteristics of unions especially affect the choice of tactics during industrial conflict: these include density of unionisation; the number of unions; non-union representation; the nature of unions; inter-union alliances at the workplace and beyond; the flexibility of union structures; and the degree and nature of politicisation of unions. Some of these factors can be illustrated by recent developments in the civil service. The civil service is represented by 9 unions, some of which are multi-grade, others of which are single grade; some organise lower-grade clerical workers, others top civil servants; they are both professional and industrial in orientation. For the purpose of general policy they are loosely associated in a Council of Civil Service Unions (CCSU) though a considerable number of workers are outside any union. When, therefore, the unions rejected the 1981 pay offer, tactics were immediately negotiated among the several unions and had to meet the agreement of all, particularly those which would bear the brunt of the chosen activity. Secondly, they were co-ordinated by a CCSU policy committee, which remained both disproportionately representative of the unions and slow-moving. However specially created local CCSUs were given operational responsibility for the dispute and indicated the civil service unions' ability to make organisational changes in response to circumstances. A great deal of the dispute, however, was conducted by activists looking over their shoulders at the less militant union members and non-union members. The continued reliance upon selective rather than all-out action was due to concern about taking the more moderate membership along. The gentleness of the picketing on the day of all-out action was due largely to a fear of losing members and further antagonising non-members; non-members therefore limited to a degree the success of some action.

Another interesting example of the way in which union organisation affects tactics is the case of multi-occupational, or general, unions in which secondary action of some sort is more readily forthcoming because both primary and secondary workers are in the same or allied unions. NATSOPA, for example, includes newspaper ink-makers and delivery drivers, as well as (semi-skilled and un-skilled) printers. SOGAT, in general printing, includes printers, paper-makers and delivery drivers. Stopping supplies in these in-dustries is usually very effectively arranged within and between unions, and picketing is quite symbolic. Similarly T & G production workers are readily supported by T & G drivers, and AUEW ma-chine toolmakers are generally supported by AUEW operators of those machines. Such co-operation may be less likely where second-ary workers in a dispute belong to a different union. In such cases secondary picketing may be the tactic needed to achieve co-opera-tion. During a local government dispute in 1980, for example, NALGO members originally worked during a NUPE strike although many were quite happy not to do so once NUPE manned a picket line. Indeed, secondary unions will sometimes not instruct, or advise, their members to co-operate unless there is picketing.

It is possible also to contrast the organisational capacity of unions to absorb change and, therefore, pursue effective tactics. The ISTC, for example, seemed unable to respond to the new forms of organ-isation or to incorporate new local leaders who had emerged during the 1980 steel strike. On the other hand, the NUM Yorkshire Area did register the impact of the 1969-72 strikes at local leadership level.

Management, of course, has its own organisational forms: industry-specific organisations such as the Engineering Employers' Federation (EEF) or the National Federation of Building Trades Employers; general organisations such as the CBI; occupational associations such as the Institute of Personnel Management. While these organisations provide political representation, information and expertise, they generally provide little active intervention in tactical choices in specific disputes. The CBI, however, in 1980 did urge employers generally to adopt tactics of solidarity in disputes. Again, during the 1980 steel strike it was the British Independent Steel Producers Association (BISPA) which took out an injunction against secondary picketing. Legal proceedings under the aegis of an association in that instance minimized possible opprobrium directed by workers against individual firms. Similarly the Institute of Directors has actively encouraged its members to resist union pressures and, if necessary, use the provisions of the 1980 Employment Act. In the engineering industry the EEF has long been an activist force and often advises its members about tactics during disputes.

The organisation of capital

While capital, therefore, may find associations useful, far more important to the prosecution of disputes is its physical, corporate, and managerial structure. Some arrangements for capital are more vulnerable to industrial action than others, and different arrangements suggest different tactics. Capital in the form of physical assets, for example, may be spread across different work sites, not all of which are necessarily in dispute simultaneously. Where production and even physical assets themselves are transferable among sites, management has a tactical advantage.

Corporate and financial organisation are also important. If, for example, there is a major interruption of normal trading at a single unassociated firm, cash-flow problems may well ensue. Whether management can locate extra finance to ensure business survival will be critical to management's handling of the dispute. If there is no immediate cash-flow crisis, the appropriate tactic could be simply to sit out a strike, assuming that the costs of industrial stoppage can be offset in the longer term. An associated company may or may not have further resources to draw upon as a result of flexible financing within the group, or group assistance in locating outside finance. Where individual managements of firms within larger companies are given responsibilities to maintain financial autonomy, certain management and labour tactical manoeuvres have clear implications. Firms in which there have been recent large capital investment may be more dependent upon a constant cash flow to service their debts. Preventing production or distribution can produce a financial crisis for such a company especially during a recession. In some of the disputes we have examined workers have not clearly understood such imperatives, believing that recent investment meant that the company was therefore thriving. As a result they have sometimes misjudged their tactics to the point of forcing redundancies and closures of plants by firms impelled to avoid financial collapse.

Management structure can have more general implications for industrial tactics. A holding company with a decentralised management structure is unlikely to constrain industrial relations policy except in very general terms, but where management and personnel functions are centralised then specific central policies will bear upon local disputes.

Picketing and secondary industrial action continue to serve as very useful forms of pressure on local management irrespective of corporate and financial structure. The extent and effectiveness of such tactics are, however, variable. They depend in part on the history of capital structures and in part on trade-union organisation. The containerisation of freight transport, for example, required enormous capital investment which was undertaken by multiple companies under the control of vertically integrated international shipping interests. The result is that any but the most comprehensive disruption may be circumvented by transfer of work, and the capacity to divert capital in the form of single container units. Whether trade-union solidarity would be adequate to resist a concerted switching of work is as yet unclear, but both secondary action and picketing would be relevant labour tactics in response to such management decisions.

Supply and distribution

Finally, characteristics of supply and distribution affect tactics in industry. First, the nature of supply into an industry whose workforce is in dispute is critical. Where several key supplies exist, considerable tactical effectiveness may result from halting the delivery of any one of them. For example, if in power stations with coal stocks hydrogen can be excluded, the coal cannot be burned. In certain manufacture oxygen is critical and can impede production though materials are to hand. The non-delivery of key supplies may be achieved by a variety of tactical means such as blacking at the producing factory or picketing drivers, although the degree of driver unionisation and solidarity and the possibility of resort to other transport is critical. Where a striking workforce is located in a key supply industry there are also tactical ramifications. For example, if the supply is from several sources, if sources are multiple, the strikers have less tactical power or, as in the steel strike, secondary picketing may be required. Where the supply constitutes a monopoly, the importance of the strike is considerable. Thus, strikes in public utilities such as water and electricity threaten devastating outcomes. While a coal strike may seem less threatening because of alternative energy sources, such as oil and gas, in fact facilities cannot often be converted from coal to oil so that power station and generators are in fact dependent upon coal supplies alone. In transport, with the growth of road freight traffic, the impact of a rail strike, though considerable, is less than it might have been previously. A more complicated situation arose during the 1980 steel strike in relation to engineering. In Sheffield, a city in which both industries are well represented, tension inevitably arose between steel-producing and steel-using unions because of the major effect of steel stoppages upon engineering employment. It may have been the critical role of steel for engineering which resulted in engineering unions requesting picketing rather than agreeing to black, and in fact a considerable leakage of steel into engineering occurred during the steel strike.

Conversely, the nature of custom for an industry in which a workforce is in dispute is critical. Whether an industry is likely to lose its customers is important, and the elasticity of custom is related to whether alternative, competitive supplies are available. Thus in a period of long-term uncertainty about oil prices and coal import controls, the coal industry and its workforce is less endangered by industrial action than in a period of low oil prices and free market energy policy. Much custom is held under conditions of specified delivery dates, which give employers a mechanism with which to discipline the workforce and the workforce a tool with which to bargain with the employer. Construction projects, for example, usually have strict completion dates. In one strike in a Sheffield sweet factory, the large order from a company known to stick strictly to delivery dates served as an incentive to both sides to settle quickly. The threat of losing customers, due to halted production or blacked output, is obviously increased in a recession where markets are scarce and closely guarded.

Whether supplies are delivered and production dispatched is especially related to the organisation of transport. Picket lines may be aimed as much, or more, at drivers as at the inside workforce. Transport may be organised as a company fleet, or by the use of external haulage firms of various sizes. The most relevant characteristic of these various transport arrangements, however, is usually the level of union organisation and the relation of the drivers' union to the union of workers in dispute. So, for example, in a dispute in a small engineering firm in Sheffield, where unionised steel workers refused to load supplies, small non-unionised haulage firms nevertheless located and drove in steel, which was also on occasion taken in small quantities into the factory by company vans. In a larger dispute, unionised drivers refused to cross picket lines with oxygen, though a few hauliers and company service vehicles were still delivering materials.

Finally, whether certain groups of workers are willing and able to strike effectively depends upon whether they can 'disaggregate' their output and target their action so as to affect certain customers and not others. While some 'selective action' is directed towards a discriminating manipulation of costs to the employer and workforce, some action is selective primarily in respect of customers or clients. Thus, health workers attempt to exempt emergency cases from their actions and the civil servants targeted powerful commercial and political interests rather than welfare recipients. The National Gas Committee of NALGO resisted an extended withdrawal of labour over showroom privatisation partly because selective interruption of gas supplies selectively on an industrial/domestic basis was extremely difficult in practice. Target-ability is especially important in the public sector where an industry or service serves a wide range of individual physical and social needs rather than private business.

Tactical choices and the state

In addition to those constraints on tactical choices created by the work situation the activity of the state may also have an effect. State activities in four main areas are important: those of macro-economic policy, its role as a major employer of labour, its provision of essential services and support for infrastructural industries and finally through its legal framework. Such activities operate upon objective characteristics of production and distribution, create other material constraints, and affect the understanding, consciousness, and will of management and unions.

In the area of economic policy incomes policy, for example, partly highlighted and partly created problems of shopfloor militancy. As the corporatist basis of incomes policy tended to integrate the union leadership into a tripartite consensus, the function of opposition was transposed to the shopfloor. As incomes policy became a virtually permanent feature of the economic scene unofficial strikes were accompanied, perhaps even superseded, by large-scale, frequently official strikes relating to incomes policy. The neo-liberal economic policy of Mrs Thatcher's government has also structured disputes and tactics. Rising levels of unemployment have resulted in disputes over redundancy, and the fact that recession has forced closures in multi-plant private industry companies has created an objective need for secondary action. However, high levels of fear and demoralisation have paradoxically discouraged such picketing. Current policy towards the public sector has to a very substantial degree concentrated disputes in that area.

The state as employer, direct or indirect, has had a role in influencing disputes and tactics. Incomes policy and cash limits have both had direct practical consequences for those in state employment. Incomes policy, closely administered in the public sector, directly incited the miners' and public service strikes of the 1970s, and the winter of discontent in 1979-80. Revisions of incentive schemes have, in the 1980s, given rise to numerous local disputes. Generally the state as employer, applying a relatively consistent policy, provides an incentive to united union action against public sector policies.

Because the state has responsibility for the delivery of a wide range of essential services and for continued production in vital infrastructural industries, the state must deal with the consequences of interruptions in those sectors immediately, not simply through general and long-term measures. The state, therefore, draws upon parts of its labour force to substitute for other parts which are withdrawn in what has come to be called 'contingency planning'. It is not possible to substitute equally effectively in all areas, and the state as policy-maker and employer carefully avoids confrontations which the state as contingency-planner cannot deal with; strikes in electricity and water supply, for example. The ease with which different public-sector workers achieved a settlement during the first three years of Mrs Thatcher's government has an uncanny correlation to the ranking of these industries on the Cabinet Contingency Committee's emergency list. However, troops have been used recently to substitute for striking dustmen and firemen. There are numerous tactical implications. First, if the state is able to substitute, workforces might either refrain from strike action or consciously plan strike action to minimise ease of substitution and maximise its cost. The 1980 fire dispute did the latter by the adoption of unannounced day-long strikes. Where substitutes are barracked in contained areas or equipment is commandeered to separate sites, secondary picketing becomes possible. In these instances, government is actively intervening to alter the 'normal' structures of production and distribution and so alter tactical responses. Such government responses are similar to certain private management tactics which alter structures. For example, when private management switches production from a site in dispute to a working site, strikers are faced with an increased need to secondary picket.

Finally, the state intervenes though the construction of legal frameworks in which disputes are conducted and tactics selected. Such legal frameworks have ideological, as well as deterrent and punitive effects. Law, as has already been suggested, does not necessarily dictate tactics. Civil (and criminal) law is not applied without large discretionary elements; it allows but does not demand that actions be taken against transgressors. This issue will be taken up time and again as we proceed with our analysis.

Disputes as process

Whilst it is important to emphasise how the organisation of production and distribution determine the range of dispute tactics available to further a trade dispute, any discussion of objective constraints must be complemented by the recognition that each dispute has its own 'natural history'. The evolution of a dispute is charted by individuals, constrained by the social and physical factors governing their work, but according to differential perceptions of circumstances and in response to changing circumstances. Any theory of objective constraints needs modification since tactical choices are in reality made according to the beliefs, goals, and interactions of participants.

Certain features of the choices management and unions make in response to one another govern the progress of industrial action. Whilst some courses of action on either side may appear to be conciliatory, others may escalate the dispute because they directly confront strikers or sharpen the pressures on management, or because they involve previously excluded workers or managements. For example, the threat to sack striking train drivers was a clear escalation of the British Rail dispute in 1982, though in the end it may have contributed, along with the refusal of the TUC to give support, to ASLEF's return to work. The intensification or extension of blacking is likewise an escalation. Because the balance of power in disputes is constantly changing, tactics employed at the beginning and end of disputes may differ radically. A chain of tactics producing counter-tactics is always a possibility, particularly in sectors where the more traditional strike tactic is held in reserve against alternative industrial action. Initial choices also foreclose possibilities. Total withdrawal of labour, for example, decreases the likelihood of subsequent limited action, such as overtime bans. Of course the use of the law itself may become an important element of response and counter-response in industrial disputes. The resort to law may be undertaken in response to the use of certain tactics, possibly those with most disruptive impact on production and distribution but possibly those which managements regard as politically unacceptable. The use of legal procedure may, however, be abjured precisely because of the subsequent disruption and mobilisation it may elicit. Other state interventions, such as the use of troops, may have a similar impact.

Unions and management which make these changing tactical choices in industrial disputes are not, however, homogeneous entities. Both are comprised of numerous decision-makers with different interests and resources. The different levels at which disputes arise and are pursued generate characteristic problems. For example, where disputes arise out of the breakdown of bargaining by national negotiating bodies, both unions and management face the problem of trying to co-ordinate a dispute from above. The aggregation of large groups of people in different contexts presents problems of agreed tactics, whilst local disputes do not face an equivalent problem of diversity and fragmented identity of the workforce. In national disputes each side may also employ a strategy of trying to maintain its own solidarity while dividing the unity of the other side. The tactics selected in a national pay campaign may well include a degree of flexibility in recognition of different local circumstances and in an attempt to maximise unity around the general campaign. Such themes have been most evident in the public sector during the first two years of Mrs Thatcher's government.

Unions, as democratic mass-membership organisations with multiple levels of autonomy, clearly illustrate the importance of internal organisation to the selection of dispute tactics. The shopfloor, the shopfloor activist, the local official, the intermediate official and the national official all tend to have different perspectives on dispute goals and tactics, especially in a locally based and politically fragmented union. Management often uses these differences to further its own interests. Private manufacturing management often pursues discussions with national union officials, actively enlisting the latter in the settlement of local disputes, sometimes against the wishes of strikers or even local union officials. We observed such arrangements on a number of occasions, and some managers were very well informed of conflict and differences within union structures that would emerge in this manner. It is not unusual for shop stewards to adopt the tactic of either allowing or denying full-time officials a platform at mass meetings, knowing full well that in order to stay within agreed procedures the full-time official is often obliged to recommend a return to normal working.

Groups of workers who take industrial action before having exhausted negotiating procedures cannot be sure of support from their union executives, and may even prefer a limited strategy which does not depend on such support being granted. Within one white-collar union, organised at a large Humberside engineering employer for example, the local branch was in breach of union rules investing substantial sums of money into a secret fighting fund. The attitude of the branch executive committee was clearly in favour of disruptive action that could force their employer to settle early, without involving full-time area officials in procedures that had the effect of delaying action and removing negotiations outside of the workplace. There are many other examples where unofficial committees, especially in the port-related transport industries, actively influence union policy in disputes through national delegate conferences.

In general we can say that union tactics will be shaped according to the locus of power within trade unions and through the sanctions that can be brought against employers in dispute. But it should be recognised that the effectiveness of sanctions will depend on unofficial as well as official support.

Management is also organisationally complex and diverse. It is important to identify which management has responsibility for which aspects of operations. The 'sharp end' rests with managers who have regular contact with the shopfloor. More removed from day-to-day industrial relations culture are financial management, which has little direct contact with the production process. These two types of management bring different concerns to disputes and may seek to pursue them in different ways, though in local disputes higher management may not be involved. It is clear that personnel managers, nearer to the practicalities of everyday industrial relations, are much less eager to use the law against workers in disputes than higher operational management and directors. They are concerned about subsequent industrial relations.

In larger companies, responsibility for handling a major dispute is often shared; the possibility for conflict between the periphery and centre therefore emerges with the final management decision resting with the board. It is here, as well as occasionally at lower levels, that special consideration will be given to the vulnerability of operations and the desire to either buy industrial peace or risk a dispute. It is here also that non-industrial relations considerations will enter into calculations. Attitudes to shareholders' interests and company reputation within the market-place regarding orders, reliability, supply of essential components, etc. may be important in shaping management response. In the course of the research one senior industrial relations director of a highly profitable British-based international engineering company remarked how he could easily understand the attitude of Sir Michael Edwardes at British Leyland, and that if he himself were responsible for a company which was making heavy losses he also might 'take the unions on'. The management attitude that the company has everything to gain from an industrial dispute is not so rare in an economic climate of severe recession where cost-cutting and rationalisation of work practices have to be imposed. Sometimes management which has traditionally acted in a benevolent way is only too aware of the need to re-establish its authority. The adoption of an aggressive negotiating stance, or abrasive style in handling disputes sometimes is adopted to signal to the workforce what is at stake in the longer term.

Tactics and the law

We have argued that the tactics employed in industrial disputes are primarily a response to structures of industrial production and their social organisation within the macro-economy. Particular tactics can achieve political prominence, and in part be encouraged by government economic policies and strategies. On the basis of this argument the 1980 Employment Act provisions would not be expected to be the major determinant of tactics. However, in the complex process of an unfolding industrial dispute, the Act may enter either as a deliberate, punitive management counter-tactic or as a general deterrent to activity which some industrial settings seem to demand. Part 2 of the book examines in detail the impact of the secondary action and picketing provision of the Act on industrial disputes during the first two years after its enactment, at least in our own research areas.

To close Part 1 the next chapter is devoted to state responsibility for policing industrial disputes. Law enforcement has its own distinct character in relation to industrial disputes and concern with the law and order aspects of picketing was an important antecedent to the passage of the 1980 Act. The past two years have not witnessed quite the same visible policing of major disputes as some previous years. Nevertheless it is important to consider recent policing of disputes since this may prefigure future activity. The relationship between the police and other state agencies, changing police attitudes to public order, the nature of police autonomy, the organisational structure of individual forces and the exercise of discretionary powers can all have a bearing on the conduct of disputes and their tactical outcomes.

5
Policing industrial disputes

If one were to search for a single event which led to the picketing provisions of the 1980 Employment Act it would be the picketing carried out by the National Union of Mineworkers at Saltley Coke Depot during their 1972 national strike. Apart from the public and political aspects the event also had a profound effect on the thinking of those agencies of the state charged with maintaining order. At Saltley the police were overwhelmed by sheer numbers. Most immediately this raised questions about the capacity of the police to provide mutual aid to each other: a question which rumbled on throughout the 1970s until the need for a more radical solution was dramatically demonstrated by the riots in the St Paul's area of Bristol in 1980. It also raised doubts about the political support available to the police during such clashes: rumours still circulate within the police about how senior Home Office personnel were 'not available' when police commanders sought advice during the Saltley incident.

Most fundamentally Saltley raised the spectre that an industrial dispute would become a threat to the state itself. Such a possibility is initially difficult to comprehend in the political context of post-war Britain – the success of a quarter century of policing had been precisely to remove such a possibility from the political agenda. Yet, the pre-eminence of the police as the only maintainers of civil order in Britain is historically much more fragile than very recent experience might suggest. Furthermore, other events during the 1970s, and especially terrorism, were to undermine seriously that pre-eminence. Saltley was seen by the police themselves as a defeat. 'Saltley' entered the vocabulary of policing as a code word for all the problems which a bewilderingly changing world was forcing upon the police. Saltley therefore came to epitomise a series of problems about how the state defended itself and maintained civil order. The police accepted the practical necessity of discussing such problems, though they were also concerned that raising such issues might signal a possible historical failure of police pre-eminence. The wider public myth of picketing, and the political momentum it generated towards legal changes, was therefore treated with caution by the police. Their desire to reassert their old pre-eminence could all too easily be thwarted by clumsy law-making or overt politicisation of their role.

The historical role of the police

The formation of the new police from 1829 onwards created a more general system of policing in Britain of which a major achievement was the depoliticisation of the control of industrial disputes. The police were structured so as not to be direct agents of the state, and they were to claim their authority from 'the law', which was presented as separate from sectional political interests. As long as this separation could be maintained and industrial disputes were controlled by the police, then such disputes posed no political threat to the state and were only a problem when breaches of the normal criminal law obtained. If industrial unrest seemed to be bordering on the revolutionary then this separation could be temporarily laid aside and the army brought in as direct agents of state power. Collapse of police control of industrial conflict, resulting in the use of troops to reassert order (as opposed to act as substitute labour), have in fact been rare: such incidents notably occurred in the period before the First World War, during the general strike, and recently during the Ulster workers strikes. Police control has always been reasserted and the separation of that control from politics reaffirmed. However, this does not mean that from 1829 onwards police control alone has, with some minor interruptions, successfully maintained civil order. First, the dividing line between police and military has been a constantly shifting one and, second, the distinction between legal order and political order has always been fragile and needed reaffirmation on a day-to-day basis. The need to maintain the distinction between police and military operations and between policing and government are the basis of police authority in Britain and therefore twin imperatives of their responses to any proposed changes in the legal control of industrial conflict.

Police and military

The question of how far the police have successfully maintained civil order during industrial disputes cannot be examined simply by looking at those occasions where the army has been called in to maintain order. A recent examination of this problem suggested that periods of industrial conflict which the state perceives as politically threatening led to an increasing militarisation of the police, and an increased role for the military in civil government (Blake, 1979).

By the 1980s the divide between the police and the military in Britain had shifted considerably. Specialised units existed on both sides which eased the difficulties of transition during emergencies. The police had adjusted their tactics of civil control so as to reduce the need for military aid but at the price of themselves adopting a more military-like posture. Finally, structures for co-ordinating police-military operations were considerably improved at both local and national level, and tested out in joint exercises.

Although the police soon established their pre-eminence in dealing with industrial conflict within each force's area, their national pre-eminence was initially hindered by the localised basis of police power. However, various legal changes, the reduction in the number of police forces, and the creation of a national police outlook through institutions such as the Police College, have increased the power of central control over the police (see Morris, 1977). Although the rhetoric of force autonomy remains, central government would now play a significant role in directing police authorities during a national industrial emergency.

In practice the continuing weakness of the mutual aid provisions was dramatically revealed during the Bristol riots when the local police were forced to withdraw to await reinforcements from other forces. The Association of Chief Police Officers (ACPO) subsequently met and recommended a number of changes in mutual aid provisions which were given further impetus by the inner-city riots in the summer of 1981.

One of the problems of mutual aid in the past had been the different traditions, organisation and even command structure in the various police forces. As it happened, central government, as part of war emergency planning, had demanded that each police force organise a stated number of Police Support Units (PSUs) to maintain order after a nuclear attack. In spite of the fact that these units were not permanently constituted, here was an organisational unit common to all forces of a suitable size for rapid deployment elsewhere and with much of the training needed for policing public disorder. As a result PSUs have become the standard unit of mutual aid between forces, and increasingly between divisions of the same force. Senior officers requesting such help will frequently express their needs in terms of so many PSUs. The increasing concern of the police with mutual aid and rapid deployment has meant that a once obscure provision of civil defence provisions has become a key structure of police planning. The number of PSUs in most forces has increased so that almost all the able-bodied younger officers belong to a unit, and have had training in riot control (euphemistically called 'shield training').

These changes in police organisation are very recent. They would undoubtedly be the basis for any future policing response to large-scale industrial disputes, and we have seen them so used in South Yorkshire and Humberside. Although in one sense they are merely a rationalisation of existing trends, such changes do demonstrate the police's determination to keep control of public order. They also, however, have potential implications for future police handling of industrial disputes. The basic *raison d'être* for PSUs and their training and equipment may produce a search for quick solutions born of rapid deployment *élan*. The mere ease of availability of such units makes simple public order solutions to events, such as mass picketing, at least a possibility in the future. In the short run the traditions of policing industrial disputes would probably restrain a police commander from seeking such a solution. However, traditions are not immutable and the local contacts on which they feed are gradually eroded each time PSUs are deployed. A serious industrial dispute which created national policing problems could destroy those traditions by the sheer inflexibility of the police response.

Police separate interest

As we have seen, the police historically have had a quite separate role from other state agencies capable of maintaining order. This separate role has been predicated on a careful nurturing of the belief that they enforce the law rather than the political will of the state.

This belief is in turn dependent upon a more general belief that the law itself is not simply an instrument of political will. Industrial legislation, aimed at altering the balance of forces between labour and capital during disputes, could all too easily undermine the delicate edifice of non-political policing. Whilst the police in general want legislation which clarifies and strengthens their position in times of conflict, this must always be balanced against the need to maintain their general authority. This balance for the police is different than that for the army, the secret intelligence services, the Home Office or the government, and in disputes over new industrial legislation the police have a rather separate interest to protect.

Police response to the 1980 Employment Bill

The Association of Chief Police Officers' (ACPO) evidence to the Commons Select Committee on Employment in March 1980, during the Bill's progress through parliament, sought to minimize police involvement with the new legislation. Generally they appeared to go along with the government's position that since the new law was of a civil nature they were not involved. This statement of general agreement was, however, only a vehicle to try and ensure that police involvement with the new law, civil or not, was minimal. Their primary concern was to exclude any possibility that the police could be involved in collecting the information necessary for civil proceedings. As they put it: 'Hopefully it is not envisaged that police would in any way be caught up in this procedure of furthering civil action on behalf of management.' They were also concerned that regardless of the government's claim that the new law was not criminal, in the end the method of enforcement was the same and carried the same danger that it could 'degenerate into police/striker physical confrontation'. We can guess that ACPO's response to the government's proposals was in fact one of cynicism since they went on to state that this dangerous possibility existed 'even though this is not the declared intention of the Government'.

In general ACPO did everything to highlight the difficulties of using the proposed legislation; presumably in the hope that nobody would, and concluded that 'the enforcement problems of the proposed legislation are daunting indeed.' As for a code of conduct they doubted its effectiveness, questioned its enforceability, and rather derisorily compared it with the Highway Code. ACPO's own position of representing the view of senior officers on matters of operational policing rather than politics prevented them from openly opposing the motivation and ideology of the new law. In fact they managed to raise doubts about both these matters by questioning the operational efficacy of the proposals.

The Police Federation's reaction was rather different. They had long held the view that successive governments' fears of antagonising the trades unions all too often left the police in situations in which they lacked the necessary power or political support to act decisively. The Federation's understandable concern with the welfare of its members, combined with a view of police politics only from the beat, led it on this as on other issues to a much more limited political stance. They wanted a limitation placed on the number and nature of pickets, to be enforced by criminal sanctions. They therefore regarded the government's proposals as 'something of a dog's dinner' and thought that 'A Code of Practice which is not backed by legal sanctions does not appear to have the authority that is required' (*Police*, 1979).

The special case of South Yorkshire police's response to the proposals

During discussion of new legislation the South Yorkshire police were the most outspoken voice in the police service against any new criminal legislation on picketing. This was ironic since the mass picketing which took place at Hadfields in Sheffield during the steel strike and during discussion of the proposals was frequently held out as an example of why new criminal legislation was needed. In part this attitude of senior officers in South Yorkshire reflected that of most senior policemen. However, the exemplary use of the Hadfields incidents by proponents of criminal sanctions made the South Yorkshire force more outspoken because it perceived this as criticism of its handling of the steel strike. Since the Hadfields incidents were, at least in part, a consequence of deliberate tactical decisions by South Yorkshire police commanders, then they had to dispute such exemplary use of the incidents. Unlike Saltley a decade earlier, the South Yorkshire force was not taken totally unawares at Hadfields, nor did it lack available reinforcements. The mass picketing was 'allowed' by police commanders as the most sensible of the options available. Any suggestion, therefore, that these incidents were examples of lack of police control which demonstrated the need for new criminal legislation had to be resisted. Hadfields had to be presented as a successful policing operation. This was the position taken by South Yorkshire officers throughout the debate and most notably when they appeared before the Common's Select Committee.

The ability of South Yorkshire police to play such a prominent role in the debate was of course made easier by the political complexion of South Yorkshire. They may have been challenging some of the ideological presuppositions of the government of the day, but they would receive nothing but support from their immediate political environment. Indeed, the politics of South Yorkshire had probably influenced their original handling of the steel strike, and the force's official attitude towards industrial disputes.

Policing philosophy, industrial disputes and the law

Whilst we cannot talk of a single police response to the proposals put forward by Mr Prior, we can discern a number of general police concerns about any industrial legislation which receive different emphasis from the different constituencies. There is a general desire to avoid any changes which may embroil the police in conflict between labour and capital, and to threaten what the police regard as their neutrality.

At the level of official police policy there is a wish to remain uninvolved in industrial disputes. Senior officers want no special role in industrial disputes and dislike industrial legislation which creates special police powers. They much prefer to depend on general criminal law designed to control public order, violence etc., rather than legislation specifically aimed at industrial disputes. Such a framework allows policing to claim to be solely concerned with any criminal behaviour, regardless of whether this coincidently occurs during an industrial dispute. This has the double advantage of providing the basis for a claim to political neutrality and also allowing for flexibility of police response in industrial disputes. Senior officers we spoke to, therefore, all have an overwhelming desire to maintain the flexibility of discretionary policing. Most lobbied hard at a political level to maintain this in 1980 just as they had done earlier when the Trade Union and Labour Relations Act was being discussed.

Much of police policy at force level towards industrial disputes is understandable as an extension of this philosophy of policing. Furthermore, for the vast majority of industrial disputes this position is viable and workable: discretion is maintained and, as we shall see later, used as part of unofficial bargaining to maintain order. The policy, however, can break down in relation to either major industrial disputes which raise serious public-order problems because of their scale, or in relation to small disputes which because of their political nature produce public-order problems. Such dangers are epitomised in police mythology as 'Saltley' or 'Hadfields', or 'Grunwick'. Such breakdowns of the normal policing of industrial disputes can be minimised as long as police discretion in handling them is maximised: specific police industrial law is therefore unwelcome. Mr Prior's proposals claimed to avoid this problem by shifting the basis to civil law, but the fact that it was specifically industrial law, aimed at events such as picketing, still raised the spectre that the police might suffer by accident the undermining of legal neutrality in industrial disputes.

The above response depends on a fairly sophisticated political vision of policing. As one moves down the command structure the vision becomes less sophisticated generally speaking – indeed the possession, or lack, of this attitude is a good indicator of the likely promotion prospects of policemen especially into the ACPO grades. More junior officers expressed the idea of police neutrality differently: the police are neutral in any dispute as long as they are only enforcing the law. This position ultimately depends on a fairly straightforward positivist legal theory, which sees properly enacted law as standing above and outside the squabbles of civil society even if it originated with them. Such a position is not simple-minded: it recognises for example that there are limits to this process and that it finally depends on no group attempting to enact utterly partial law. However, such a position does assume that in contemporary Britain these limits are not breached, and the threat to the police's position does not come from that direction. Instead the threat to neutrality comes from unclear rules and inadequate methods of enforcement. This is frequently seen cynically by junior police officers as an attempt by politicians to avoid making hard decisions by leaving the police to deal with conflicts without clear rules. Codes of Practice and the like are especially resented as devices for evading the government's proper function of laying down rules and sanctions, and so leaving the police without the necessary power to deal with incidents.

The desire to protect the political neutrality of the police can then lead to contradictory demands within the police service. On the one hand, those who wish to defend neutrality through general laws with discretionary application and, on the other, those who see defence via specific laws with certain application. This conflict is largely mediated by the fact that the two views are contained by formal hierarchical authority, although this may not always be the case. The explanation of this differentiation of view may partly be a straightforward situational response: constables in situations of large-scale public disorder are likely to cherish the idea of clear and unambiguous rules for the particular game since rule-bound 'games' are less dangerous than 'mobs'. However, the hierarchical distribution of the views suggest that they may also be a consequence of organisational structure and this is discussed later.

There is also a general police concern that whatever laws exist their intention should be clear to the potential deviant. This sense of 'clarity' does not conflict with a desire for discretion and generality, so that one senior police officer even described the 'sus' law as a 'model of clarity' in this sense. Clarity of purpose is usually seen to go together with practicality of enforcement. Once again differences as to the practicality of enforcement are discernible between junior and senior ranks, but this time the difference is judgmental not conceptual. The Police Federation would have liked a numerical limitation on the number of pickets to be criminally enforceable in the 1980 Act, because they believed this would have been both clear and enforceable. Senior officers were less clear on this proposal since, whilst they agreed it was clear in purpose, they had doubts about the practical difficulties of enforcement. As one senior officer during our research put it: 'How do you arrest a mass picket and how do you process them afterwards – by hiring a football stadium?'

We found similarly a shared concern that whatever the civil nature of the new law its implications for policing should be recognised. The government's ideological gloss which tended to hide this fact was therefore generally resented.

Police policy and operational control

Ideas as to how industrial disputes should be policed may vary between senior and junior officers, but the location of these different views also reflects the organisational structure and recent history of the modern police. The most visible change in police organisation is that the 117 police forces which existed in England and Wales in 1966 have now shrunk to 43. The divisions of a modern force are frequently bigger, in both geographical area and manpower, than the old borough forces. Changes of these dimensions have necessarily had some important implications for organisational and command structure.

The office of Chief Constable, his deputy and assistants and their staff, have expanded into a managerial headquarters staff. These ACPO level officers usually have no day-to-day command function and see their jobs as planning and management. Divisional Commanders (Chief Superintendents outside the Metropolitan Police) are now responsible for a unit so large that they also are increasingly locked into a managerial function, leaving day-to-day command to sub-divisional commanders. Some forces, such as Humberside, have acknowledged this increasing managerialisation of divisional commanders by articulating a new management and command structure.

These changes, however, are recent and still being worked through by most police forces. There are still plenty of men who remember the old ways and are unhappy about the changes. Sometimes there is resentment of the ACPO officers and their staff: as remote bureaucrats by junior officers and as irrelevant 'tea boys' by commanders on the ground. There is no doubt that modern large police forces need managerial structures and skills, but these are not easily fitted into a hierarchy that historically developed out of the needs of command. ACPO officers, and increasingly Divisional Commanders, may largely carry out managerial functions, but it remains the case that they are also senior command officers. Once an industrial dispute escapes the geographical or resource limits of a sub-division or division then these are the men who begin to exercise control. The career pattern that these men have had to follow to develop the necessary managerial skills means that some of them have had remarkably little command experience. In the inward-looking world of the police service such facts are known and noted. There is then in the contemporary police a cultural divide between the old and the new ways. The divide is mainly age based and so will decline, but it is not entirely so since it is also a divide about the philosophy and purpose of policing.

These differences have implications for the policing of industrial disputes. It is the new men who are most likely to adopt a response to trade unions reflecting national political concerns. The old guard tend to resent in principle the idea that trade unions as such should be treated differently from any other group. At first sight the attitude of some (older) commanders sometimes seems nearer to that of junior officers referred to earlier. In fact all commanders cherish flexibility of response, but the old style responded to immediate, local, events, whilst the new is more concerned with a broader politics. The old style has its origins in smaller forces and home-produced police commanders who knew every nuance of their areas from years of street experience: their methods may sometimes appear rough and crude but are based on a local cunning which usually makes them acceptable. There are still commanders in this mould; the sort of man who during our research stood in front of picket lines and began his policing by saying – 'You know me and I know you.' The new police forces, however, are producing a new type of commander. He is likely to see his career in the police service as a whole, and not just within a small local force. He will have moved jobs frequently and at ACPO level will almost certainly have served in more than one force. Such men think naturally in terms of a national politics of policing, and in any case lack the sort of detailed knowledge on which the old style depended.

For most industrial disputes which have some police involvement, differences such as these are of little importance since they are contained within a single command unit, although we did occasionally observe conflicts within a division, or even sub-division, on how a dispute should be policed. The differences do, however, mean that one cannot generalise about the precise police response to industrial disputes. Different police forces are at different stages of the organisational changes consequent upon amalgamation, and within a force there will be clear differences between different commanders. Such differences can be quite visible and trade-union activists have clear, if not necessarily accurate, views of them.

Differences become most clear during large-scale industrial action which needs response at a force level. On such occasions differences between senior and junior officers, between ACPO officers and commanders in divisions and between new and old style officers can emerge. ACPO officers' attempts to maintain a political flexibility of response may all too easily be seen as vacillation, buck-passing and uncertainty due to lack of operational experience by commanders in divisions. The historical tradition of divisional commander autonomy is not easily overthrown by the new ACPO level, although divisional commanders will ritually defer to the senior officers. Frequently Chief Constables, Deputies or Assistants guide operations by hints and allusions whilst leaving divisional commanders in operational charge on the ground. The final policing of a large scale dispute emerges out of this curious balancing of interests, powers and ideas. A Chief Constable's ideas on how an industrial dispute should be policed may be the most important element, but the final result is unlikely to be simply a product of orders passed down a chain of command. For example, during the steel strike in South Yorkshire the attitude of the Chief Constable and the Assistant Chief Constable (Operations) set the general tone of how the very long dispute was policed. The general policy was not, however, accepted with equanimity by all operational commanders but they were constrained from rebelling on any scale by the knowledge that they would then be 'left to carry the can'. Occasional breaks in the general policy did occur. These were most likely when a relatively junior officer commanding on the ground was left to use his discretion without understanding the subtlety of policy at senior levels.

Policing industrial disputes: the normal case

The vast majority of industrial disputes do not involve the police. Indeed, the only tactics used during a dispute which are likely to involve the police are picketing, demonstrations or marches and certain forms of public lobbying. Furthermore, in spite of the political attention given to it recently, the majority of picketing is not regarded as a problem by the police. It is useful to examine this non-problematic picketing in order to understand how picketing can become a problem for the police.

Police forces do not, in our experience, maintain any regular, systematic intelligence-gathering operation about industrial disputes. Except for rare events, they do not depend on information provided by Special Branch or non-police secret intelligence agencies. Their day-to-day knowledge of industrial affairs is most commonly gleaned from reading newspapers. Apart from this general knowledge, the first specifically police information is usually when a patrolling officer reports the existence of a picket line. Sometimes, although by no means always, this is preceded by a telephone call from the management and very rarely indeed from a trade union. Assuming that this initial contact does not raise immediate fears of violence (and most picket lines do not), then the local police commander's primary need at this stage is for information. This initial search for information is aimed at deciding whether it is a 'normal' dispute which will not present policing problems, or whether there is a danger of its 'going naughty'.

The beat officer first making contact will try and find out about the nature of the dispute, and will often seek the name of a strike leader. An unknown group of pickets is worrying but an identified leader suggests organisation, and organisation can be channelled into co-operation. In fact we often found that this need by the police can lead them to over-emphasise the organisational and planned aspects of many picket lines. This initial contact will be followed by a telephone call to management, or even sometimes a visit, and perhaps a contact with the local trade-union official. If the dispute seems 'normal' then the police response is likely to consist of little more than beat officers keeping a regular eye on the picket line. Additionally both sides of the dispute may be instructed on how they should conduct themselves to keep the dispute 'normal' – e.g. pickets may be told how and when they should picket, and management may be told not to be provocative by driving dangerously through picket lines. For the majority of the picket lines we observed during our research this is the extent of police involvement.

A normal dispute for the police is restricted to an argument solely between a management and the workforce over terms or conditions of work. Picketing is a legitimate tactic within such a dispute providing it is conducted in certain ways. Policing of such picketing will be primarily aimed at maintaining it within this acceptable framework, by building up personal relations with the strikers. Police and pickets will easily fall into a stoical acceptance of the event as just an unfortunate part of their jobs. Both will present the picket as a consequence of forces outside their immediate control (senior officers, management, union officials or the 'system') to be borne with shared patience. The normal picket line of our research was a small group of strikers and policemen standing together, trying to shelter from the rain or snow, with the tedium occasionally relieved by the arrival of a delivery lorry. The archetypical conversation was of a policeman explaining to a picket how cooking foil placed in the boots helped keep feet warm!

A number of things can upset this normality, and some will set positive alarm bells ringing for the police. Any dispute which seems to be political worries the police. This can mean two different things: either that the dispute is not straightforwardly about terms and conditions of work, or outside influences are attempting to politicise a dispute. The most common example of the former concerns disputes about union recognition. The police know that in such cases neither side is likely to give way easily, and picketing is not simply one tactic within an ongoing bargaining process. In such cases picketing may well go on for a long time and pickets may become increasingly frustrated. Such disputes are especially likely to become political in the second sense. Outsiders on a picket line always worry the police. Outsiders for the police, however, are not defined in the same way as 'secondary action' or illegal picketing under the 1980 Employment Act. The police resent any pickets who do not seem to them to have a legitimate reason for being involved, and legitimacy for the police essentially resides in being an employee of the company being picketed. Since the 1980 Act defines illegal picketing in relation to 'place of work' rather than employer then, ironically, the police will sometimes accept as legitimate picketing which is illegal under the Act. Non-employees are 'outsiders', they are not part of the dispute, and their motives can only be to create trouble. Any such outsider will almost invariably be challenged by the police to explain 'what's it got to do with you?' The historical attempt to de-politicize the role of the police in Britain, and the police's own desire to rely on a criminal law which they can present as non-partisan means that they will vigorously resist any attempt to involve an industrial dispute in any broader notion of political action. Industrial disputes for the police ought only to involve employees and employers, any other involvement appearing to be necessarily politically motivated. Outsiders, therefore, worry the police both because their actions are less likely to be constrained by existing relationships with the company and the issues of the dispute, but also because they threaten to undermine the police ability to act neutrally as between capital and labour.

This everyday police concept of who may legitimately be involved in a dispute is different from that underlying the 1980 Act in one important respect. The Act accepts that trade unions, as organisations, can be involved legitimately in disputes, and that certain designated union officials may legally be on a picket line. When conflicts are in industries where unions are clearly identified as parties, for example a national mining or railway strike, then police will accept the presence of union officials. However, in industries such as engineering where small-firm localised disputes predominate then the appearance of a local union organiser on a picket line will often be resented and treated with suspicion by the police. Officially senior officers will accept the political judgment enshrined in the legislation, but most policemen will privately respond on the basis of the everyday police notion of legitimacy. It is hardly surprising then that union officials sometimes complain (and occasionally make official complaints) that the police have objected to their presence on a picket line.

The presence of outsiders was nearly always resented as political interference on the picket lines we observed. The more overtly such people were attempting to politicise a dispute – whether as party politicians or representatives of more extreme groups – then the more police were likely to regard the particular picket line as crossing the borderline between a normal industrial dispute and one which presents special policing problems. Other facts can also potentially have this effect. Large numbers of pickets relative to the numbers being picketed even if there are no outsiders; picketing in a way which causes other policing problems such as on a main arterial road; attempts to block entrances, etc. can all worry the police. How far they do in fact create a new problem depends upon whether the police can quickly negotiate a solution with the pickets. At the heart of the police notion of a normal picket line is an event whose scope and form they can negotiate. Normality both resides in, and is to be judged by, the extent to which pickets and police can negotiate how the picketing is to be conducted.

If a dispute seems a normal one then the police will lay down what they see as acceptable forms and dimensions of picketing. These will vary depending on the type of workforce (they are especially sensitive about picketing of a predominantly female workforce), the location, number of entrances, size of workforce, etc. However, as long as there are no other signs that the dispute is about to 'go naughty' then such matters are negotiable up to a certain point. At a mundane level the negotiability is frequently presented by the police in the form of willingness to allow divergence from what they ought to do in return for co-operation from the pickets. We observed them turning a blind eye to braziers which could be deemed to obstruct the highway; not objecting to slightly more pickets than they had originally asked for and in certain circumstances even ensuring that lorries stopped safely whilst pickets put their case. In this way the police present themselves as reasonable people willing to compromise: compliance is achieved at the psychological level by binding the pickets into a co-operative enterprise with the police. Police control the normal picket line not by enforcing legal rules but by negotiating reasonable compromises. Rule enforcement is, however, always held out as the alternative mode of control which will be adopted if negotiation breaks down. The police desire for flexibility in legislation has its reflection in their mode of handling the normal picket line. Flexibility is the means by which picket lines are maintained within the police concept of the 'normal'.

The 1980 Act, and more especially the Code of Practice on Picketing, was in part aimed at defining acceptable picketing as against unacceptable picketing. We have already noted differences between the police's working notion of 'normal picketing' and the Act's definitions of illegal picketing. Certain aspects of the Code of Practice's definitions of acceptable picketing are, however, much closer to the police notion of the normal: hardly surprising since it was to some extent based on their comments. One aspect of the Code – the suggestion that pickets should be limited to six persons rapidly entered the folk memory. Both management and many workers we have talked to on picket lines believe that this is a restriction in the Act itself and furthermore that it is enforceable by criminal sanctions. The police do not go out of their way to disabuse pickets of such misapprehensions and indeed on some occasions, we have observed, have fostered such beliefs by vaguely referring to 'what the new law says.' Given the complex nature of the 1980 legislation such actions may, of course, have been as much due to ignorance as deliberate attempts to mislead. Generally if pickets believe that they should limit their numbers to six then in most cases it pragmatically suits the police not to disabuse them. However, this does not mean that the police necessarily welcome the existence of the

Code. Its suggestion on the practical aspects of picketing in part reflect the kind of suggestions the police would have traditionally made for the average normal picket line (such as restricting pickets to, say, half a dozen), but not all cases are the average. Although legally speaking the Code may be only offering advice, its form and origin make it look suspiciously like law to strikers. There is a danger then that the Code may undercut the flexible negotiation based upon reasonableness by which the police control normal picketing. The Code may even on occasions threaten the reasonableness of pickets in a normal dispute – it is surprising how many strikers we talked to wanted picket lines of seven since the 1980 legislation! Apart from the cases where pickets themselves act on the basis of the Code as discussed above, the police largely ignore the Code and act as they have traditionally done. Ironically, the most common reference by the police to the Code, in the disputes which we have observed, has been as part of those rules which will have to be enforced if negotiation does not produce a reasonable solution : 'Well the Code says six but as long as everybody behaves sensibly I will allow one or two more as long as it doesn't get out of hand.'

Other aspects of the Code such as advice on picket leadership, armbands, etc., if followed, would demand a form of organisation or equipment which would necessarily involve union officials in picketing; but such involvement in many cases is precisely what the police wish to minimise. Indeed, such involvement in some cases would move the picketing out of the normal category for the police as already explained. These aspects of the Code, because they reflect a view of industrial disputes as being between politically organised labour and capital, are antithetical to the police desire to maintain as much picketing as possible in their normal category by keeping it de-politicized. Legislation, because it is generated out of a national political process, will respond to those unusual disputes which are abnormal precisely because they in some way threaten the political balance of the state. By legislating for such events governments run the risk of unintentionally undermining police ability to prevent the vast majority of industrial disputes ever becoming abnormal in this sense.

The abnormal cases

Not all industrial disputes and picketing fit within the police notion of the 'normal'. Some disputes break the boundaries of the 'normal' because the police are unable to maintain a successfully negotiated framework. Other disputes are so large or political in nature that they cannot be handled in the normal way. The police's greatest fear is that a dispute may shift to this later category in the way that the Grunwick case did. Some police commanders talk as if these are stages in a progression which only successful policing will prevent, and all policemen know that any dispute is a social process which can alter its form and, as already explained, will carefully watch for what they regard as indicators of change.

If any signs emerge that a dispute is beginning to 'go naughty' then the police will respond by replacing negotiable suggestions with firm instructions and will increasingly refer to rule enforcement. This firm attitude may also be reinforced by deliberate displays of strength, and the appearance of more senior officers at the picket line. In such cases we have seen both union and management representatives called to the police station and told how the police expect them to behave in the future. The object of this activity is initially to try and force the behaviour of workers and management back into the police category of the normal.

For the police the most obvious sign that a dispute is no longer 'normal' will be when outsiders appear on picket lines, or when mass picketing takes place. Mass picketing not only means that the dispute is taking on a political dimension but it presents the police with an unpredictable policing problem. Allegations of police over-reaction or heavy-handedness most frequently relate to mass picketing. Operationally police intelligence about likely numbers is often surprisingly poor, and, in erring on the side of caution, sometimes accept at face value the inflated rhetoric of the mass-picket organisers. Organisationally the police commander will often respond to a planned mass picket by requesting extra men and in many police forces these will come in quite large units with public order training. He may for example be sent a Police Support Unit, or part of a headquarters special group (called various things in different forces such as Special Patrol Group, Technical Support Echelon etc.). The result can be that a small industrial dispute may have a mass picket of twenty people heavily outnumbered by police.

The danger is that special group police units can develop a danger-ous hard-hitting *esprit de corps* and may not share the local police's interest in returning to flexible control. Some forces are very well aware of these dangers. South Yorkshire police, for example, does not have a separate headquarters division but instead uses small support units based on operational divisions, and Humberside changes the membership of their special unit regularly to prevent the build up of any elite identity. Even if successful such measures still do not obviate the fact that in small local disputes such police units are still seen as outsiders. Tactically a police commander will want to be able to handle any eventuality during a mass picket, and conventional police wisdom is that if arrests are to be made in such situations the police should ideally have a 2:1 superiority in num-bers. The effect for the pickets can sometimes appear to be a formidable display of police force.

Arrests are quite likely to occur in such situations if only because the police have the capacity to effect them: something they fre-quently do not have in the day-to-day policing of picket lines and another reason for the negotiating style of achieving compliance. Whether arrests do occur will depend very much on the senior officer on the spot. Why arrests are made is often very difficult to explain. Excluding the very rare cases of, say, outright serious violence then many arrests on picket lines are for obstructing either the highway or a police officer in the execution of his duty. Both of these charges could be made on all sorts of occasions during a picket. From what has already been said it is clear that the picket must in some way have diverged from the police view of the 'nor-mal', and that the senior officer must have enough men available to effect arrests with safety. Beyond that the missing element is that the senior officer on the spot feels that 'something isn't quite right' or 'something is going to happen.' Such feelings do not lead to a deliberate decision to make arrests, but rather to a decision to take firm controlling action and if necessary arrest those who will not co-operate. Arrests will then frequently follow and be justified on the basis of the pickets' behaviour.

Not only is the process leading to arrests on picket lines often difficult to explain but, by the same token, it can be difficult to predict. Pickets are often mystified as to why on one occasion their behaviour will produce a negotiable response, and on another, and to them similar occasion, will produce a display of force and end up with arrests. The difference may, of course, simply reside in the number of police available in the two cases, but more often it is a result of the different understandings which the two sides have and the shared misunderstandings which can result. Fellow union members joining a picket line will not necessarily be seen as in any significant way altering the situation by pickets, but for police they are outsiders who radically change the policing problem. A small 'mass' picket may be a simple show of solidarity, but to the police it is a dangerous change for which they can see little purpose except to intimidate those attempting to cross the picket line. Not all such signs are misunderstood: many pickets will turn away offers of help from students or left political groups knowing what the effect will be on the police response. However, the possibility of misunderstanding is great enough to mean that any misinformation can radically change the policing response.

In spite of the allegations of telephone tapping and the work of the Special Branch, police intelligence about strikers' intentions can often be very limited. Management put much greater effort into discovering strike plans, and in some disputes we examined had actually planted their own men in the strike organisation. In some cases then management is the best source of information for the police, but not necessarily of impartial, or reliable, information. We observed clear cases where management fed misinformation to the police in an attempt to produce (not always successfully) a particular police response. Obviously the police are well aware of this danger and will sometimes become highly sceptical of information coming from some employers. However, the general point is that the police frequently lack reliable information and often act on the basis of rumours built out of strikers' bravado. The police will sometimes see danger signals which later information would have dispelled. Although some senior police officers will claim to have good contacts with trade unions these claims almost always turn out to amount to very little. Most trade-union officials have virtually no contact with the police and regard them with suspicion.

Police contact with management is often better than with trade unions, partly because the organisational structure of companies is more like that of the police themselves and so easier to liaise with. Police commanders have no difficulty identifying who is in charge of a company's response during a dispute. The democratic basis of trade-union structures, on the other hand, can make it difficult to

identify such a figure and indeed no individual may possess equivalent authority. We often found local commanders frustrated by the
difficulties of identifying who was 'in charge' on the union side of
a dispute and suspicious when local union officials were unable to
give commitments about future actions. Yet their ability to forward
plan in terms of manpower or support requirements is seriously
impaired if no information exists on likely numbers of pickets.

More generally there is a feeling among trade unionists that when
things begin to get difficult on a picket line then the police lean
towards the interests of management. The easier communication
with management partly explains this. Certainly we observed some
management quite blatantly attempting to use the police for their
own interests: for example, by making telephone calls exaggerating
the scale of picketing, etc. to try and elicit a police response which
would deter the strikers. Police commanders, however, were well
aware of such tactics and usually did not react. They especially
resented some management's enthusiasm for arrests made during a
dispute and later refusal to appear as prosecution witnesses once the
dispute was concluded. On occasions we know that police commanders firmly lectured some managements on their future conduct.
Such extreme management behaviour is rare but, of course, precisely likely to occur during the most bitter disputes.

The civil nature of the 1980 Employment Act has made it easier
for the police to refer management to legal advisers if they complain
about picketing *per se*. However, once legal action is pursued it is
very difficult for the police not to be involved. The serving of a writ
under the Act, against mass secondary picketing at a Yorkshire
company, involved a very large policing operation as a precaution
against possible reaction. In such a case the resort to law, from the
police point of view, may actually be provocative and for the police
the disadvantage with civil law is that they do not exercise the
discretion over when it will be used. Similarly, the issuing of writs
to terminate a factory occupation depended, to some small part, on
intelligence provided by the police. More generally all the police
commanders we spoke to accepted that they would in the end have
to respond to a management request for assistance in lawfully getting
goods in or out of a factory. This would also apply to maintaining
certain minimum public services such as the free movement of
supplies or ambulances in and out of hospitals during a health
workers' strike, for example. Such access may be a legal entitlement

but pickets are likely to see such an involvement as against their interests. In order to avoid open confrontation the police will sometimes help management gain access at unusual hours or by subterfuge. Such help is the very stuff of which stories of police bias are built. In the end some trade-union tactics, if effective, are unlawful and, in the end, the police will enforce the law. The limits of the neutrality available under the rule of law depends on whether law is seen as partial or not.

Policing the *causes célèbres*

Most of the policing of industrial disputes discussed so far has not included the kind of events which become the *causes célèbres* leading to industrial legislation. It was the very large mass picketing at Saltley or Hadfields, the potential volcanoes such as Grunwick, or the flying pickets of the miners, the building workers, or the steel strikers which played this historic role. However, these sort of events present quite different policing problems from other picketing and are also very rare. For example, although the steel strike lasted for four months in South Yorkshire Police area, and 173 premises were picketed in that period, nearly all were handled in the ways already discussed. On only two days was a very large mass picket organised, and even then not for the whole of each day.

These kinds of events primarily pose all the problems of large-scale public-order policing. They will necessarily involve large bodies of police, many of whom will have to be borrowed from other forces under the mutual aid provisions. The command of such an operation will almost certainly be taken by the Assistant Chief Constable (Operations), if not by the Chief Constable himself. Operationally the greatest problem for any force will be providing the logistical back-up for such a large body of men.

The great problem for the police in dealing with such large scale events is a tactical conflict over whether their primary emphasis is to be on enforcing the law, or instead on maintaining order. On a number of such occasions the police have been heavily criticised, especially in parliament, for not enforcing the law rigorously enough. Some MPs seem to have mistakenly believed that this was because the law needed changing so that arrests would be made. This in fact has never been the problem. The 1,648 pickets, who the South Yorkshire police estimated as being present in Vulcan

Road during the mass picketing of Hadfields on St Valentine's Day 1980, were all potentially liable to a charge of obstructing the highway if nothing else. There are in fact numerous laws that the police could use in such situations. The problem is not whether an arrest is technically possible, but rather whether it is desirable and tactically feasible.

Chief Officers of Police will always define their primary task as 'maintaining the Queen's peace'. Essentially this acknowledges that rule enforcement must always be discretionary within the overall purpose of maintaining civil order. In spite of popular beliefs large crowds, such as a mass picket, are by no means necessarily violent. Many senior police officers will decide that the first goal of policing in such a situation is to achieve a stability which minimises the risk of large scale violence. Police and picket lines will be drawn up and the physical arrangements of numbers of police at strategic points will take precedence over that of dialogue, but the primary task will still remain that of containment. Any attempt at large-scale arrests would be counterproductive, and almost certainly produce a violent confrontation. In fact large-scale arrests are almost always tactically impossible. If the arrests were to be carried out with safety huge numbers of police would be necessary, and certainly more than those being arrested. During the steel strike South Yorkshire Police borrowed men from seven other police forces yet the maximum manpower available was never much more than a thousand. On the day when 1,648 pickets were present in Vulcan Road the total police manpower in the whole of South Yorkshire was 952. Even if large scale arrests were carried out a similarly large number of police would be needed to process those arrested, and the logistics of jailing or bailing such numbers would be formidable. Such a policy is quite beyond the normal resources of any police force, and would only be achieved as a result of co-ordinated planning between a number of forces over a lengthy period. By their nature the kind of events we are discussing do not give this sort of advanced warning. The only other tactical alternative would be a clearing operation which used police to charge pickets and force them away. Such operations always carry high risks of injuries on both sides, and can themselves create a very serious public order problem. The locations of picketing often make such operations very dangerous – Vulcan Road for example is narrow and next to a motorway. In any case most Chief Officers have regarded such operations in relation to industrial disputes as improper. They have thought such policing methods as acceptable only in response to serious violent public disorder which has already broken out. They resent the political pressures to use such methods in industrial disputes, and fear such tactics would destroy any chance of them maintaining a degree of impartiality.

The tactics of containment have been the preferred solution because they link with the police view of what impartial policing of industrial disputes under the law is about. They fear that because in such *causes célèbres* political postures are clearly adopted by all sides, and especially government, that aggressive policing would certainly be seen as a political act. Such tactics would therefore threaten the form of impartiality which the police have historically tried to maintain, to say nothing of the damage it may do to their future relations with their local community. This latter aspect can be especially sensitive: South Yorkshire Police found that officers from other forces were treated with great suspicion by local steel workers during their strike.

Containment policing then is often the only practical solution for normalising picket behaviour. Many of the methods used in such operations are very similar to those of smaller pickets. Negotiable flexibility is still extensively used. Chief Officers start this process if possible well before with union officials and picket organisers: in some rare instances this can be so successful that police will stay in the background leaving union appointed marshalls to exercise control. The process continues on the ground with local officers to the fore to create a good-natured banter with the pickets. Football jokes especially abound: 'Keep behind that line or I'll make y' go and watch Owls (Sheffield Wednesday) next Saturday', and camera crews and newsmen provide both sides with entertainment and a target for jokes. Such tactics are designed to reduce the possibility of violence occurring, and the majority of police manpower will often be kept in reserve. This does not mean that arrests will not be made: at Hadfields on St Valentine's Day 22 people were arrested and all charged with threatening behaviour. Indeed a successful containment operation will mean that policemen will not be opposed when they do move to arrest a member of the crowd. However, arrests will be deliberately curtailed. This can be appreciated if we set the 22 arrests made at Hadfields on St Valentine's Day against the 115 made at the same picket line during the rest of the steel strike; and the fact that Hadfields was a continual flashpoint can be seen when we realise that of 159 arrests made by South Yorkshire police during the whole of the steel strike 137 were made at Hadfields. For these reasons South Yorkshire police would regard their policing of the mass picketing at Hadfields on St Valentine's Day as a highly successful example of containment. In spite of this, the television scenes of Hadfields were referred to by the prime minister, during the debate which led up to the 1980 Employment Act, as justifying the need for further legislation. The police know that such mass industrial demonstrations need the mass media, and that brief periods of ritual confrontation will provide the basis for news-clips. They do resent judgments of their policing being based upon such brief scenes rather than an evaluation of their overall policy.

How far legislation could affect these *causes célèbres* is doubtful except possibly by delegitimating such tactics in the eyes of trade-union members. However, as we argue elsewhere, tactical choices are deeply rooted in the structures of particular industries and therefore will not easily be changed. The present organisation and structure of the British police makes certain styles of policing operations very difficult to mount, and so far such alternatives have been opposed to the existing British police philosophy of maintaining civil order. How far any of these factors are changing, or are capable of being changed, is something we shall return to later in the book.

PART 2

6
Nationalised industries

The Conservative Government led by Mrs Thatcher is generally committed to reducing the industrial state sector for two main reasons. First, it argues that much state enterprise takes the form of a monopoly. Therefore, unable to benefit from the cut and thrust of competition, nationalised industry is inefficient and bureaucratic. Even where state industry is not a complete monopoly, government funds buffer it from market forces: competing private enterprise is therefore placed at an unfair disadvantage and starved of some of the investment it would win in a free market. Second, such industry is a drain on state expenditure, potentially putting pressure on the money supply and contributing to inflationary spending. Government economic policy therefore points to a reduction in the state sector, and economic goals fit well with the populist side of the government's politics which has harnessed a general resentment against nationalised industries. As we shall indicate, these matters, little and large, have had a major impact on the industrial relations of those industries – much more so than the impact of the new law.

However, the neo-liberal theories from which government policy has drawn inspiration do recognise certain conditions under which a state sector will have to exist. First, there are services which only the state can properly supply, which are connected to its duty to defend its territory against external aggression and to maintain civil order. Second, there will be a permanent need for the state to provide some services which the private market will not be able to offer. Hayek gives the example of emergency services which, he says, generate insufficient demand most of the time to justify their private provision. He warns that such cases must be strictly and pragmatically limited since otherwise the argument becomes a general case for state socialism (Hayek, 1979). Third, there may be an historical need for the state to assume control of a declining industry where the effects of uncontrolled decline would be very damaging for the national market. Railways would traditionally have been seen as such a case in Britain. Fourth, there may be a temporary need for the state to help the early development of some form of enterprise which can be rapidly handed back to the market. With the exception of the first of these the rest are all seen as temporary, limited or 'unfortunate', and the job of good government is believed to be to withdraw the state as quickly as practically possible.

Whilst this approach may have been the underlying philosophy of Mrs Thatcher's government, it inherited a national economy where state enterprise had variously been used over a thirty-five year period in attempts to halt industrial decline and regenerate industry. De-nationalisation therefore was not an easy policy to pursue quickly in spite of philosophical inclinations. Indeed, the government pursued less direct de-nationalisation of major sectors than some previous Conservative governments. What little de-nationalisation has occurred has taken place outside key productive and infrastructural sectors; the National Freight Corporation, for example, was de-nationalised but large sections of British Steel were not. It must be added, however, that a number of 'hybrid' developments, mostly operating under the 'Phoenix' label have occurred. They have produced various mixes of capital as between the private and public sector with attendant implications for jobs.

Private capital would not, in current circumstances, want certain key productive nationalised concerns because they are unprofitable and losing market shares, due to a combination of long-term decline, cyclical recession, and lack of industrial modernisation. Added to these economic constraints on de-nationalisation there were political ones. Not all aspects of the nationalised industries were completely unpopular with their customers, as the government discovered when it announced its intention to sell off the gas showrooms. More importantly the level and consequences of resistance which could be expected from the trade unions involved varied considerably. The Conservative leadership was well aware of these differences in attitude even before it took office. A report written by Mr Nicholas Ridley in 1978 examined the different strengths and weaknesses of the various unions and suggested those against which an early confrontation might be won, as against those who would resist and had the capacity to inflict serious damage. The rankings in that report

matched fairly closely the order in which major disputes have occurred in the nationalised industries.

The general philosophy was to de-nationalise as much, and as
quickly, as possible, but with regard to these constraints. Where
de-nationalisation was not possible then the aim was at least to place
industries or sections of an industry on the road to de-nationalisation
and subject them as much as possible to market forces. What was
innovative in this thinking was that the state sector was no longer
necessarily conceived in terms of the traditional categories of the
nationalised industries. Instead, sectors were re-organised to create
de-nationalisation, or parts of industries were examined for their
suitability for 'privatisation'. For both economic and political
reasons the government had to pursue a pragmatic and differentiated
policy towards nationalised industries. Whatever these pragmatic
constraints, however, the general policy was clear and the tactical
implications of the shift it signalled from the previous post-war
policy was not always quickly appreciated by some of the unions
involved.

Although the steel industry had been de-nationalised by previous
Conservative governments, the world recession in steel meant that
the British Steel Corporation was no longer likely to find a private
buyer. Steel, however, is vital for a number of other British industries from engineering to aerospace. Whilst much of this demand
could be met by the world market, there remained residual military
and strategic considerations in some cases. The medium term strategy was therefore one of restructuring and attempting to render at
least sections of BSC profitable and competitive, making British
Steel suitable for privatisation. The relative weakness of the steel
unions, the traditionally co-operative stance of ISTC towards management planning, and their inability to threaten the health of the
whole economy meant that the government did not fear a confrontation. The steel strike of 1980 was one of the first major confrontations between the new government and the state sector unions and
one which the government had less reason to fear than some. At
British Leyland rationalisation and demanning were also being demanded in circumstances where the retention of a volume British
car market was less important to the new government than it had
seemed to its predecessors. The unions in both these cases failed to
notice that their industries had moved significantly down in the
importance the new government attached to their continued exist-

ence, at least in their existing forms, for the good of the national economy. Yet the unions' traditional strength and tactics depended on that assumption.

In contrast, infrastructural industries, such as power and water, coal and railways are not candidates for (major) privatisation, though in the latter some hiving-off has occurred. Both coal and railways, however, are open to an erosion of market shares. The government seems eager to diminish the role of coal by substituting nuclear and other energy, and the rundown of the railways will open freight and passenger traffic to private road transport. In most of these industries at least an important section of the workforce is well-organised and likely to resist strong measures of marketisation or privatisation. However, the rail unions were slow to realise that the development in road transport had severely eroded the arguments for state maintenance of rail as an infrastructural industry: that their tactical strength was badly weakened.

In the gas and communications industries major hiving-off and partial privatisation is being pursued. The government has trod carefully in connection with privatisation of the gas showrooms, selecting perhaps the least well-organised workers in gas as a target, backing off when the whole of the industry threatened strike action. The Ridley Report identified gas as one industry in which major strike action should not be fought. The response to the threatened privatisation of the British Gas Corporation's gas and oil extracting activities – where workers are extremely poorly organised – remains to be seen but seems likely to be weak. The splitting of post from telecommunications, and the increased entry of private business into both telephone equipment and telecommunication services, has fractured the power once available to the unions in the industry.

In all of these areas, though at different paces and with different intermediate goals, the government has been pursuing its general 'marketisation' policy and cutting public expenditure. The primary method of enforcement has been a strict limit on cash aid, that is cash limits. Cash limits were to be used progressively to decrease levels of government investment and to press industries to become more self-financing. In some of these industries, such as coal and rail, which are dependent upon stable and large-scale investment, management and unions have greeted such measures with concern and, in the case of rail, management has used the need for investment to bargain with the unions on productivity. The Ridley Report suggested that nationalised industries be required to borrow from the exchequer at market rates of interest, but made no gestures in the direction being urged by the chairmen of some nationalised industries that they be allowed to borrow on the open market. The government also wishes each nationalised industry to achieve a set rate of return on capital employed. There is, too, a strong move to lower wages in the nationalised industries sector, partly through these indirect means which are often used in bargains over wage levels as when pay and productivity, or pay, productivity and investment are linked. The concept of wage comparability is rejected, and the criteria for wage payments are, instead, the manpower situation in the industry or service (if possible considering the *local* labour market) and the vulnerability of the nation to a strike. Thus power, water and mining wages have remained below the rate of inflation but relatively high, steel wages have been depressed, and Telecom apprentices have taken wage reductions. Finally, aggressive medium-term managerial planning and day-to-day operations have been encouraged in most industries, and 5-year rolling corporate plans have continued with a good deal of rapid restructuring envisaged. In steel, for example, the 1980 McGregor Plan represented a more ruthless version of the 1979 proposals, aiming to reduce the nationalised steel industry to a single profitable bulk steelmaking corporation through investment, large-scale demanning and real wages cuts. As a consequence BSC is being reorganised into separate businesses for specific product ranges.

The tactical response to this strategy has, of course, been uneven. Strongly placed industries, with strong unions, have so far resisted the imposition of strict market criteria. The NUM, for example, in 1981 successfully resisted the imposition of cash limits which would have led to pit closures only by initiating strike action. On the other hand, as the government expected, the resistance in steel collapsed after the 1980 strike. A coherent oppositional stand by what the government regarded as a weak union was made even less likely by later government moves: the McGregor plan was presented as a *fait accompli* without consultation, the already existing climate of fear was exacerbated by threats to close more plant if the unions were not compliant, and BSC sites were divided from one another. The unevenness of union response can be gauged by the fact that whereas the whole industrial labour force responded together in the face of threats from the British Gas Corporation, the management of British Rail were faced with division and disarray from the union side.

Several general features of tactical responses in the public sector are notable. First, the 'marketisation' policy of the government has reduced the differences in economic and financial conditions between private and public industries. Because nationalised industries are not unambiguously located within the market, 'market discipline' does not operate as strongly in, for example, wage claims as in the private sector. However, increased exposure to market criteria has made workers more sensitive to market pressures. Where unions have recognised the political nature of finances, their target has often been the government and its cash limits. This has, on occasion, meant all-out strike action in an attempt to pressure the government by using allies outside the particular public industry. However, because of the diversity of employments, union structures and also the deliberate diversity of government policy towards the unions, concerted opposition has been difficult. A shared location in the public sector – with both production interdependence and shared policy effects – has, however, provided the framework for some attempts at joint union tactics, as in the Triple Alliance between the NUM, NUR and T & G. The pace and seriousness of change in the public sector has meant that union tactics have had to change, yet tactics to resist privatisation and job loss have been generally slow to develop.

The rest of this chapter discusses dispute tactics and the relevance of the 1980 Employment Act in four nationalised sectors: steel, railways, water and coal. In each, government policy has contributed to a substantial measure of dispute and discord between management and labour. The response to disputes in these industries has depended less upon the state of the law than other, more structural matters.

Steel

The public steel industry in South Yorkshire was of course the site of much militant picketing during the 1980 strike which influentially affected the provisions of the Employment Act. None the less in the two years since there has been no large-scale activity in the industry in this area. This again indicates less about law than about the fact that matters such as mass and secondary picketing episodes occur in specific historical circumstances and are not necessarily industrial routine.

The secondary picketing during that strike was the result of highly particular factors. While in some quarters the strike was presented as a mere pay dispute, it was widely believed that the government intended to restructure BSC in preparation for privatisation and to restore profitability partly by holding wage rises far below the inflation rate. The Ridley Report provided specific evidence of such intentions. Therefore, for many trade unionists, the dispute was more than a trade dispute with their own employer; it was a fight with the government about the future of BSC. The resort to secondary picketing to create maximum impact must be seen in this context. The political organisation of steelmaking into private and public sectors was reflected in the unions' reluctance to call out private sector workers behind the BSC claim. Union members therefore resorted to secondary picketing to win the support of private sector steelworkers in resisting government strategy. The particular sites of mass secondary pickets were chosen for specific reasons. One such site in Sheffield, which had been in commercial difficulty, was seen as a clear rival to BSC and had announced its determination to continue production through the dispute. It was believed to be taking on BSC work, which other private firms had promised not to do, and was therefore a target of strenuous picketing.

The announcement of an all-out strike by the two main steel unions in 1979 gave the industry three weeks' notice in which they had the opportunity to build up stocks. Immediately a division arose between the national leadership of the union, which had exhibited little foresight about the difficulties of successful industrial action or made plans for the conduct of the strike, and determined rank-and-file organisations in such areas as Yorkshire. The union leadership had, in fact, co-operated with management in the long-term contraction of the steel industry and had no real experience of executing large-scale industrial action. The ISTC leadership predicted a short-sharp strike in the hope that a compromise settlement might quickly be reached. In fact, steelworkers and the district committees which found themselves left with responsibilty for strike organisation began slowly to realise that for the strike to be effective more action had to be taken than merely halting their own production. In order to make a significant impact on steel supplies barriers had to be placed on private sector production, imports, and distribution from stockholders. The official union decision not to call out the private steel firms was in conflict with these local understandings and so secondary picketing became a feature of the strike.

This secondary picketing involved the police in the dispute. For instance, at Scunthorpe the ISTC divisional organiser faced a police division well-prepared and sensitive to the way the dispute was being conducted because of previous experience of picketing which had resulted in an accidental death. In order to prevent the same happening again, the local police were prepared to stop lorries on behalf of the pickets, so long as the strike organisers did not produce more than a handful of pickets. In Grimsby, on the other hand, despite visits to the police by the ISTC organiser the police were unwilling to stop lorries. Instead they asked for six days' notice of picketing and offered 'gentle' policing in return.

In South Yorkshire, as already discussed in Chapter 5, steel picketing resulted in the largest ever policing operation during an industrial dispute. This very large-scale picketing was to provide the context for much of the subsequent industrial action during the following two years. For the police it reinforced their belief in certain tactical responses to picketing, and these became part of their accepted procedures. Furthermore, South Yorkshire Police became acknowledged experts in large-scale industrial disputes and passed their experience and conclusions on to other police forces. For the unions some of the hostility generated over secondary picketing of engineering companies, and the activities of left political groups, continued to rumble on. These arguments, however, were part of a broader demoralisation inflicted on a local labour movement with a proud and militant history by their defeat in the steel strike. Their confidence in the success of large-scale industrial tactics to fight unemployment and government policies was badly shaken. The result was a continuing hesitancy to use some tactics, and a less innovative approach to finding new tactics to combat redundancy in, for example engineering, than was shown in some other areas.

In the course of the dispute, private steel companies took legal action to prevent the ISTC executive from calling out members in the private sector (*Duport v. Sirs, supra* Ch. 3). The refusal by the High Court to grant an injunction was reversed by a Saturday morning hearing of the Court of Appeal. The injunction was obtained under the banner of an association, the British Independent Steel Producers Association (BISPA), not a company. Associations are by their nature divorced from operational decisions and responsibilities and therefore less constrained by longer-term industrial relations consequences of legal confrontation.

There was the feeling amongst managers and directors alike that as all other tactical options had been exhausted, the law had to be used to remove the pickets for financial reasons, particularly in view of the dismal commercial situation of the private steel producers. Whilst this 'last resort' view of law was common among management, within BISPA individual companies had very different views of the strike in general and the legal action in particular. Some were mindful of the industrial relations consequences of recourse to law and even wrote letters justifying their actions to the workforce. Other firms had no such compunction, continued to defy mass pickets, and solved their own cash-flow problems by doing work normally carried out by BSC.

For the unions a crucial tactical element of the strike was the support that could be obtained from other workers. The ISTC required the assistance of other unions, such as the T & G, which organises dockers and lorry drivers involved in steel distribution, as well as BSC technical unions and private sector steelworkers. Because of the selectivity of the ISTC/NUB strike call, there was some difficulty in ensuring this external support. For example, lorry drivers could see steelworkers continuing to work in the private sector and so sometimes crossed picket lines. On the East Coast ports, NUR lockgate men and docks railway staff similarly had to be persuaded to black steel imports. The limits of partial action in steel are similar to the difficulties encountered by some selective strikes in the public service discussed later.

Many of the difficulties of organising successful resistance to government plans apparent during the steel strike have continued in relation to proposals for demanning under the McGregor plan. Nowhere in the course of the steel strike did the official union negotiating stance explicitly link pay with the defence of jobs. In fact, the final wages settlement contained an acknowledgment of the need for future job losses. The continued slump in the market for steel and lack of any union leadership offering strategies for the industry has meant that workers have largely accepted closures, redundancies, and wage freezes in the public and private sectors.

Interestingly, since the strike the steel industry seems to have reverted to its past pattern of consensual industrial relations. This

consensus has partly been facilitated by a highly centralised negotiating system, with weak union accountability to its grass roots.
Historically there has been a close co-operative relationship between
national union officials and the 'captains of industry'. The hierar-
chial structure of the steel union is, in turn, related to the hierarchy
of tasks and system of job seniority in steel production. However,
localised unofficial strikes have been a steady undercurrent in the
industry and account in part for the organisational skills displayed
at local levels during the national steel strike. While, therefore, the
steel industry has not been the site of large-scale industrial action
since 1980, the absence of industrial conflict is almost certainly not
reducible to the effects of the Employment Act but rather to deeper
economic and industrial relations matters.

Rail

British Rail provides an example of a nationalised industry which
historically has been regarded as an essential infrastructural service.
More recently, with the growth and potential further development
of road transport, the government seems willing to endure short-
term disruption of the railways and also to forego their long-term
development. While some of the highly profitable enterprises on the
periphery of BR's main activity have been privatised, the major
industrial relations confrontation has occurred over the terms of
government funding of the railways. Government policy has emphasised large-scale productivity improvements involving demanning and low wage increases in exchange for capital investment.
Many of the demands on the rail unions have been precipitated by
the introduction of new technology, such as single-manned engines.
   In the railways, the conflict over the terms of government financing has occurred between a centralised management and two centralised unions, ASLEF and the NUR. Nationalisation unified the
assets owned by 125 different railway concerns, and this centralisation of ownership and management means that the unions were
under considerable pressure to develop their own centralised structures. The result is that all major industrial relations issues in the
railways – particularly wage negotiations – are dealt with at a national level.
   The near monopoly position enjoyed by organised labour in the
railways has conferred considerable power and disruptive capacity

upon the railway unions. While there is high density of union organisation in the industry, however, railway workers are organised by two unions structured differently and with different political complexions. ASLEF, currently the more left-wing of the two main unions, organises the highly skilled and traditionally craft-conscious footplate staff and has a small membership. At a local level, its departmental committees see to a variety of tasks, many of them, such as rostering, apparently technical and managerial but also incorporating a strong element of job control. The NUR is more an industrial than a craft union and has a recent history of stronger co-operation with the Board and less opposition to technical innovation on the railways. While for the NUR such innovation may mean some job and membership loss, for ASLEF such innovation means rapid loss of a high proportion of its members.

The recent disputes over flexible rostering have been a stark illustration of the uneasy relations between the two unions. While the NUR Secretary publicly agreed to flexible rostering without seeking his members' approval, the ASLEF Secretary was mandated by union conference to oppose it on the terms being offered by the Board. The NUR, with a large, non-driving railway membership which stood to suffer from a prolonged dispute, no doubt pressed strongly against TUC approval of the ASLEF strike.

The tactics employed by the two unions during the long-running dispute over the 1981 pay and productivity settlement were to bring the railways to a halt through an all-out national strike in order to achieve more favourable terms. Prior to the first national strike, however, there was a clear effort not to allow other local issues to develop into serious and long-running strike action. In centralised unions there is often pressure not to allow local disputes to assume great importance. For example, the threatened closure of the Manchester to Sheffield Woodhead line – part of more widespread economies in services – provoked a limited strike strategy which would minimise loss of wages to members and maximise public sympathy. The NUR calculated that because of industrial recession, withdrawal of freight services would not have much of an impact on the Board nor would it have made the public aware of the threatened closure and NUR opposition. The NUR also sought to minimise inconvenience to the travelling public. They thus chose not to collect fares. Suspension of a guard refusing to collect fares resulted in supportive withdrawal by other guards, a temporary return to work over the Easter holiday, and subsequent selective action by signalmen before the dispute finally ended. In respect of selective action in the railways, signalmen are generally in a strategic position, especially as signalling has become more automated and centralised. Selective action in the railways, as elsewhere, however, risks dividing the union and minimising external support from other workers.

The two national strikes over the pay and productivity award were all-out actions. In the first, the NUR and ASLEF acted together, minimising the need for picketing and secondary picketing. ASLEF itself is in a strategic position to interrupt the railways, because it organises an overwhelming proportion of drivers. During the second strike, in June 1982, many NUR members worked, including a very small number of drivers, together with an even smaller number of ASLEF drivers. The importance of these few working drivers was not that they could ensure a significant and efficient service. In the war of nerves between government and management on the one hand and ASLEF on the other, a single strike-breaker was presented as evidence of division in ASLEF's and union ranks, a weakening of the strike, and a victory for 'sensible' workers who saw the future of their jobs as tied to improved productivity in the railways. Management and government thus created a need for secondary picketing to overturn these symbols of ASLEF's defeat.

In their all-out strikes, ASLEF and the NUR depended upon some secondary action. For example, the railway unions depend upon the miners refusing to load coal on to lorries where it normally travels by rail. The co-operation of lorry drivers in other industries and in passenger transport is also important and often cannot be guaranteed simply by national agreement with the T & G. Therefore local contact must be made, and ASLEF pickets are sometimes deployed to cover lorry or coach depots. In Sheffield during the 1981-2 disputes ASLEF made approaches to the T & G over freight, though it is not clear to what degree these were successful. In South Yorkshire and Humberside, local T & G members did refuse to operate additional buses to meet the extra passenger demand. In the disputes in which the NUR was involved, the support of NUR bus drivers who service rural routes, such as in North Lincolnshire, was solid. The unexpected support in August 1982 of the electricians in the newspaper industry over the publicity given to alleged misconduct by ASLEF drivers was the occasion for a 1980 Employment Act injunction: print workers of course are not within the protective ambit of the new law (currently unreported).

The most striking point about tactics on the railways is, perhaps, that about the growth of alternative forms of freight and passenger transport: the railways are viewed by the government as a merely desirable national asset, which can certainly be complemented and perhaps even replaced by other forms of transport. When the railways constituted the main form of freight and passenger transport and in so far as industry depended upon coal, industrial action by footplatemen could paralyse the railways and the economy as a whole. Indeed, in the past government had used emergency powers and the military to maintain rail services. The growth in alternative transport has meant that people and goods are less dependent upon the railways. In this context, prohibitions on secondary picketing and secondary action are quite relevant to what might constitute a maximalist ASLEF strike strategy. Such a strategy would attempt to stop not only the railways but the growing alternative means of passenger and freight transport. In such an event public and private employers of labour in such industries might be tempted to have recourse to the law.

Water

The water and power industries represent necessary infrastructural industrial services, are currently among the three industries in which a strike makes the country most vulnerable, and are well-organised by trade unions. Consequently, government strategy has been not to privatise these industries but to try and hold down wages whilst avoiding serious strike action. In both the 1980-1 and 1981-2 wages rounds the industries have settled above the wages 'norm' for the public sector. The 1980-1 water wages round illustrates the use of tactics and counter-tactics in an essential well-organised public service industry.

The government's tactic in the water industry's 1980-1 wages round was to contain wages to as near the public sector norm of 6 per cent as possible without provoking serious strike action. In addition to influencing wage bargaining through general economic and political developments and ideology, the government undoubtedly brought considerable pressure to bear through the industry's negotiating structure. The main administrative unit in the industry is the Regional Authority which then sends representatives to the National Joint Industrial Council, which is responsible for wages and conditions in the industry. The Regional Water Authorities are comprised of a majority of local authority appointees (usually a majority of only one), with the Chairman and rest of the members appointed by central government. However, the dominance of local authority representatives is superficial. Local authority representatives are appointed from among numerous, widely disparate authorities with authorities often sharing representatives. Because of this fragmentation, the low visibility of water service work, and the absence of any real accountability to local authority constituencies, the initiative in the authorities passes to government appointees and officers. The National Joint Industrial Council (NJIC) is comprised of representatives of these regions and of the National Water Board, with a government-appointed chairman. Therefore, government influence on negotiations through its own appointees, through sympathetic local authorities, and through financial and other policy controls is strong.

In the 1980-1 wages round there was strong pressure on the NJIC to make and hold a 6 per cent offer. The 'first and last' offer of 10 December was regarded by many involved in the negotiations as out of character for an employer which had shown considerable flexibilty since the 1950s. The coincidental publication of the *Green Paper on Trade Union Immunities* with this offer was seen also as a deliberate attempt by central government to influence negotiations. In addition, negotiators on both sides have reported that local councillors, especially from rural areas and the south of England, supported the inflexible and low offer. In the south, especially in the Southwestern Region, not only did Conservative councillors try to keep the wage rise to or near 6 per cent for political reasons, but they also stood to lose less from a strike due to the presence of private water companies and the smaller scale of service. As with the fire service NJIC, the number of votes that regions held on that body is not proportional either to the number of workers in each regional jurisdiction, or to the size of population served.

While in water no formal comparability agreement similar to that in fire or the civil service existed, two comparabilities were in conflict during negotiations. Rather than a clear conflict between prospective saving and retrospective formal comparability, the water authority negotiators faced an established conflict between informal comparability to gas and electricity and comparability to local authority services (in whose jurisdiction water originally fell). Clearly, in this case local authority comparability was a 'cheap option', as local authority workers were relatively weak and expected to settle within the 6 per cent, while electricity and gas workers with considerable industrial muscle were more likely to breach the norm. However, the powerful position of water workers resembles that of gas and electricity more closely, and a pragmatic policy towards the nationalised industries yielded a settlement akin to those in the other national utilities. The 6 per cent offer was improved and the final agreement amounted to an overall increase of about 12 per cent.

Because of the devastating effects of an all-out strike in water and the threat of public resentment increased by the timing of the Green Paper, water workers were considering both selective and all-out tactics. The manual side of the industry has been a closed shop for several years, and the four unions sitting on the NJIC (GM, T & G, NUPE, NUAAW) and NALGO, representing supervisory grades, all co-operated in discussing and developing strike tactics. This was important since an earlier dispute in South Yorkshire involving sewerage workers had been tactically undercut by supervisors continuing to work in spite of picketing.

Selective action might have centred on withdrawing distribution workers (such as those engaged in repair and maintenance) concentrated on large urban depots, instituting overtime bans, removing standby arrangements, picketing chlorine tankers, withdrawing sewerage workers, or launching short surprise strikes. However, because of its more powerful effects and avoidance of dividing unions and union members, an all-out strike was seriously considered.

The impact of industrial action, particularly an all-out strike, in the water service is extremely serious for two main reasons; viz. the rationalisation and integration of water services, and the technological and skill requirements in the service. Rationalisation and integration of the water services – supply, distribution and sewerage – means that disruption in limited geographical areas or in particular parts of the water cycle has ramifications elsewhere. Particularly as the water grid itself is an integrated system this interdependence is marked. In fact, the rationalisation and integration of the water cycle since 1974 had been largely responsible for moving water from fifteenth to third on the Cabinet Committee's civil contingency list.

Before April 1974 water supply was provided by 198 separate water supply undertakings (68 local authorities, 101 joint water boards, 33 private companies), sewerage and sewage disposal was undertaken by 1,300 county boroughs and county district councils and 24 joint sewerage boards and conservation of water was handled by 29 river authorities. In 1974, ten Regional Water Authorities, public corporations, took on all these functions. Their administrative structures matched the water cycle, and their boundaries followed natural watersheds. However, some private water companies remain, especially in the south. The existence of large integrated units makes the potential effects of stoppages much more powerful.

The devastating impact of a water strike is due also to technological developments and skill requirements in the industry, combined with the social solidarity among staff and manual unions. If NALGO supervisors were willing to supervise troops, some navy engineers could possibly operate pumps. However, NALGO supervisors were unwilling to supervise troops or contractors. The only alternative left to the government and contingency planners was, therefore, to take over whole works. However, the Cabinet Contingencies Committee apparently came to the conclusion that the armed forces did not have sufficient expertise to do so; controlling and monitoring pressure and water levels would have been particularly problematic. On the other hand, because technology in the water service remains uneven, some substitution possibilities of a limited nature do exist. For example, in Yorkshire, some supply stations in the Pennines are relatively simple and depend largely upon gravity. At some of the most highly technological sites, a few key computer personnel and higher management might possibly be able to continue operations in the face of a strike. Police planning for a possible strike consisted, therefore, of plans to escort military water tankers (probably the 'Green Goddesses' once again), or guard rationed stand pipes. The great difficulty of maintaining supplies in an all-out strike meant they were more concerned with possible civil disorder as a result of shortages, or forcefully entering water plants.

The role of picketing, and certainly of secondary picketing, is therefore limited in the water industry. As a service industry, or provider of a utility, water works do not manufacture commodities which are stored and distributed separately from production. Water is essentially a monopoly, though the existence of some private companies might provide cause for secondary picketing. Government attempts to use troops to maintain some services would certainly have provoked picketing and confrontations. These were the confrontations the police most feared. The unevenness of technology also provides some potential for secondary picketing. Certain selective actions, e.g. picketing of chlorine tankers, might involve secondary picketing, and therefore the 1980 Act. However, water service drivers are in the same union as many water workers, the Transport and General Workers' Union, and other forms of solidarity action might be substituted for picketing. In fact, in the water industry, as in other powerful industrial services, the use of picketing and secondary picketing was never tested during the first two years of the 1980 Act.

Coal

Nationalised in a state of extreme technological backwardness highlighted by the requirements of the Second World War, the coal industry now appears to be a stable monopoly, segments of which, however, might be hived off. Government strategy towards coal has reflected its public expenditure cutting priorities. Unlike the water industry, the coal industry has supply competitors, both in the form of imports and alternative energy sources, and functions in discrete units. Consequently, the government has been able to pursue a two-pronged strategy of significantly reducing investment by closing units and of attempting to depress wages; the mechanism for both has been cash limits. However, just as in the water industry, the government has tried to enforce such measures without occasioning a strike and the employment of tactics which would endanger energy supplies and perhaps the government's own legitimacy.

Union tactics in the coal industry were well tested in the 1970s, and partly inspired the government's picketing legislation. They clearly led to the current government strategy of discouraging confrontation. It was only in the late 1960s that large-scale strikes, beyond a single coalfield, began to occur in the NUM. Prior to that time, due to a fragmented wages structure and the persistence of regional union autonomy within the shell of a national union, strikes in the coal industry were short, small-scale stoppages. Only occasionally, such as in 1955 in Yorkshire, did strikes spread among pits. So-called 'secondary picketing' did occur occasionally within the coalfield, but it was relatively 'invisible' in an industry whose industrial relations were isolated and idiosyncratic. By 1969 and 1970 'secondary picketing' was a well-established tactic, but it was only in 1972 that it played a publicly key and controversial role in an official national strike. The mass picket at Saltley became a celebrated incident within the union and a particularly important symbol of left-wing success. More than any single event of the 1972 strike, it was seen as a victory for union solidarity and some consolation for the defeat of 1926 which even at that time still rankled.

To the Conservative Party, Saltley became a symbol of its own inability to govern. When the miners again struck officially in 1974, secondary and mass picketing were less prominent, but the strike provided the occasion for Edward Heath calling an election, in which his government was defeated. In the Tory mind, Saltley and the election defeat seem to have merged, and the particular successful tactics associated with the 1972 dispute became a focus of concern. Secondary picketing was beginning to be seen as a particular threat to Conservative governments. Further, it represented a politics of social power and mobilisation, rather than of parliamentarism and articulated well with Conservative concern for 'law and order'. The result of an attempt at economic management through controlling incomes, it perhaps also stood as a symbol of the failure of Keynesian economic management.

As in other industries, tactics in coalmining – including the need for secondary picketing and action – are structured by the organisation of production and distribution in the industry. Several basic factors affect the possibility of a complete withdrawal of labour in coalmining strikes: the near monopoly position of the NCB, the degree and type of unionisation in the industry, and management's incapacity to substitute for withdrawn labour or to supervise substitution. However, because coalmining produces a stockable commodity, simple withdrawal of labour does not necessarily halt the distribution or use of coal, and secondary picketing assumes particular importance in coalmining strikes.

The NCB is for all practical purposes a statutorily recognised monopoly producer of coal. By far the greatest proportion of its coal is deep-mined, and in deep-mining the NUM organises 100per cent of the workforce. There are strong social pressures among miners to adhere solidly and loyally to union decisions. The overmen in the industry are organised by the National Association of Overmen, Deputies and Shotfirers, a traditionally moderate union. However, because of the labour-intensive, highly co-ordinated, and skilled nature of mining, as well as the considerable physical exertion it demands, deputies are unable to substitute for miners or to supervise substitute labour. The social and political traditions of the coalfield, founded upon the organisation of production and work, make it unlikely that a decision to substitute labour would ever be taken. Deputies, occasionally old or injured faceworkers who live in the same communities and sometimes the same families as miners, have little incentive to strike break. In an official strike, therefore, all pits producing coal stop completely.

Picketing is important, therefore, not to stop production but to prevent the movement and use of coal with sympathetic action fulfilling similar functions. Though there are alternative energy sources available, only coal can be used for certain purposes such as steel production, and many facilities cannot be switched quickly from coal to oil. Coal may move from several sources:

(1)*Pithead stocks*. In the 1974 miners' strike there were no significant stocks at pitheads and no picketing at pits. In 1981 pithead stocks were considerable and miners planned to picket the main point of access to pits, usually a lane or narrow roadway. Such picketing may have discouraged the movement of the small proportion of coal transported by lorry. Pickets would not only have served to discourage lorries from entering but also to gather information for any necessary blacking. As many coal lorries are regular transporters of local coal, the threat of blacking is a very effective one. However, many stocks are held on NCB property away from entrances, and loaded mechanically onto slowly moving railway trucks. One or two people work the loading machines at the pit, but management could operate the machines. Therefore, the co-operation of ASLEF or the NUR is important to the NUM. The rail unions have in the past co-operated with official strikes, mainly by refusing to cross picket lines, which have often consisted of single pickets with placards on railway bridges or crossings. In 1981 the NUR was a member of the so-called Triple Alliance and itself fighting closures and redundancies due to government policy. The more militant ASLEF was also sympathetic and there was a close personal relationship between the left of the NUM, and Arthur Scargill in particular, and Ray Buckton, the ASLEF General Secretary. Furthermore, it is not possible to alter the mode of transport of stocks at short notice should either train or lorry drivers show unwillingness to move coal.

(2) *NCB and private stockyards*. The NCB holds its own stocks not only adjacent to collieries but also wherever else ground is available at reasonable cost and convenience. Coal cannot be stacked vertically without limit because of the problem of spontaneous combustion. Therefore external stockyards are numerous and sometimes fairly small. In Yorkshire the NUM knows exactly where these yards are and has plans prepared to picket them.

(3) *Stocks within the perimeters of power stations and other facilities*. Because of both the recession and the dangers that became apparent during the miners' strikes of the early 1970s, coal stocks inside power stations were fairly high in 1981. National stocks were at 15 million tons, which under normal weather conditions is 2 months' burn. It is this national figure which is important as the electricity grid is interchangeable. If miners wish, therefore, to have an immediate impact upon power generation, they would have to resort to one of two tactics.

First, they could try to stop other supplies entering power stations. Hydrogen is essential to power generation and has been a target of picketing in the past. Since the last miners' dispute most large power stations have the capacity to manufacture hydrogen on the premises, and there are contingency stocks. It is not clear whether materials to manufacture hydrogen are stocked. Oil is often necessary for flame stabilisation, and oil is certainly stocked although it is not clear how long stocks would last. It is delivered by private tankers, drivers of which may or may not be unionised. The NUM even has plans to block food and toilet supplies and the CEGB accepts that these could be important for industrial relations. Water too is essential for cooling purposes, but is often taken from nearby rivers or the sea. Purer water, however, is required for boilers, and this is often taken from town mains, though stations often have their own treatment units run by electricity unions. Interruption of these supplies would clearly have proved crucial.

The second tactic is one of sympathetic action by CEGB manual workers. Coal-burning power stations are located within coalfields, and there is considerable personal contact between the two groups of workers. In coal-fired power stations, work resembles that of pit-top facilities. The Enginemen, Firemen, Mechanics and Electrical Workers' Union used to organise both in power and mining, and the former EFMEW General Secretary, Roy Ottey, became the Secretary of the NUM Power Group in 1967, when EFMEW was fully merged into the T & G. However, these connections do not create automatic sympathy and co-operation between the two groups of workers. Sympathetic action by manual workers, moreover, would not necessarily shut down the grid; it is likely that supervisors and managers would run the stations, and power rationing would be introduced. If, however, supervisors did not do so the situation would be very serious since the military is no longer capable of safely running modern power stations. For this reason the power stations are regarded as the greatest potential problem by the Cabinet Civil Contingencies Committee, and emergency supplies and safe shutdowns in places depend on the rather crude use of old aero engines.

(4) *Coal imports*. To halt the distribution of coal imports, the miners would both picket the docks and ask the dockers not to unload (or load) coal. The dockers have co-operated in the past with such requests and would have done so again in 1981. Though the halting of imports is more important to the NUM, the disruption of the export trade also pressures the NCB, which, in a period of oversupply, is trying to maintain and extend export markets.

A maximum official strike strategy would, therefore, have succeeded in halting production in all British pits due to the NCB's position as a monopoly employer in mining. The difficulty for the NUM is to halt distribution and consumption rather than production, but they could probably have succeeded in largely checking the movement of coal through a combination of picketing, blacking and sympathetic action. Due both to the requirements of effective industrial action in coal and to the traditions of such action, secondary and mass picketing of sites external to pits would have been used in cases of non-co-operation by other unions. With broad official labour movement support, such tactics may have been unnecessary. But it is highly likely that the left wing of the Union may have encouraged such tactics at the slightest justifiable opportunity in order to discredit the 1980 Employment Act had the opportunity presented itself.

The unofficial strike which broke out in February 1981, on the other hand, followed a slightly different pattern. In this case the main tactic was 'secondary' picketing of other pits. Militancy among and within coalfields has always been uneven for a variety of reasons, and pickets have often travelled from more to less militant areas and pits to spread industrial action. For this reason such 'secondary' picketing is characteristic of unofficial strikes.

We are convinced that solidarity tactics would have been particularly prominent and effective in the threatened 1981 pit closure strike. First, as a dispute defined clearly as over jobs and employment, the general labour movement would have been likely to provide solid industrial support where required and possibly would have engaged in additional sympathy action. With 2.5 million unemployed and hardly a sign of industrial resistance in sight, the labour movement could well have used such a dispute as a rallying point. The NUM chose to make its stand on jobs rather than wages partly because it understood the stronger resonances of the former and the divisiveness of the latter within the larger labour movement. The NUM also felt itself involved in a struggle for jobs in general, since the coal industry has suffered the consequences of closure in other industries such as steel.

The NUM political left was particularly determined that an uncontested decline would not occur again in the coalfield. To this group, picketing, and especially secondary picketing, were critical to an effective industrial resistance, and Arthur Scargill, in particular, had recently organised such action successfully in the 1972 dispute and risen to prominence because of it. This same group was publicly determined not to be deterred by new trade-union law and hoped to discredit it. The unanimity among miners that pit closures had to be fought may have been affected by the fact that, in a Union Presidential year and in view of the fact that a 'fundamentalist' Tory government was responsible for the closures, moderates would certainly not wish to be left behind on the issue of jobs.

It was, therefore, not surprising that as the determination of the miners became clear and against the historical background of government defeat, the government made available the resources to forestall the pit closure programme. The NCB had no choice but to work within the financial constraints established by the government. Ironically perhaps, at the same time that it was revising its plans to meet new government cash limits, it also sought to apply pressure on the government to change its plans. Its own long-term production-based rather than financially-based plans were in jeopardy. In an alliance of interest with other nationalised industries the Board protested against unreasonable and unexplained external financing limits. The positive purchasing policies of nationalised industries meant also that British industry in general, and particularly British mining equipment, would be hard hit by government plans.

With the NCB opposed but constrained to follow government financial guidelines and the NUM opposed to the effects of financial limits, it is clear that there was a limited coincidence between NUM and NCB interests. It seems a bit too simple, however, to say that the threat of a strike was the result of an NUM/NCB alliance. The NCB's statutory responsibilities and ties to government prevented it from openly discussing a strategy of opposition with the NUM. Certain kinds of joint appeals to public opinion were impossible. There was uncertainty on both sides about what the other would do, and on both sides there was a certain lack of control. The timing of announcements of closures separately in each Area, with York-shire at the end, indicated that if the Board did want NUM resist-ance for its own purposes, it wanted it at least cost to industrial production and order and at most expense to the NUM left. It may therefore be more accurate to talk about an unspoken coincidence of interests between the NCB and NUM moderates, or about the NCB manoeuvering between the NUM and government. The gov-ernment, faced by a range of effective tactics including secondary picketing and action, backed away from the confrontation.

An all-out coal strike would undoubtedly have meant a testing of the new picketing laws. The 1980 Act was seen by the union as an attack on the 'rights' of working people to picket. Scargill and others in the NUM also recognised that the legislation would have a vari-able effect upon unions, and that the NUM would be especially badly hit due to the importance to them of picketing as a tactic. However, it is unlikely that either the CEGB or the NCB would have used the law against the miners. The NCB in particular was fully aware of the strong union traditions in the industry and the importance of maintaining positive industrial relations.

Nationalised industries vary in terms of their strategic importance to an economy in recession, and are also internally differentiated by the capacity of their workforce to engage in disruptive action. Although the range of tactical choices in each of the industries described is wide and effective selective industrial action can be mounted, it should be noted that the threat of an all-out strike and subsequent confrontation with the government seemed to be the preferred alternative of the single industry unions. The impact of a future law, which seeks more sharply to distinguish politically motivated action from 'pure' trade disputes, is therefore likely to be given ample testing in the public sector where government policy can be a direct cause of disputes. Picketing and secondary action will no doubt continue to be seen as important by some of the unions involved in circumstances where their proscription might well be thought to be partisan and inflammatory.

7
The public services and industrial disputes

The public services have been an important focus for disputes over the last two years because of deliberate government strategy to diminish the resources dispensed, because the sector is buffered from certain of the difficulties of the private sector, and also because of changing ethics of employment within the public services. While some disputes have been local in nature, there have been three major national disputes with ramifications for the South Yorkshire and Humberside area: in the fire service in 1980, in the civil service in 1981, and in the health service in 1982. They each afford an occasion for the examination of selective tactics and for the role of the law in controlling such industrial action.

Government strategy towards the public services

Government strategy towards the public services has, in recent times, been to reduce the resources they use and the number of functions fulfilled. One important element of the objection to a large public-service sector is the monetarist view that public services bloat public expenditure and therefore contribute to inflation. Public services, in this view, consume a disproportionate share of resources and function inefficiently because they are subjected to market competition even less than the nationalised industries. Because services not exposed to market competition are necessarily inefficient one way of increasing the efficiency of remaining public services is to expose them to competition from the private sector where, naturally, wages are subject to market forces. Such services also need to be strictly subjected to cash limits, and to productivity improvements through mechanisms such as incentive schemes and more efficient working practices. The pulling of public services towards the market has also been justified on the grounds of neo-liberal political theory.

The public services are, however, of concern for neo-liberal monetarists in an additional sense. They are basically unproductive: that is, they do not produce commodities that can be bought and sold, nor do they earn profits or trade in international markets. Not only are they themselves non-productive, but they support non-productive individuals, thereby destroying the incentive to work at market rates.

The present government has resorted to a variety of means for reducing public services and public-service expenditure, which measures have produced tactical responses from the trade unions involved. While most actual privatisation has occurred, or been threatened, in nationalised industries – segments of British Rail and gas showrooms, for example – a great many moves in the direction of privatisation have also occurred in the public-service sector. Some of these have been direct, such as the introduction of private street cleaners in the London Borough of Wandsworth and the divestment of heavy goods vehicle testing stations. In other cases, the government is reducing the level and conditions of service in the public sector, thereby creating the conditions for the growth of private enterprise. Perhaps the clearest example of the latter is the health service, in which trade unions fear for the increasing privatisation of ambulance and other services, oppose the encouragement of private medicine, and are discomforted by decreased entitlement to free NHS treatment. The low wages offer of the 1982 round has also been seen as contributing to a deterioration of morale and standards in the health service.

Short of privatisation, the government has tried to achieve its ends through the exercise of its powers as direct and indirect employer, mainly through the devices of cash limits and 'returning pay to the market'. The government's tactics as direct employer are evident in recent developments in the civil service. In the post-war period the guiding principle on civil-service pay has been that civil servants should not be paid according to the changing policies of successive governments, but on the basis of external comparisons. While pay comparability, established through the reports of the Pay Research Unit (PRU), has not always ensured prompt payment of wage increases, most civil-service unions have defended the system as essentially equitable. However, in the 1981 wages round the government unilaterally suspended PRU on the grounds that cash limits of 6 per cent had to take precedence over comparability.

Shortly after the successful implementation of a low award – despite months of industrial action over the suspension of PRU – the government began talking consistently about returning civil servants' pay to market determination, ideally to *local* market determination. An arbitration award in 1982 was followed by the report of the Megaw Inquiry, which strongly endorsed market as opposed to comparability mechanisms. While retaining the form of pay inquiry and analysis, Megaw – closely reflecting government concerns – recommended that information relating to wages should be collected mainly to ensure that the government as employer pay civil servants enough to recruit, retain, and motivate them to perform efficiently. This was heralded as a model for all public-service pay. Meanwhile, the Civil Service Department has been placed under stricter and more direct Treasury control and can be expected to be more consistently subject to the government's overall economic plans.

When central government is an indirect employer, it has exercised increasing control through the imposition of cash limits, on intermediate negotiating bodies as in fire, health and education. This has been done even where there existed prior comparability agreements. However, differences among intermediate negotiating bodies have had significant consequences for government and union strategy. For example, in the fire service the management side of the negotiating body is comprised of 30 representatives of local authorities, representing the Association of Metropolitan Authority (AMA), the Association of County Councils (ACC), the Greater London Council (GLC), the Committee of Scottish Local Authorities (COSLA) and Northern Ireland. Local authorities are of course independently constituted political bodies accountable to local electorates with their own revenue-raising capacities. Correspondingly, government control is best exercised through sympathetic local authorities, in this case the ACC, and through cash limits on the rate support grant, which still accounts for a large portion of local revenues. In the 1980 fire service dispute the imposition of cash limits of 6 per cent and the abrogation of a comparability agreement which indicated an 18 per cent rise was more acceptable to some local authorities than to others. The early 18 to 12 division on the management side was between the ACC, exercising a 'three-line whip' and the GLC, on the one hand, and the AMA, COSLA, and Northern Ireland on the other. The ACC's attempt to run the employers' side created tensions and threats of walk-outs. London was thought to have voted against the agreement only because of internal organisational problems, and some members of the ACC were not pleased with their instructions.

The ACC may have had reasons in addition to political allegiances and pressures for feeling that they could oppose the 18.8 per cent. Rural areas have a larger proportion of part-time firemen, and in the counties the part-time firemen are often members of the Retained Firemen's Union (RFU) which announced that it was prepared to fight fires during a strike. However, in London, the most densely populated area on the National Joint Council (NJC), there are no part-time firemen. Therefore, the coalition against the 18.8 per cent was fragile. The main union, the Fire Brigades' Union (FBU) whilst aware of its own weakness realised that with no majority block formally committed to the government it needed to pursue a strategy dedicated to altering the balance of view within the management side.

In health, the management side of the Whitley Council(s) is composed of the Department of Health and Social Security (DHSS), the Regional Health Authorities (RHAs), the Area Health Authorities (AHAs) and the Board of Governors of teaching hospitals. RHAs and AHAs are not political bodies in the sense that local authorities are, and the DHSS represents government directly. The Treasury, which provides over 80 per cent of NHS funds, is not a party to collective bargaining. Therefore, there is little possibility of the (multi-) union side altering balances in its favour against a determined government, and union strategy during the 1982 pay dispute, for example, was clearly directed unequivocally at central government.

Disputes in the public services during the first three years of the Conservative government, therefore, have on several important occasions grown out of the conflict between the prospective saving implied by cash limits and retrospective comparability. In fire, the nine-week strike of 1977-8 was ended by an agreement that firemen's pay should be linked to a formula which equated firemen's earnings with the level of earnings of the upper quartile of male manual workers. However, on the eve of the 1980 negotiations the government announced that it was imposing a 6 per cent pay limit on local authorities by limiting the rate support grant and employers agreed to award only 6 per cent, despite the 18.8 per cent comparability.

Similarly in the civil service, the 1981 PRU report was subordinated to cash limits.

In fact, this rigid application of cash limits in the public sector resembles the 'traditional' discriminatory treatment of public sector services under incomes policy, and some of its industrial consequences are similar. As with the incomes policies of the 1960s and 1970s, the present government attempted to use the public sector to set an example of cost-containment to the rest of industry. Be that as it may, these devices have represented a potential source of disputes which have, because of the general coherence of government policy, been broadened into larger political concerns. Cash limits are joined to a clear policy of holding down public-sector spending, especially in 'non-productive' services, and of reducing the public sector at large. Resistance to cash limits, therefore, often involves themes of defending the public sector and the delivery of welfare services. As a primary site of services in the post-war welfare state, local authorities' campaigns against cash limits and cuts have involved these broader themes. As part of an integrated monetarist neo-liberalism, however, cash limits on the public services lose some of their negative discriminatory aspect. With the private economy in deep recession and job losses mounting steeply, public-sector workers are said to have relative security of employment and so enjoy a relatively favourable employment position.

Nevertheless the application of cash limits in the public sector has not treated the public sector as an undifferentiated whole. The government found it politic to 'buy off' stronger groups and held firm against the weaker, both among and within services. 'Strength', in government calculations, has consisted of importance to their general political stance (e.g. police), industrial muscle (e.g. the miners), or contingency threat (e.g. water, electricity). To a lesser degree, the government has made small concessions to groups with strong appeal to public opinion such as nurses. The small concession to the nurses in the 1982 wages round has, however, been seen more as an attempt to divide the nurses from ancillary workers and to create disagreement among the nurses themselves. The general consequence of this strategy has been a growing gap between 'weaker' low-paid workers, often in public services, and certain key groups with unusual power.

In summary, then, the government has pursued its goal of a reduced public-services sector through encouragement of privatisation and low wages awards. The latter have often been imposed despite and against operating comparability agreements and have occasioned important public-service disputes in fire, the civil service, and the health service. These disputes have occurred in the context of a post-war history of changing industrial relations in the public services.

Changing industrial relations in the public services

Many public-service workers have a history of deference, professionalism, dedication or discipline which have historically militated against the development of strong trade unionism which is often associated with vulgar self-seeking. In the fire service there has been a strong tradition of military-like discipline with a hierarchy of officers and men. Hierarchy suggests an ordered community, rather than separate organised groups in conflict so that within the service trade unionism has been subordinated to command-obedience relationships. Health-care occupations, on the other hand, have traditionally been characterised by altruistic ideologies, and NHS health-care staff often refer to the existence of an ethic of 'dedication' especially for nursing and paramedical grades, or of 'the spirit of the service', especially for administrative and medical grades. Dedication has involved an identification with patient needs, an ideal of public service, and a willing acceptance of personal disadvantage. In nursing and paramedical grades, dedication has been reinforced by a conservative professionalism accompanied by an acceptance of professional hierarchies (Berridge, 1976, pp.48-9). Here again trade unionism was a weak growth, and one commentator has described industrial relations as an 'old colonial system', varying 'quite a lot from a mixture of deference and indulgence, traded by some time-served ancillary workers, to the often rather high-handed treatment of student and junior nurses by their superiors' (Bosanquet, 1979, p.3). In education too there has been a sense of professionalism, of public service, and of identification with the client – in this instance the student. The school community has been seen as a consensual one with teaching itself an activity into which bargains of the 'cash nexus' should not intrude. For many in teaching, the union has served mainly as insurance against claims of mistreating pupils.

The breakdown of these traditions has occurred slowly, and incompletely, over the last twenty years. A relative decline of dedication and discipline are clearly traceable to the consequences of post-war incomes policy, cash limits, changes in technology, scale of operations and so on. In the fire service, the strike of 1977-8 was the result of frustration over low pay that had been building for years, partly due to incomes policy. There had been a number of investigations into fire pay: the 1962 inquiry, the 1970 Holroyd Report, the 1973 McCarthy Report, a 1974 joint job evaluation between the National Joint Council (NJC) and local authority employers, and a 1975 report, which suggested a 22.5 per cent increase but was overridden by the 'social contract'. The sustained suppression of wages in the service seems clearly to have led to the determined use of the instruments of trade unionism.

The first national fire-service strike in history went far to destroy the inhibitions of a previously obedient workforce against industrial action. Similarly, in 1962 there was a dispute between the nurses and Ministry of Health. The 1968 National Board for Prices and Incomes (NBPI) report on nurses pay also helped to encourage change through the 'Pay As You Eat Scheme', by which nurses were to exchange free meals for higher pay. An NBPI report on pay among local government and NHS ancillaries alleged low productivity and recommended more rapid introduction of incentive schemes. They spread slowly, bolstering local activity and creating bitterness about low pay. By the 1970s, local and national industrial disputes in the health service were not uncommon, with a large ancillary strike occurring in 1972-3 and a nurses' strike in 1974. Incomes policy and repeated delays in payment of comparability awards also led to increasing 'trade unionism' in the civil service.

Simultaneously, several public services have seen the introduction of new technologies and the development of large-scale employment sites. In the civil service, large 'factory offices' have developed, especially at key computer centres outside London. At these sites, there are large groups of low-status and low-paid workers. These workers have little chance of promotion in a service in which promotion has traditionally been important to career-minded entrants and in which promotion sometimes compensated for low pay. Such promotion prospects often served to deter members from becoming involved in trade-union activity. At the same time the process of computerisation has also meant the emergence of key groups of workers with considerable bargaining power. These countervailing tendencies have both in their own ways contributed to breaking down traditional hostility to trade unionism.

Elsewhere changes in technology have brought their own accompaniments. So the introduction of more technologically sophisticated fire-fighting equipment has made firemen as a whole more powerful than formerly since troops would now be less able to commandeer their equipment. In the health service too changes in technology have meant that occupations have become more complex and varied, and the bargaining power of certain groups has consequently increased. Thus, following the reports of committees such as Salmon (Ministry of Health, 1966) and Zuckerman (DHSS, 1968) the restructuring of occupations functioned

(1) To emphasise a new reward structure based upon organisational and managerial abilities, (2) To provide new bureaucratic control methods to replace the internalized code of 'dedication', (3) To show that mainly senior professional practitioners were involved in operating the bureaucratic mechanisms and climbing the hierarchy, with its graded and interrelated rewards of pay, status, and authority (Berridge, 1976).

However, the conflict between professional/service ethics and trade unionism remains. In the civil service there has been a slow evolution of trade-union attitudes, while there is no longer a strong feeling of loyalty to government, 'Crown', or 'nation'. Yet professionals, and those in departments involved in social security, are still reluctant to embark on industrial action. In the health service there remains a strong sense of responsibility for patients and teachers still identify strongly with the well-being and success of pupils. However, the professional ethic is not necessarily incompatible with trade unionism, especially where government is not adequately rewarding professional skills or not providing resources adequate for professionals to do their job to high standards. Here, 'professionalism' may positively encourage trade unionism, even if outright industrial action is still regarded cautiously.

In the public-service sector there exist a number of independent unions exhibiting differences in organisation, ethos, membership interests etc. None the less, in recent times the developments which we have been describing have begun to produce concerted action.

For instance, after an action in 1979 in which there was some serious disunity, the civil-service unions made unity a key theme in the 1980-1 round with the Council of Civil Service Unions (CCSU) assuming a leading policy and operational role. The CCSU is comprised of 63 members from 9 civil service unions and, while it provides leadership and co-ordination on pay and conditions, leaves individual unions with the autonomy to pursue their own claims. During the recent dispute the CCSU central co-ordinating committee met twice daily, though individual union's HQs also had their 'action rooms'. It was nevertheless the CCSU which took the initiative in establishing local action committees to wage the strike. These were comprised of two representatives of each union, and one full-time official, and built strong links among unions at local level. In Sheffield the local action committee during the 1981 campaign even included members of the First Division Association, due to the presence of Manpower Services Commission headquarters in the area. This form of multi-union organisation was able to keep at bay many of the differences which might have led to a fragmentation of union action, such as the different interests of lower and higher paid, the disproportionate burden of strike action placed upon certain unions and so on. In the end, the union action was unsuccessful due to a general lack of will rather than because of a splitting of ranks so that at least we can say that government policy has left a legacy of potential solidarity within the civil-service unions.

Similarly, several developments between 1977 and 1980 in particular led the National Association of Fire Officers (NAFO) to announce sympathetic action with the firemen in November 1980. Not only had some officers fought the 1977 strike as FBU members and felt strong allegiance to the union as a consequence, but the FBU had also come to include a larger proportion of officers which development probably influenced attitudes of officers in general. These and other developments have led to the position where there has even been some discussion of a single federated union in the fire service.

In the health service and education, the TUC and its committees have performed an important co-ordinating role. While many CCSU unionists in the 1980-1 wages round said that they expected little assistance from the industrially oriented TUC, the Trades Union Congress assisted in achieving a unified settlement date in the health service and provided a forum for strategic and tactical planning in health and teaching. With the dwindling of its industrial base and the threat to a broad range of public services necessary to trade unionists and the unemployed, the TUC has not surprisingly undertaken to support and co-ordinate public service unions.

Tactics in the public services

More than in any other employment sector, public-service workers have recently tended to rely upon selective industrial tactics. That is, they have manipulated resources in a more differentiated way than is usual in the traditional all-out withdrawal of labour. The heavy reliance upon such tactics is substantially due to the nature of the public services: they are run by the state to serve the general public or particular groups within that public. An all-out withdrawal of labour in the public services thus affects, in the first instance, the satisfaction of a wide range of individual physical and social needs rather than the accumulation of private profit. Therefore, unions have been especially conscious to select the effects of their action, directing penalties and inconvenience away from the most vulnerable and towards those areas most likely to make an impact upon the government itself. Thus, the civil-service unions, since they were aware of the government's concern with the Public Sector Borrowing Requirement (PSBR), have made revenue-collection a central target of their collective action. By pulling out computer operators, they halted payment of VAT, PAYE, and National Insurance. However, the CCSU made it clear that it would be unacceptable to use the old, the sick, or the unemployed by denying them benefit payments. In addition, CCSU identified certain areas of international commerce for action, namely British-Irish trade which involved sensitive Common Agricultural Policy payments and recent incidents of fraud and British-EEC trade in general. A third group targeted by CCSU was 'public servants' not themselves employed in the civil service but having high political connections. Judges, barristers, and parliamentarians were hit by court actions and the withdrawal of statistical services from parliament. Defence was another area thought sensitive and CCSU took out staff at various Ministry of Defence establishments, on one occasion attempting to disrupt NATO exercises. In the health service, selective action, e.g. the use of ancillaries and clerical staff and continued provision of emergency cover, is an attempt to target hospital administration rather than harm the sick. The threat by the FBU to embark upon unofficial one-day strikes was also an attempt to manipulate cost factors occasioning least harm to the public and the FBU's own members.

The possibility of effective selective action in the public services, at little cost to union members, is often created by the technology and organisation of production. The centralisation and computerisation of public revenue collection and disbursement has created a strategic group of workers in a few civil-service computer centres at Southend, Shipley and Cumbernauld. Similarly the technological division of labour that has been introduced in some areas of customs has facilitated additional industrial action. Goods coming into Britain must be cleared through customs by an agent at ports. Historically, all duties have been paid before goods have been cleared. However, some areas have now adopted a computerised Electronic Processing Unit system, which seals cargo at ports and inland clearance depots without collecting payment; a monthly account is then issued by the computer at Southend or a local site. By ensuring that these computers were shut down the unions sent customs into chaos especially as substituting management, while able to send out accounts, did not know how to handle incoming payments. Subsequently, the Southend and Manchester EPUs were pulled out. In the fire service, as well, the technological complexity of the current generation of engines has made troop commandeering virtually impossible. However, the efficacy of these selective strategies, both in customs and in fire, also depended upon social solidarity among workers who refused to substitute. In the fire service, officers have refused to drive engines, and civil servants refused to cover for striking colleagues.

While selective action, involving few strikers for maximum effect, had positive strategic value, selective action also fits well with the 'reluctant unionism' present in some parts of the public services. Teachers, to avoid harming pupils, tend to withdraw their 'goodwill', rather than their teaching. Rather than embark on all-out strikes they tend to refuse to undertake after-hour supervision of pupils, to attend after-hour meetings, to supervise lunch breaks, to cover for absent teachers, or to teach over-sized classes. The health service has, in its turn, relied upon non-nursing staff to carry its industrial action; laundries, sterile supplies, and accounts and records were targeted in both South Yorkshire and Humberside during the health workers' dispute. Finally, the civil-service action depended upon preliminary canvassing of personnel in the key computer centres to ascertain their willingness to embark upon a long selective action. Shorter-term disruptive actions were undertaken only where there was strong support.

This being said, particular problems nevertheless stem from the use of selective tactics – not least the possibility of divisiveness within the union or between unions and possible limits on external solidarity. In those selective actions in which certain groups of workers are relied upon to carry the burden of action, resentment against non-participants or against official decision-makers who fail to bring disputes to a successful conclusion is possible. Thus, in the civil-service strike the Inland Revenue Staff Federation (IRSF) – whose members were out on long-term selective strike at Shipley and Cumbernauld computer centres – were at some stages most vociferous in urging escalation of the civil-service dispute, and, on the other hand, there was reluctance of court staff, certainly in the Sheffield area, to be used again as they were in 1979, as a major focus for the dispute. In order to decrease these problems of selective action, unions often combine short-term *all-out* action with longer term selective activity. Short all-out action builds solidarity among all sections and spreads the burden of action; it mobilises broad sections of the workforce and serves as a warning to the government of the possibility of stronger action. Of course, with an exceptionally determined government as employer selective strategies may simply not be 'strong' enough to win disputes. It is a combination of this weakness, the phenomenon of workers in dispute working and/or being paid while external workers lose pay, and the foreignness of selective tactics in many traditional industries that may limit external support. Hull dockers, for example, involved with customs and excise civil servants, were sceptical about the civil servants' action on all these grounds. However, miners and other workers have demonstrated that selective action in services can be supported by significant selective action outside, though the success or failure of the health-service campaign is unclear at the time of writing. The nature of the health service renders the original selective strategy more justifiable, and the relationship between miners and health workers made support more likely. However, by limiting the impact of action at any one moment in a dispute, selective action may result in long campaigns which are difficult to sustain.

One of the issues which emerges from the foregoing is that the need for picketing in public-service campaigns which rely largely upon selective actions is limited. We have already noted that whether the output of production is a commodity or service critically structures tactics in disputes. Where a service is offered we have also seen that the moment of production is also that of distribution and consumption. Picketing therefore is in the public services necessary to stop production but not to prevent a separate process of distribution. In addition, where selective actions are relied upon, picketing may be less necessary than where 'stronger' action is taken in that carefully selected groups of strikers are to a degree self-selected and self-disciplined. However, picketing may be used on limited-duration all-out strikes which are often combined with longer term selective strikes in order to halt supplies as well as staff entering the premises. Because these one-day actions are often meant to show solidarity with a smaller group of strikers, they also invite outside solidarity, i.e. 'secondary picketing'. While this sort of picketing was limited in the civil-service dispute, it has been more marked in the health-service action. It should also be noted that due to the unevenness of militancy and the operational life of sites within services, workers in dispute often picket at other than their own place of work. While all picketing has a symbolic component, public-services picketing is often clearly a public demonstration that a dispute is in progress, rather than a strong attempt to halt the movement of people and goods. Demonstrations themselves also assume considerable importance. Finally, the tactics of the government as employer often create a need for picketing, even secondary picketing, which otherwise would not have existed.

These points can be illustrated by discussion of the long civil-service pay campaign. The basic form taken by the civil servants' campaign was a general one-day stoppage followed by sustained selective strike action, mainly at computer centres, and other disruptive action. During the initial one-day strike there was considerable primary picketing, in the South Yorkshire area at least. Certain sites were closed but at others staff tried to enter offices through picket lines. Though the majority of pickets were at their own places of work, some demonstrably were not. People picketed their own place of work because it was more convenient to organise the lines that way, because it was customary, and because picketing was a continuation of attempts at persuasion that had been going on for some time in workplaces. In certain cases, pickets were used to convey to the public information about altered procedures at a particular site, e.g. signing on at unemployment offices; therefore, knowledge of the site and its business was essential. Interestingly perhaps, in addition to turning away some staff, the pickets also succeeded in stopping postal deliveries. In general, co-operation from the Union of Communication Workers (UCW) was good throughout the strike, and since mail represents a key 'supply' to the civil service this relationship was particularly important. Furthermore, because the picketing was undertaken under the CCSU banner rather than in the name of individual unions, there was an easy mixing of pickets and consequent difficulty in identifying either their places of work or their union. Local union representatives, also identified as CCSU, circulated freely.

After the one-day strike the action took the form of selective strikes at revenue-collecting computers, as well as 'rolling' disruptive action elsewhere. The Shipley and Cumbernauld computers, employing 1,000 people and collecting £100 million revenue per week, were key targets. It became clear early in the dispute that the government was having management collect Shipley mail and extract the larger cheques for manual processing. Management also tried to switch processing to Sovereign House (Sheffield) and Bush House (London) without manifest success since both sites more or less blacked the work, with middle management also refusing to 'strike break'. Higher management then set up 'secret' processing centres, one of them in Leeds, in order to process the cheques. This resulted in the picketing of the centre at Leeds and approaches being made to the unions involved with the Leeds premises. Further, banking unions were asked to black Inland Revenue cheques in spite of the difficulties posed by incomplete unionisation in banking. Finally, a picket of CCSU members was mounted outside Sovereign House to keep the blacked cheques *inside* the building and away from the bank. The success of that picket was unclear. What is of particular interest then is that the perceived need for secondary picketing was actually created by government or higher management intervention.

In the health-service campaign, picketing had been confined to the short all-out stoppages and used to dissuade staff, turn away supplies, and inform the public. The South Yorkshire evidence is that primary picketing was effective on all three counts. In fact, uniformed nurses were placed towards the front in many picket lines, no doubt to enlist public sympathy as strongly as possible which they attempted by leafletting passers-by and patients. On those days of all-out action external groups of workers joined the lines. The nurses themselves also went to other places of work to explain their case and urge support with the result that some health-service unionists proudly referred to them as 'flying pickets'. Some trade unionists also travelled to other hospital sites to boost picket lines. However, in both the civil service and health service the withdrawal of labour itself interrupted production/consumption decisively, though selectively. Nevertheless there were countless infractions of the 1980 Act in circumstances where neither the government nor the police showed any signs of taking action.

In the civil-service dispute we have described limited secondary and mass picketing especially in connection with Inland Revenue matters yet again the government neither took action under the Act nor publicly threatened to do so. In some areas civil servants openly entered into negotiations with the police which legitimated picketing of Crown buildings whether or not the pickets worked at the particular sites being picketed. There are various reasons why the government may not have acted. First, it may not have had accurate information about where such picketing was occurring. Again since some of this picketing was short-lived and unpredictable, the legal process would have been of little use, and there may have been a realisation of difficulties defining 'place of work' in the civil service. The Minister in charge of the civil service, a traditionalist in political terms, may also have opposed the use of law fearing further exacerbation of an already difficult industrial relations situation. Of interest nevertheless is that when civil servants expressed a willingness to take action in support of the health workers during the summer of 1982 the then Minister for the Civil Service, a relative newcomer to that position, pointedly advised them that such action might well breach the 1980 Act. At the end of the day, however, what almost certainly proved conclusive was the fact that picketing was not the main tactic upon which the CCSU relied; the withdrawal of key workers being infinitely more important. It should also be borne in mind that other sanctions were available to the government: suspensions, blockage of promotion, decreases in pension entitlements and so on. On one occasion it was even moved to initiate a prosecution under the little-known 1875 Conspiracy and Protection of Property Act.

In the health workers' dispute secondary and mass picketing were much more publicly visible but again were not central to the main action affecting the hospitals. In fact, much of that 'secondary' picketing was specifically aimed to undermine and discredit the 1980 Act and the 1982 Employment Bill then passing through Parliament. In the Trent Regional Health Authority, there was some discussion of possible legal remedies against picketing, and government spokesmen emphasised that the picketing was 'illegal'. However, no legal action was initiated.

Both primary and secondary picketing in the public services are, of course, subject to police supervision under the general criminal law. Not unexpectedly, the police appear to pursue different tactics in different public-service settings, but in none has their presence been as strong in numbers as we often observed in relation to smaller picket lines in the private sector. A rare and most notable exercise of 'aggressive' police power occurred at the courts, where police forcefully forbade pickets to approach judges and tried rigidly to enforce the picketing Code thus demonstrating their traditional deference to judges, although we have no evidence to suggest that this was an instruction which emanated from command level. Their relative absence from health-service picket lines and their generally tolerant and distant attitude towards pickets in ambulance and fire disputes, on the other hand, probably owes something to an affinity and trust among the uniformed emergency services. Where ambulancemen or firemen are involved in disputes what seems to have happened is that the police have walked a thin line between maintaining public order and safety and strike breaking, a tension clearly perceived by the police themselves. The latter phenomenon exhibits itself in, for instance, ambulance strikes, where police use their own vehicles for emergency transport, and in strikes in the fire service where they play a co-ordinating role, escort and guide troop-driven vehicles, and generally supervise fire sites.

Government policy, therefore, has played a central role in initiating numerous public-service disputes over the last two years, including national conflicts in the civil service, fire service, and health service. In none of these disputes has 'secondary picketing' or action played a major role and the 1980 Employment Act's provisions have not been resorted to. What has resulted is a high level of industrial activity in the services, with selective action the central tactic. Partly as a result of these disputes, public-service unionism shows some interesting signs of change. With sharply diminishing resources and the increase of market pressures in the public services, trade unionism shows every sign of being a solid implant, with prospects for growth and change towards unionism and away from 'associationism'. This change, while attributable to a long process of erosion of 'dedication' and discipline and of discriminatory wages treatment, has been accelerated in the present period. The result may presage the future integration of the public services into the broader labour movement and a resort to more traditional, less selective, tactics. In fact, the history of disputes of this period itself may discourage selective and encourage more complete industrial action. The long selective strategy in the civil service ultimately proved unsuccessful and the unions may well have learned its limits. It is noticeable that already the old moderately inclined CPSA Executive, which was partly responsible for the conduct of that dispute, has been displaced by a more left-inclined group of unionists. Another effect of the disputes has been the growth of local union activity in a traditionally highly centralised industrial relations sector. For instance, in South Yorkshire and Humberside civil-service unions have met since the conclusion of the campaign, civil servants have stood on local health-service picket lines, and some branches and workplaces have seriously taken up issues such as new technology; while in many areas joint health-service committees have functioned. This growth of local solidarity unionism also has potential implications for the future. On the one hand, centres of local union power with co-ordinating abilities may either initiate action or press national levels to initiate action. On the other hand, national centres can now rely upon sophisticated local knowledge and co-ordination in either selective or all-out national action. As the local committees are inter-union, practical solidarity is more likely in spite of the persistence of inter-union tensions.

Although the impact of the 1980 Act has been minimal in this part of the public sector it will be interesting to observe whether the newer proposals now passing through parliament, and which are centrally aimed at weakening trade unionism *per se*, will prove effective to impede these embryonic developments.

8
Government policy and the private sector

Monetarist neo-liberalism conceives the market as a sphere of competitive but free exchange which maximises the production of wealth and guarantees individual liberty. It therefore aims to maximise the free market by reducing the state sector and state interference. Market mechanisms of supply and demand, pricing and profit-making will themselves, in this view, ultimately result in modernised and restructured industry. Because the concept of the market is premised upon individual exchange, trade unions are seen as interfering with the workings of the free market and decreasing management's right and need to manage in response to the market. Further, monetarist neo-liberalism suggests that the national economy must be integrated into international capitalism in terms of trade and investment rather than protected by tariff barriers. A consequence of international competition is regarded as more efficient industry with larger national and international markets.

Government policy towards the public sector has had various actual effects for private industry. Perhaps the most significant has been the contraction of demand from public-sector manufacturing and construction. In the South Yorkshire economy, for example, steel and engineering firms have been badly hit by the decline in aerospace, construction and motor manufacture. In addition, energy prices have risen due to the government's revision of terms of reference to monopoly public suppliers in the interests of the public-sector borrowing requirement. Heavy energy users such as steel, refractories, concrete and glass have consequently suffered. Again, the rise in interest rates has had a general deflationary effect in the private sector.

The national pattern of industrial rationalisation resulting from the general depression of demand has been in evidence in both South Yorkshire and Humberside where rationalisation has taken the form of cutting costs for survival rather than investment and technical innovation. This has largely taken the form of demanning in conditions where prior lack of investment had already left industry uncompetitive. In industries where labour costs are disproportionately large it scarcely needs saying that labour bears a heavy weight of cost-cutting. Traditionally 'overmanning' has been, at least to an extent, the result of managerial attempts to retain labour in periods of full employment and not simply a question of union restrictive practices. Unions which have not effectively controlled manning levels now find it impossible to do so.

The other main method of holding down labour costs, of course, is through small or nil wage rises which can in the present climate be enforced effectively due to high unemployment levels. The rates of redundancy in engineering in Sheffield, for example, have increased markedly over the last three years, reflecting the trebling of unemployment in Sheffield as a whole. A further indication of demanning in Sheffield is the number of firms which, formerly characterised as 'large' by numbers of employees, have become medium-sized. In Humberside, redundancies have meant not only closure but also severe job losses in larger companies. Rationalisation has also involved the prominent listing of shop stewards in redundancy announcements, the unilateral suspension of procedure agreements and resistance to new forms of unionisation. Against the background of a government-encouraged low wages strategy, management has usually been able to impose low wage increases. While it is difficult to evaluate the degree to which such developments represent a departure from previous practice, it is our very clear observation that government policy and general economic developments have encouraged more aggressive management styles, especially in engineering, and in many cases new management seems to have been employed primarily to make cost savings and productivity improvements. The ability to shed and strictly to contain the costs of labour may, however, only be an adequate strategy in certain firms. Where investment has occurred recently, the government's deflationary policy may paradoxically be placing serious pressures on just the sort of firm government would like to succeed. The evidence from South Yorkshire is ambiguous, but logic would suggest that while older, more traditional firms can shed labour and wait, more dynamic firms with recent debts might be placed under serious financial strain.

In addition, government policy seems to have accelerated types of restructuring which have characterised the last ten years. Nearly all engineering (and steel) firms in Sheffield have become part of large national or multi-national firms. In heavy industry the scale of investment required and the slow rate of turnover make it virtually impossible for small single companies to carve out niches. One-product firms have, either by diversification or takeover, become part of multi-product operations. Some mergers and takeovers have been executed mainly to capture order books. As well as acquiring units, companies have also been divesting themselves of manufacturing sites which in the current depressed market has most often taken the form of closures. Remaining single-line firms are most usually subcontractors, dependent upon larger firms for their success and some small firms have received a fillip from the disposal by larger firms of their ancillary workers and the increase in subcontracting which has been part of general cost-cutting.

The government's attempt to use international competition to revive the economy has simply reinforced rationalisation and restructuring as general international recession has been allowed to influence economic demand and as Britain's internationally competitive position has not noticeably improved. Increased import penetration has hit some sectors, such as special steels and hand tools, particularly. Some foreign-based companies with British subsidiaries or plants can be observed to have sacrificed British concerns to the needs of the foreign centre or other manufacturing units. The strength of the pound – due to monetary policy and oil exports – has also meant that exports have not boomed in the hoped-for way though they have so far held reasonably steady.

Government policy, therefore, has fostered certain types of rationalisation in industry which have resulted in high social costs to labour and union organisation. These types of rationalisation have defined the nature of disputes in private sector industry. The structure of ownership and control and union organisation have determined the forms that disputes, created by this intensified industrial conflict, have taken.

Industrial disputes in private-sector industry : engineering in South Yorkshire and Humberside

While disputes arising throughout private industry have been similarly affected, different employment sectors have shown different patterns of disputes and dispute tactics due to different industrial structures. The South Yorkshire and Humberside engineering industries provide a useful focus for the examination of disputes in the private sectors for a number of reasons. First, the industry is a significant traditionally dominant industry in South Yorkshire, particularly Sheffield. Second, engineering presents a useful contrast to other, especially public, sectors in terms of types of disputes that arise and the tactics used to prosecute them. Third, the diversity of forms of ownership and production in engineering offer a broad canvas for study. Finally, the relative frequency of disputes in engineering provides sufficient material for examination. Let us now turn then to the structural issues which, we have argued, help to determine the form which disputes tend to take.

Structure of ownership and control

The most striking characteristic of ownership and control in engineering is its diversity and fragmentation. Large numbers of engineering workers are found in both the public and private sectors, in small and large companies, in national and multi-national firms. Workers organised by the Amalgamated Union of Engineering Workers (AUEW) are found not only in metal-working but in nearly every industry which employs complex machinery. The situation is similar in much of private industry. With bargaining structures and union organisation which reflect this fragmentation, engineering disputes, like those in much of the private sector, tend to be local or even sectional.

It is possible to distinguish three modes of operation in engineering, and probably much of the rest of private manufacturing, though any one firm may have features of more than one type. All, however, are subject to the constraints of market profitability and recession has put more pressures on firms to adopt strict financial criteria.

First, new, financially oriented capital tends to be large-scale and mobile, though of course small companies may also conform to this style of operation. Such firms are usually run by a controlling group of professional managers and accountants whose skills are professionally acquired and general. The style of such management is impersonal and exhibits little commitment to either the industry or local community in which operations are based. Associated with this form of enterprise is 'multi-layered' management, where there exist fairly long lines of managerial responsibility. Criteria for decision-making and negotiations are relatively clear-cut, i.e. they are financial, and managers are less concerned about whether concessions erode traditional authority than with whether they fit into costing and financially determined authority. They tend to work more on the basis of the commercial self-sufficiency of production units or divisions than the old industrial type of firm.

Traditional industrial firms, on the other hand, regard their power base in the local community and status and authority relations in the firm as important. Here 'finance', according to one union official we interviewed, 'is almost secondary.' Companies within a group dominated by this culture are probably engaged in considerable cross-subsidisation.

Lastly, entrepreneurial firms are dominated by individuals without power bases or traditions in local communities yet without the consistency or professionalist orientations of financial capital. While some may be small-scale and paternalist, others may be quite large.

Linked to differences in general mode of operation are differences in the roles of managerial personnel in companies. Clear differences exist between managing directors or personnel directors and personnel managers over a wide variety of issues; the conflict is perhaps best summarised, if over simply, as a tension between concern for overall operational efficiency and concern for harmonious industrial relations. In financially oriented firms we have noted that the personnel function is clearly subordinated to financial calculation. Especially where such a company is large, the main financial decisions are taken at the centre, while operational responsibility, including industrial relations is devolved to local levels. In traditional industrial firms, the personnel function may have more importance and there may be closer integration of decision-making. In a recession there is the tendency to fuse styles so that the personnel function may, in all types of firms, begin to be subordinated to financial considerations. Certainly the recession has submerged the incorporative style of personnel management which emphasised co-operation with and welfare concessions to the workforce.

Ownership in engineering, and elsewhere in private industry, has recently changed frequently. As certain traditional companies are bought out by new finance-oriented concerns, labour's understanding of company practice is likely to become blurred. Changes in the structure of and the sheer complexity of financially oriented capital itself are bound to cause confusion. For example, in South Yorkshire, the acquisition of a traditional small engineering firm by a European-based multi-national company made it difficult for the workforce to understand company strategy and led them to misjudge management's intentions and future actions. In other cases, workers have mistakenly regarded the good fortune of a group of companies as safeguarding their own. Conversely, the movement of workers from large to smaller, more paternalistic or entrepreneurial, firms has sometimes led to misplaced expectations of rationality and orderly bargaining on clear criteria. The wave of rationalisation in the 1960s and again the developments in ownership in the 1970s, reinforced by current government policy, have no doubt increased such problems.

Union organisation

Strong autonomous ('unofficial') shopfloor organisation reflects the fragmented and decentralised nature of control in the engineering industry, as well as itself contributing to the importance of domestic bargaining in the industry. The situation is similar in other parts of the private sector. The existence of the shop steward as bargainer in the post-war period has rested upon several factors. Collective agreements leave scope for workplace supplementation and improvement, and national collective agreements are less important than domestic bargains. Disputes procedures have been a key factor in the development of domestic bargaining and where no disputes procedures exist, workers have less chance of building up workplace organisation. Incentive schemes too continue to play an important part in the organisation of work and the response of workers to stewards. Within engineering at large employers themselves have tended to resist detailed outside regulation and free entry of full-time officials into the workplace.

All this contributed to the effectiveness of shop stewards, especially in the 1950s and 1960s, when high levels of employment and consequent labour scarcity have been reinforcing items. Such traditions do not easily evaporate so that in engineering – as elsewhere

– shop stewards remain important in spite of the fall in employment levels over the last decade. This feature has been reinforced by recent trends to expand domestic collective bargaining.

None the less, in spite of the continued centrality of the shop-steward movement organisational defects have become evident. Thus, development of group shop-steward structures and combine committees reflects the growing awareness that individual workplace organisations are not necessarily adequate to cope with the new and complex problems of large companies. While combine and group committees have been most important for exchange of information, they have occasionally also been involved in co-ordinating industrial action. Such committees, however, face many difficulties in unity of action. Workplaces usually cover a diverse product range and diverse markets, and shifts in world trade may produce dissimiliar conditions at different sites. Work sites are often managed relatively independently, and work may be moved to one site at the expense of another. However, the information function remains important, and the combine or group committee aggregates the experience of a number of sites. Co-ordinated political action is thereby also possible. It has been noted that in some cases full-time officials are suspicious of combine committees although mistrust is far less common where full-time officials have themselves risen through a group committee and where the official structure incorporates prominent members of those committees.

In the AUEW, the steward is subjected to the formal control of the District Committee, which itself enjoys exclusive control over wages and conditions in the District. The District Committee, while including elected representatives from the quarterly shop stewards' meeting, is comprised mainly of representatives of paired branches. Many branch delegates are also conveners and, according to one Sheffield AUEW official, branch delegates who are conveners must often be reminded that they serve on the District Committee as representatives of their branches, and not workplaces. Stewards may also make representations to the General Purposes Committee of the DC and directly to the District Committee itself. The (mainly geographical) branches, which provide the majority of representatives on the DC, are themselves in decline due to the break-up of traditional working-class communities tied closely to a small group of local factories; the full-time employment of craftsmen on single sites; the appropriation by the state of certain provident functions and the centralisation of union administration. The DC, therefore, represents a separate official structure which is none the less responsive to shopfloor concerns, including actual and potential domestically generated disputes. The DC may ratify constitutional or unconstitutional action taken at a local level and pass resolutions critical of national positions to the Executive. The DC may also provide organisational and financial assistance. However, there is no formal contact between stewards and branches, and the contact between stewards and DC is, by many accounts, inadequate to integrate stewards into the life of the union in an orderly and efficient manner. While shop-steward autonomy may, therefore, increase stewards' responsiveness to the shopfloor, it may exact a price in communication, consistency and unity of action. In most places where the union organises it does not, in any case, enjoy exclusive bargaining rights; thus, joint shop-steward and group committees have developed as almost independent bodies, often engaging in negotiations and policy-making outside the structure of the union. Combine committees exhibit some of the same properties only on a larger scale.

The pivotal local official in the AUEW is the District Secretary, who is the full-time agent of the DC *and* responsible to the national Executive. One central function of the District Secretary is negotiation, and as the volume of domestic bargaining has grown, the pressure on the District Secretary has increased. The secretary also provides general assistance to the membership. The District Secretary has a continuous and important role in disputes, often supporting domestic disputes and maintaining their objectives, sometimes imposing certain objectives or procedures upon them. However, as a single official covering a widely diverse and fragmented membership, the District Secretary can only play a limited role. In an industry where numerous problems particular to individual work sites arise, both the District Committee and District Secretary must make strategic choices about where to employ resources. Because of the fragmentation of ownership and diversity of production and autonomous shopfloor organisation the involvement of political groups during disputes especially at less experienced workplaces is not surprising. In lengthy engineering disputes in South Yorkshire and Humberside, such involvement was not unusual.

The District Committee has the authority to make a strike official, but only the Executive Committee can pay benefit. A strike, as noted, may be declared official before procedure is exhausted, though there is pressure from the Executive to keep to official procedure. Exhausting official procedure has become more usual since this procedure has been shortened. The authority of the DC, the negotiating structure and strike-pay procedures all create the potential for considerable official supervision of disputes.

The course of disputes is, of course, greatly influenced by financial resources available to strikers. Strike benefit, paid by the Executive, £12 per member per week, is often paid only six to nine weeks into the strike. District levies may be applied by the DC, though administration of the levy takes nearly two months. Consequently, stewards take collections from other factories, often while they are also organising blacking. While this form of voluntary funding is independent of national official decisions, it consumes local resources of time and energy and is subject to local constraints, such as the financial stringency accompanying short-time working, primary management's attempts to discredit the dispute, and secondary management's willingness to admit stewards on to premises. In Humberside an address book of trade-union contacts and organisations which have made fighting-fund contributions previously is passed among strike committees. In the first crucial weeks of disputes, resources come from local and unofficial rather than official sources.

Dispute tactics

Tactics adopted in engineering, and other similarly organised parts of the private manufacturing sector, reflect the fragmentation and complexity of ownership, union organisation and bargaining. Engineering firms, it has been noted, are both privately and publicly owned, and owned by many different types of capital whilst the industries in which engineers are employed involve a myriad of unions. In South Yorkshire, weak or moderate unions, such as the Boilermakers and ISTC, for example, share workplaces with the better organised AUEW. Not all workplaces are fully unionised, and the two-tier bargaining structure can create a great many domestic and sectional disputes. There are also possibilities for labour substitution, since some engineering production processes are not as finely skilled, labour intensive or interdependent as those in some other industries. Therefore, engineering workers ordinarily have to rely upon picketing to stop production as well as distribution.

A useful contrast can be drawn with the mining industry. Mining is a publicly owned, centralised and highly rationalised industry. It is organised by a single industrial union with 100 per cent unionism and a strong tradition of solidarity. Since 1966 the bargaining structure has been highly centralised, and in consequence significant disputes tend to be national in nature. Because mining is labour intensive, skilled and involves a complex, interdependent production process, for which substitution by supervisors or the military is nigh impossible, picketing to halt production is unnecessary. Yet, in both engineering and mining, which are industrial processes which produce (stockable) commodities, picketing is necessary to halt distribution and consumption. Both these industries contrast with service industries and public services, such as the fire service and health service, in which, as we have noted, the moment of production is also that of consumption.

The limited *extent* of disputes in engineering leads to heavy reliance upon blacking rather than picketing as a form of secondary action. As engineering sites often manufacture components for other manufacturing processes or for widespread final consumption, their products have multiple destinations, yet because of the small scale of engineering disputes, strikers' physical and financial resources are few. Blacking products is a tactic which demands not physical presence by workers in dispute but selective action, self-administered by secondary workers, who may belong to different trade unions. Blacking where the blacked product is a major input into production, however, requires extensive co-operation, self-discipline, and sacrifice by secondary workers, and so on certain occasions is difficult to sustain. However important blacking may be, it is, none the less, difficult to assess its effectiveness due to its self-administration, physical distance from the dispute, and the possibility of alternative outlets for the blacked product. Yet, when it is effectively organised it has very serious repercussions for employers, particularly in a recession where blacking threatens precious markets. In one engineering dispute in South Yorkshire for example the company concerned admitted that it could not have survived another two weeks of blacking, a matter clearly not appreciated by its workers. The threat to the viability of the company stemmed from a combination of its precarious finances and the effectiveness of the blacking so that ultimately the tactics of management were dominated by the urgent necessity of a solution which would remove it.

Blacking is organised from both workplace and official levels. In engineering, the District Committee generally circularises local shop-steward committees with lists of products and contacts the District Confederation of Shipbuilding and Engineering Unions (ConFed). Both District and ConFed may request blacking at national level and send letters to other unions requesting assistance. More usual is that both District AUEW and ConFed rely upon issuing official letters of introduction which individual members of strike committees can carry with them when making personal contacts with stewards. Both Sheffield and Humberside AUEW prefer to avoid sending letters to full-time officials because requests 'get lost'. It is more effective for strikers to go directly to stewards to make their appeals, and such activity is financed through the strike fund. In this regard, the way in which blacking is organised reflects the way in which engineering and related industries are organised and avoids relying upon union officials who, in many industries, have limited contact with their membership. Calls for blacking, in fact, rely heavily upon inter-union and workplace solidarity of a particularly informal kind built through past experience, reciprocity, and the exchange of favours among activists. This informal element increases the uncertainty concerning its effective implementation, but also may make it particularly recalcitrant to formal control – such as by legal intervention.

The structure of ownership in engineering – multi-company or multiple-factory groups – creates an objective reason for secondary action, including secondary picketing. Where ownership is extensive, as in many engineering companies in Sheffield, pressure on the employer may be exerted not only at the site in dispute but elsewhere. Where there is production duplication or possibility of transfer of production within the group there is added incentive. Against the increasingly extensive and complex ownership in engineering, however, must be placed several factors which tend to confine industrial action to 'primary' sites: the separate managerial structures of many group firms, the emphasis on domestic bargaining, and the relative weakness of cross-site organisation. Some of the reorganisation which has been taking place throughout the industry in response to the recession increases the difficulty of effective joint action in multi-site companies. The most obvious local example is the McGregor reorganisation plan for British Steel. By increasing the amount of plant-level negotiation this reduces the capacity for company-wide action.

One particular set of current economic developments which is relevant to secondary picketing (and secondary action) in engineering is the closure of plants in multi-site or multi-company firms in a general economic recession. In engineering there has been a large number of individual plant closures which have been fought as local rather than as national issues. However, the closure of a single site in a multiple-site company provides a reason for secondary picketing since only limited pressure, such as obstruction of the disposal of assets and public protest can be exerted at the site of a closure.

The paradox is that as closures make secondary picketing more necessary, the economic recession makes it more difficult for 'inside workers' to accept secondary picketing, and for unions and individuals to gather the financial resources and morale to mount and sustain a secondary picket. In the case of one small engineering firm in South Yorkshire, inside workers at a secondary site were afraid of losing their own jobs and were correspondingly unsympathetic to the resistance of a closure which had probably saved their own jobs, at least temporarily. In another dispute, workers from a Manchester engineering site were unsuccessful in attempting to prevent inside workers at the parent company in Doncaster from working. They too were concerned about their jobs, they lacked strong trade-union organisation and had only recently become part of the same company as the Manchester workers. In both instances then strikers were faced with mounting secondary pickets at some distance from their home bases at inhospitable hours and in poor weather conditions. The financial difficulties of doing so were considerable, especially as the disputes had endured for some time and, in the case of the Doncaster company, as official backing had been withdrawn.

The anticipated fight against redundancies at a large Sheffield steel site of a steel and engineering firm also illustrated the problem of inside workers. Despite the formation of a special Steel and Engineering Committee to support such a struggle, the workers directly involved were apparently unconvinced that workers even at other sites within the group would support them. When the joint shop-stewards committee visited the key Manchester site, they were greeted by a 'dismal response'. The site had recently been reduced from 2,000 to 180 workers, and the remaining labour force was not keen to take strike action in support of the threatened site.

While engineering, and other private sector tactics are structured in this general way, tactics in any particular dispute in the industry are dependent upon a variety of factors, many of them – such as organisation of production, management strategies and tactics, domestic union support and organisation – are variable from site to site. In addition, different levels of the union or different political groups in the union may arrive at different assessments of such variables and advocate different forms of action. In a union where official and rank-and-file levels are not closely articulated, these differences may emerge in action.

For example, domestic union organisation and practices often determine how picketing is pursued. In 1982 engineers at a glass factory in South Yorkshire struck over a pay award offered to both shift and day engineers. Only a token picket against glass production workers was mounted at the start of the official dispute, in the expectation that other (unionised) workers would shortly come to a decision to support them. Picketing against deliveries and removal of supplies, however, continued throughout the dispute. On the other hand, at a small firm producing razor and other light cutting blades, union pickets had to picket strongly against a large number of non-unionised workers who continued to attend work, and regular mass pickets were mounted to discourage their entering the premises. With non-union labour continuing to produce, the picket against delivery of supplies and blacking took on great importance.

In another engineering dispute in South Yorkshire, union officials had a different view of management strategy and the possibilities for successful action, with perhaps a more accurate understanding of management plans, than the rank and file. The AUEW District Secretary urged acceptance of what was admittedly a very low wages and conditions offer, in the hope of averting what was understood to be likely closure. The workers, not understanding the new management and influenced by a Socialist Workers' Party steward, chose to fight, doubting management's intention to close. The workforce saw the new manager as similar to previous weak, ineffective and possibly corrupt managers. The rank and file pursued its own course of action which included an all-out strike, primary and secondary picketing, and occupation without the active support of the District

Secretary. In the end the factory closed and all the workers were made redundant.

The EEF and dispute tactics

Of course the Engineering Employers' Federation (EEF) acts nationally as a representative of its members to government on a range of issues, including employment legislation, But it is at regional and district levels that the Federation plays a more central role in industrial relations terms, especially since the shortening of the bargaining procedure has contributed to a greater role for local levels of the EEF. In fact, a general effect of renegotiation of the National Engineering Agreement has been an increased reliance by some managements upon the resources and expertise of the Federation, including legal advice, especially where, as in Humberside, firms tend to be small. Whatever role the Federation plays, it will stop short of actual decision-taking. The EEF does, however, have an active policy of dissuading members from taking any major action, especially legal action, without contacting the Federation first. Federated firms may, therefore, be expected to act differently from non-federated firms where legal action is possible. The EEF also organises mutual support among federated firms. This has taken the form of temporary relief for payment of accounts and suspended contracts for employers in dispute. However, in third party disputes involving secondary action from outside engineering (for instance steel, road haulage and docks) there is little the EEF can achieve through such methods. In these cases in particular, engineering firms may find it useful to seek injunctions against workers other than their own.

Dispute tactics and the law

A large variety of legal provisions, going well beyond the traditional torts may influence the initiation of and forms of industrial action. Perhaps the most obvious example of relevant law beyond the traditional torts is the law governing redundancy. When redundancies are threatened, fears that statutory payments and *ex gratia* additions may be lost may deter workers from taking industrial action. Dismissal of strikers or deeming them to have dismissed themselves is, of course, common in strikes, and such action may result in loss of statutory redundancy. In one case, management threatened that favourable terms might be withdrawn if there were difficulty, with the result that no strike occurred. The law of redundancy can also sometimes be a hindrance to the settlement of disputes. At one stage of a long engineering dispute, an offer of jobs was made to some workers if they would return redundancy payments. The workers, however, had spent the money.

In South Yorkshire engineering disputes the traditional torts have often been committed in relation to picketing and sit-ins. Nevertheless, in the instances in which these were relevant the law did not prevent workers from mounting action. It could be argued that workers who take industrial action in the present economic climate are particularly determined and unlikely to be deterred by a law which anyway may not be invoked. Perhaps more important is the fact that the primary determinant of action in disputes is not the legal framework established by picketing and trespass law but the structures of production and distribution themselves.

Given that secondary picketing and sit-ins continue to occur and that the legal remedies against them lie in civil law, it is necessary to evaluate when employers are likely to resort to law. Actions against both occupations and secondary picketing are more likely to be used when factories are closing, the offending workforce is being dismissed and materials are badly needed. Furthermore, the picketing provisions of the 1980 Act are more likely to be used in engineering than in some other sectors. This is because the fragmented nature of ownership and control in engineering and the diversity of employers mean that there are more individual points of autonomous decision. A traditional explanation for reluctance on the part of employers to take legal action against their own workers has been the seriousness of industrial relations consequences. However, the different modes of operation within engineering mean that such a reductionist analysis is inadequate. In the case of financially oriented capital a decision to proceed to law may be taken as a strict financial calculation, especially since it is unlikely to be the decision-taker who must live with the consequences of such a decision. She or he does not have to negotiate with the defendants or their fellow trade-union members and capital may always be relocated and a new workforce employed. Again, entrepreneurial firms are likely to involve individual decision-makers of strong personality who may be prepared to take on a workforce in legal battle. It is in traditional industrial firms where the personnel function has been important and where the firm attaches importance to its local base, that the industrial relations consequences may be given greater weight. Even in such firms, in a recession, financial considerations may be paramount. In addition, in the engineering industry, where ownership is fragmented and unionisation incomplete and locally based, the consequences of legal confrontation are less severe than those in differently organised industries.

Two cases from South Yorkshire and Humberside illustrate some of these relationships. The first dispute occurred at a small engineering firm, the parent company of which was a European-based financially oriented multi-national corporation. A second company plant was located outside the area. The dispute began when the workforce struck, against official advice, over a wages and conditions offer, with the result that it was dismissed *in toto*. Two days later they began a factory occupation and within five days a writ was issued seeking possession of the works, which, on service, was immediately respected. At a hearing in the Manchester Crown Court the defendants, 7 named stewards and 54 other workers, did not appear and were not represented. The plaintiffs were granted an order that the defendants vacate the premises. By the date of the hearing the strikers had already reverted to a primary picket. Though the secondary site had been picketed several times, the secondary picketing provisions of the 1980 Employment Act were not used, since the Managing Director anticipated that legal action would intensify the picketing and create additional tension. However, had the secondary picket had any lasting effect, the Managing Director was prepared to use the law. The use of the law against the occupation was a strict financial calculation intended to free badly needed assets at the primary site, at a time which in industrial relations terms was also judged to be ripe. The strikers' decision to leave the factory was also influenced by the full-time AUEW official, who had made it clear that the union would not provide defence or further support unless the strikers obeyed the order.

A second dispute began with a declaration that a large Manchester factory would close. At a mass meeting the workforce voted to take over the factory. The AUEW District supported this action, but the AUEW Executive withdrew its support after some weeks. Several months later the Managing Director was granted an order for re-possession of the factory, yet in this instance the strikers remained and were only evicted after four months. They subsequently mounted a secondary picket against the parent company's head office and factories in South Yorkshire and an injunction against six named pickets was ultimately granted under Section 17 of the 1980 Act. Before the hearing, however, the secondary picketing had ceased not so much because of the writ as the general lack of support the pickets were receiving. At the hearing the defendants argued that because their factory was closed their 'place of work' was the head office and contiguous factories. The judge disagreed, and the injunction was granted. In this instance the motivation for the use of law seems not to have been a mainly financial one, as the secondary picket was proving ineffective and was collapsing prior to the use of law, but an exemplary action by a tough, and slightly maverick, entrepreneur. The defendants, already isolated from the union, initially defied the order, but eventually complied because of lack of support.

Two further points related to the impact of law emerge from these two cases: a point about workers' perception of the picketing law and a point about the non-decisive impact of the law. The statement of the AUEW official in the first dispute described that unless the writ were obeyed no defence would be provided was so influential because workers are not eager to face the law, in unknown and hostile territory, alone. Rank-and-file response to the 1980 Act, and often other law, is a combination of ignorance of its mechanisms and fear. The social reality of the picket line also blurs the distinction between criminal law enforced by the police, and civil law available at the behest of an injured party. Much of the 1980 Act is nevertheless perceived as 'police law'. Because it sometimes suits the police to play on such beliefs, the misconceptions and illusions are reinforced. The confusion among engineering workers in Sheffield may have been greater than that in other industries or in engineering elsewhere. AUEW officials in general tend not to be in close contact with a fragmented rank and file because of the disjuncture between official and unofficial structures. In addition, the AUEW took a deliberate decision not to take measures to explain the 1980 Act or to issue picketing guidelines. Because of scarcity of information from official sources, strikers in certain cases have relied upon information from far left newspapers and activists.

In both of the cases cited, however, the legal actions themselves were not decisive in the collapse of the disputes. In the case of the first engineering site, management strategy was firm and workers refused to respect the secondary picket line. While blacking was well-organised and strikers felt it was having some effect, its actual severe consequences were not as apparent to strikers as to management. The sit-in had simply been a more comfortable execution of a primary picket of limited effect.

In the second case, support for the strike decreased steadily over several months. Not only had national officials withdrawn support, but other factories in the group continued working. Where the secondary picketing occurred, the entire workforce crossed the line. In view of the continuation of work, the NUM, whose industry received as much as 60 per cent of the production from some group factories, was unable to institute a general blacking of the group's products. The NUM did agree to black material brought through picket lines, and in view of this assurance, secondary pickets were important. However, with low levels of financial and physical support, picketing five geographically dispersed factories, especially in cold, snowy weather was impossible.

In both cases the workers lost their dispute less because of legal action than because they enjoyed low levels of support, even inside the companies involved. Economic recession in privately owned and fragmented industry creates a strong tendency to increased division of the workforce. The implication of this for the use of law against engineering workers is that it is, in a recession, less necessary, and the law is less likely to be resisted when it is used.

9
Regulated employment and disputes

Most work situations are governed by a host of legal regulations other than those contained in the 1980 Employment Act, or indeed any law consciously designed to influence industrial conflict. These other legal frameworks may also have an impact on dispute tactics, or in some way modify the impact of the 1980 Act. To examine such influences this chapter looks at disputes and tactics in three related transport industries: the docks, merchant shipping and road haulage. In each of these industries there are unique legal and other regulatory frameworks.

The strategic importance of transport underlines some of the special regulations in the various sectors of that industry. The military significance of the merchant fleet and merchant seamen was recently highlighted by the Falklands war. In the past the Merchant Shipping Acts have, in part, sought to ensure that industrial relations did not undermine the industry's ability to play a strategic role in both military and trading terms. Legal regulations of industrial relations in the docks, on the other hand, was granted in order to achieve the co-operation of the dockers during the Second World War. What has emerged in merchant shipping and the docks are two distinct regulatory frameworks which govern employment. In road haulage employment is also governed by a distinct regulatory framework but in this case deriving mainly from safety, rather than strategic considerations.

Although these industries have distinct regulatory frameworks, they are interrelated. For example, cargoes loaded into metal containers will link distinct groups of workers: dockers, merchant seamen and lorry drivers. Such interconnected freight has special tactical significance. Secondary action can be a very powerful way of giving support, and picketing can interrupt the market circulation of commodities. Effective industrial action in each of these industries, therefore, often depends on support and solidarity from workers in the rest of the transport sector. How far regulatory frameworks influence such joint action is an especially interesting question.

The docks

The trend toward dismantling the long-standing dock labour scheme, or 'deregulation', is clearly understood as a threat by the traditional registered dockworker in this country. The contraction of employment on the docks, and the vulnerability of dockwork to fluctuations in trade, has reinforced the dockers' resistance to threats of abolishing the National Dock Labour Board Scheme operation in 78 of the estimated 600 ports in Britain. In fact in June 1980, the T & G National Docks Group formulated a policy based on the extension of the NDLB Scheme. This means that the docks are a potential source of conflict over the issues of state regulation but also because they have a more general history of industial militancy which has previously challenged government attempts to reform industrial relations.

The NDLB scheme

The 'Scheme' has its origins in the needs of the wartime economy and established the permanent decasualisation of dock labour by the Act of 1946 followed by an Employment Regulation Order in 1947. A measure of protection from the competition of casual labour was obtained by allowing only licensed employers to employ registered workers to do 'dockwork' in those ports, and to perform jobs listed under the scheme. The scheme is administered by the National Dock Labour Board through local dock labour boards. These boards have equal representation of dockers and employers and so increased the bargaining power of dockers. However, the principle of 'registration' relies upon a legal definition of dockwork which has become a contentious issue in its own right and is a question around which the dockers have pursued a greater share of control over their labour market. On the other hand, both employers and different governments have preferred to view the scheme as a policy response to earlier problems of casual employment on the docks. In spite of much divergence the scheme has meant that in negotiations dockers represent a fairly self-sufficient section within the ports industries.

The unofficial dockers movement

The National Dock Labour Scheme imposes a financial levy on port employers to provide for a 'fall-back pay' when there is no work available, for welfare facilities and other amenities. Combined with the outlawing of casual labour on the docks, these provisions of the scheme mean that the historical necesssity of participating in a more widely based general industrial union temporarily declined. Whilst the dockworkers union, the T & G, did not aggressively pursue dockers' demands in the 1950s, the dockers themselves were able to exploit their new stronger bargaining position to great effect. Indeed, they were to find themselves in conflict with their own union precisely because of increased wages militancy. The extent of unofficial action over wages issues in the post-war period finally led to a substantial number of dockers leaving the T & G for the competing 'blue stevedores union' NASDU. The end result was the expulsion of NASDU from the TUC. The subsequent government appointed inquiry under Lord Devlin in 1965 eventually led to the permanent allocation of individual dockers to port employers finally to end casual employment. Although the port employers could have taken over all the functions of the Dock Labour Scheme and then in theory dispensed with it at some later date, they did not do so. The conclusion seemed to be that they were prepared to buy in-dustrial peace by supporting the National Dock Labour Board. An accompanying step was to fashion industrial relations into a more orthodox structure of shop-steward participation in the hope that there might be fewer lightning strikes and that dispute procedures would be observed. This initially failed to have the desired effect since the introduction of shop-steward committees included the appointment of both T & G and NASDU members. In doing so these committees inherited functions from former rank-and-file committees controlled by previous elected dockers under an un-official banner. In the eyes of employers this new shop-steward system was dominated by militants. In effect the new committees only perpetuated a wholly unofficial element and thereby reinforced the dockers' own strategic independence of action. Wages militancy and the introduction of new technology followed in the wake of the 1967 reforms leading up to the historic conflict of 1972.

The 1972 docks dispute

Whilst the dockers successfully pursued higher wages, the employers were introducing new technologies. Revolutionary methods of containerisation, palletisation and roll-on, roll-off (Ro-Ro) led to new inland depots located outside of the control of the Dock Labour Scheme. These eliminated at a stroke the twin evils of the levy and high wages which employers associated with registered dock labour. This was the escape route which small employers in particular had been looking for, and they developed with alacrity new container-handling facilities in the unregistered ports and wharves. These developments precipitated for dockers a crisis in security of employment and relative bargaining strength. The changes meant the loss of employers and work to the unregistered ports and depots, where wage rates were lower, and the beginning of a serious surplus labour problem. Furthermore, attempts were made to place registered dockers on something termed the Temporary Unattached Register. The TUR was originally an interim device for making subsistence level payments to dockers who were either suspended for disciplinary reasons or awaiting permanent transfer to a new employer. However, some employers tried to use TUR as a device for reintroducing casualisation.

Hence the industry changed rapidly between 1966 and 1972 from a position where both sides pledged permanent employment and no compulsory redundancies to a situation where registered employers were faced with the rising costs of surplus labour and the need to make redundancies, or at least alleviate costs through the TUR.

The development of tactics

In this context the 1972 National Docks strike may have seemed inevitable. Given what we have said about the causes of the conflict the tactics will be no surprise. The dispute began with unofficial blacking of containerised cargo which brought the dockers into conflict with individual road-haulage operators. From a tactical standpoint the dockers' monopoly control over freight movements through registered ports could be exercised with immediate total effect and to the severe long-term disadvantage of individuals in the road-haulage industry. Selective blacking of hauliers also engendered a selective response from employers who were prepared to use the National Industrial Relations Court and the provisions of the Industrial Relations Act 1971. The persistent unofficial actions of the dockers in defiance of the NIRC went far to discredit the idea that unions could be coerced into controlling their stewards, or that a legal remedy could be applied which directly constrained individual activities. Blacking continued throughout the 1972 dispute and after, with some firms even to this day permanently blacked and prevented from entering on to the docks despite the illegal nature of such actions. Enforced, rigorous discipline by dockers in applying a selective black-listing of firms is, therefore, the key to the effectiveness of this tactic which is wielded both as a deterrent and punishment.

However, blacking exacted a price for the labour movement: it put great strain upon the internal T & G solidarity which could be expected between the road transport sector, which worked the rival container depots, and the dock section. The logic of the dockers' section of the T & G strategy was to stop the growth of non-registered dockwork at source. This not only required a picket of the unregistered wharves to stop them working but also meant that lorry drivers confronted by pickets faced the threat of future blacking on the docks. The response of lorry drivers in some instances was to organise 'reciprocal picketing' around container firms where dockers were employed. The greater the resistance to the dockers' campaign the more important became picketing, particularly the mass picket when it was only through sheer strength of numbers that the movement of cargo could be stopped. This led to a fiercer kind of confrontation, this time with the police (Turner, 1980). The imprisonment of the 'Pentonville Five' dockers by the NIRC became a *cause célèbre* for the whole labour movement and the TUC called for a general strike. Meanwhile the vulnerability of the country to a national dock strike became apparent. The Heath Government sought emergency powers, but the seriousness of the economic disruption was never put to the test given the outcome of the dispute under the Jones/Aldington agreement of 1972. Voluntary severance payments were increased to induce surplus dockers to leave the industry, and the employers agreed to the dockers' demands that men in the TUR should be allocated to other employers.

The 1980 docks dispute and the TUR

The intervening years saw relative peace in British dockland despite the failure of parliament in 1977 to place unregistered ports within the scheme. Nevertheless two problem areas, definition of dockwork and surplus labour, have persisted into the 1980s, and in some ways provide almost an identical re-run of the antecedents to the 1972 dispute. Interestingly though, overall strategy and tactics involved are now completely different.

The main change in circumstances has been brought about by the effect of the world economic recession and the downward trade spiral. In recent times whole ports have been placed in jeopardy – a fact forced home by the early closure of Preston in 1980. The overheads of dock employers have not fallen off with decreased trade but have become burdensome in view of the levy to finance surplus labour and the costs of meeting voluntary severance payments. The consequence has therefore been that the industry has needed to shed labour faster than ever before. At the same time the combination of no compulsory redundancy and no TUR has prevented this from being achieved quickly, and the employment policies of the Dock Labour Board have prevented employers from using labour more flexibly, as had always been the case under the old so called 'Pen' and 'Blue Eyes' system.

It is hardly surprising then that some employers have succumbed to the inevitable. In fact a crisis was reached with the closure of two Liverpool firms in September 1980 which meant that 178 registered dockers either had to be reallocated to remaining port employers or become effectively redundant through staying on the TUR. The Liverpool employers refused to take on the extra men and the response of the organised labour was swift. Support for a national stoppage immediately emerged. The T & G was already committed to call a national strike if the TUR were ever used again for shedding labour but first they sought government intervention unsuccessfully at the outset.

The response of the NDLB was to secure a promise to loan £1.8 million for further severance payments from the Department of Employment. As the strike date loomed nearer, union negotiators were insistent that dockers' jobs took precedence over voluntary severance, especially as the dockers were not covered by the Redundancy Payments Act or the Employment Protection Act, but by the NDLB Scheme which would be undermined if the TUR were used again. At the eleventh hour agreement was reached confirming the reallocation of the Liverpool men, recognising that the Jones/Aldington agreement should continue to be observed, and accepting that the TUR would not again be used except for the strict purposes of administering disciplinary procedures.

The outcome, viewed by dockers as a clear victory, had wider implications for tactics. The action taken by employers was seen as a test, to which the dockers felt the need to respond by the threat of a strike call. This seemed to import either a long and bitter struggle with uncertain consequences for the future of the industry as a whole, or government intervention in the form of financial help aimed at buying another round of peace. This analysis would indicate the possibility of future disputes over the same issues, disputes whose course it is interesting to speculate upon. It might therefore be useful to consider what might have happened if a strike had occurred in 1980.

Our information suggests that the balance of tactics was in favour of dockers who, unlike 1972, could expect the support of substantial numbers of T & G members who work the larger unregistered container ports such as Felixstowe. The economic recession had clearly threatened their own jobs and in certain areas of specialised work they were no longer in competition with the work of registered ports. Instead, secondary picketing would have been primarily at the non-docks wharves. For the port of Hull, to take one example, this would have meant picketing points along the rivers Trent and Ouse. Picketing and blacking goods at other locations was inescapable since cargoes once contracted for have to be unloaded at some destination or other. In the event of a mass picket being necessary, the Hull dockers again were in no doubt about approaching the neighbouring Yorkshire coalfields for assistance from miners. Calls for solidarity from other groups of workers such as lockgate men and other NUR members at railway ports had already been made in preparation of the September strike action. Politically, the industrial situation was unusual in that any government strategy aimed at weakening trade unions' influence through threats of unemployment was just the kind of device which would necessarily create further solidarity amongst dockers. There are also the employers' tactics to consider. In the event of strike action or selective blacking the threat of suspension of pay is available to employers. It is interesting to note that whether dockers lose pay helps to determine their attitude to other groups of workers. During the civil-service pay dispute, for example, dockers were not prepared to risk being put off pay as a result of refusing to handle certain goods, at least as long as the civil-service unions still had their own members in the customs-and-excise section working on the docks. In the event of all-out strike action in the docks management's recourse to the law as a tactic against secondary picketing would be of doubtful use. Even though employers might seek injunctions against secondary picketing of wharves, there is little likelihood on the basis of past experience that they would be effective. Docker's leaders are in fact quite used to receiving writs, especially from foreign firms who clearly place more faith in such methods than do their British counterparts. The response of dock leaders is almost always, in our regular observation, to consign all legal documents to the waste bin.

Fascinating as it is to speculate on the industrial action of labour in the docks, the interests of the dock employers must be borne constantly in mind. Here it is vital to recognise the need for unity and lack of dissension which seemed to characterise their response in 1980 to the revised issue of the TUR. In a real sense the dispute was not so much between the dockers and the port employers as between the latter and the NDLB so that employer unity was of the essence. If the employers had been able to convince the government to dismantle the NDLB then perhaps the events at Liverpool would not be replicated and port labour relations would have looked very different. Indeed, even if they wished the National Association of Port Employer (NAPE) would have found it difficult to resist the dockers' demands as long as the government was buttressing the Scheme. In the near future governmental attitudes will remain crucial.

Shortly after the settlement of the Liverpool TUR issue, another problem over surplus registered dockers – this time in Grimsby – arose and again a national stoppage seemed a possibility. This stemmed from legal questions concerning the definition of dockwork in relation to fish dockworkers, known colloquially as 'lumpers'. The Grimsby Fish Merchants Association appealed against a previous Industrial Tribunal decision on the grounds that the local definition of dock labour work contained no reference to the loading of fish into road transport as opposed to rail. The GFMA then offered the 'lumpers' new contracts of employment with no loss of pay provided they were willing to forsake their registration and the attendant protection of the NDLB Scheme. Some conceded and some took severance payments. Nevertheless some 37 men wished to remain under the protection of the Scheme and were consequently reallocated to other Grimsby employers by the NDLB. Thirty of the men were promptly accepted by their new employers but seven were not. This was more serious than the Liverpool action for a number of reasons. First, the reluctant Grimsby employer was not a member of NAPE, and consequently not subject to their control. For the dockers it was serious because the issue had gone one stage beyond the Liverpool situation without a prior strike call; men had been made effectively redundant, had lost their dockers' registration, and had no TUR as a fallback. It was a threat to the NDLB Scheme which neighbouring Hull dockers would never have allowed.

The dispute was only finally resolved when the local Dock Labour Board revised the reallocation of the seven to remaining employers in the Scheme. The dockers were nevertheless very unhappy with this resolution of the problem since they perceived it as a backdoor method for employers to abandon the Scheme. The way in which this dispute was resolved was therefore unsatisfactory both in the eyes of employers and dockers in registered ports and illustrates that the surplus labour problem, and the definition of dockwork, are increasingly intractable problems given the state of the industry and its overlap with so many other unregulated areas.

Another interesting dispute recently arose outside of Hull docks on the river Hull itself, where a number of wharves exist. At one is a firm specialising in bulk imports of animal feedstocks where dockers had been previously taken on to do the work in the days when labour was hard to find and dockers easy to get hold of. Other port employers had repeatedly pointed out the danger that the dockers would come to regard the wharf as if it were registered dockwork. This is precisely what occurred when a new owner of the wharf employed non-dock labour. Despite a tribunal decision which had gone against them the dockers argued that a principle was at stake: the loss of jobs. The dockers, therefore, proceeded to picket the narrow entrance on to the riverside wharf in circumstances where they were clearly contravening the provisions of the Employment Act since they were not employees of the firm itself. Interestingly, the legal position did not enter the thinking of the employer in any strategic way since this was unofficial action, and it was possible to continue doing business despite the picketing. The strength of the dockers' action relied very much upon other major employers and customers realising the consequences of having their own lorries blacked throughout the port if they were to service this firm. The employer, however, responded with a letter to all customers to have no fear, since instead of them coming to collect, they would receive their goods delivered by a third party. This was feasible since the services of road hauliers who did not mind being blacked were readily obtainable.

A second example reflects a different employer's attitude towards the law. The location of the dispute in the expanding fish catching industry of Grimsby is important since it involved the use of 70 casual labourers to do the work of the registered 'lumpers' who had withdrawn their labour in support of a pay claim. By their action they were in breach of the law on two counts in that they were neither licenced employers under the Scheme, nor did they hire registered labour to do the work.

Significantly, pressure for prosecution of the firms involved came from the T&G which had the effect of forcing the local Dock Labour Board to instigate legal action. However, this urge to use the law backfired to an extent in that the Dockwork Regulations clearly authorised the local Dock Labour Board to allow unregistered employers to use non-registered labour to perform dockwork. Although the employer concerned had not complied with the requisite procedural requirements the magistrates were moved to grant a conditional discharge.

Whilst these two examples are in themselves minor they suggest, like the outcomes of the threatened national strike, that industrial initiatives belong less with employers through use of powers under the Employment Act 1980 or elsewhere, than with government in relation to its policies on the future of dockwork in general and the Scheme in particular. It is on precisely this issue that some of the most recent developments concerning dock labour have emerged. So, for instance, the NDLB has recently withdrawn proposals for reorganisation of the Scheme into fewer boards and services after dockers had threatened another stoppage. The dockers clearly wanted any proposals to be the subject of consultation between the T&G and Government. What is noteworthy, however, is the fact that it took the threat of further industrial action before government was prepared to begin talks with the union over the future of the Scheme. This new-found strength is none the less easily sapped in times of fierce competition and general economic recession. When this is allied to governmental policies which seek to alter at least part of the regulatory framework of the industry, then the tactical implications for the conduct of disputes become particularly complex.

Road haulage

Port-related transport by road has played a vitally important role in the development of containerised cargo. The vast majority of all containerised freight is now carried by road which provides the link between port and destination with least transhipment of cargo onto different forms of transport. Except for certain bulk items, such as coal and raw materials which can be delivered by rail direct to the consumers, it is also the cheapest and quickest means of transport.

The growth of container firms reliant on road hauliers was both the backdrop to the 1972 docks dispute and the impetus which gave lorry drivers a new-found bargaining strength within their own industry. However, a few historical antecedents might be appropriate in order to appreciate the context in which the industry operates.

In 1947 the Labour government established the Road Transport Executive as an integral part of its plans to nationalise the bulk of long-distance haulage and thereby largely excluded private hauliers from operating in this area. Denationalisation occurred in 1953 with an attendant encouragement for small fleet operators to move in. The post-war period then has been characterised by varying degrees of state involvement in and regulation of the industry. In fact in the 1960s a whole new set of policies produced controls over vehicle licensing which were directed at ensuring higher standards of safety and operation. At the same time mechanisms were introduced for securing better co-ordination between road and rail.

The foregoing also needs to be viewed alongside a longstanding record of state intervention in wages and other conditions of employment. Thus as far back as 1930 legislation had introduced both a fair wages formula and a limit on hours worked. An Act of 1933 then linked the granting of licences to compliance with these requirements on basic terms and conditions of employment. The culmination perhaps was the 1938 Road Haulage Act which established statutory wage regulation by joint boards. This operated as the basis for bargaining in the industry until the 1980 Employment Act removed its fair wages provisions. A consistent pattern of state concern with the industry then can be observed though the structure of operations in road transport has to a considerable extent frustrated the various designs which successive governments have sought to impose.

It has always been the policy of the Road Haulage Association to have a nationally negotiated wage structure, but the unions have consistently resisted this. In their view a national RHA negotiating body would be as unhelpful as the old wages council, whose rates were thought to be abysmally low. The reasons the RHA wanted negotiations through a national JIC are obvious – a national body would even out competition between different employers and prevent union negotiations from dividing employers against each other through testing the weaknesses of local members of the Association. In this context both the RHA and the unions have problems in organising the small establishments which operate between 5 and 10 vehicles only and make up the vast majority of the industry. Union officials in particular have to overcome the close relationship between the small operator and his employees which often precludes interest in a union.

Road haulage itself is not very strike-prone for several reasons. First, 'the chap that drives his own vehicle likes to be on his own', and disputes imply collective action. Second, because the capital structure of the industry is highly fragmented and contracts are often time-bound and short-term, a strike means rapid loss of work to competitors. Third, because of the divided nature of the workforce, issues of discipline or sackings that might cause a strike elsewhere can occur without the knowledge of fellow workers. Finally, the nature of driving is itself complicated and legally rule-bound, which can give employers a high degree of formal control with which to discipline their workforce. This constitutes a type of industrial law quite different from that generally considered in the present book.

However, when drivers do strike or when they decide collectively to pressure their employers, they can be extremely powerful. The clearest example of organisational effectiveness on a large scale came in early 1979 when drivers organised themselves nationally, mainly through the T&G, for a pay rise and cut in the working hours. The strike was significant for two main reasons. First, it placed lorry drivers in greater contact with each other and through their shared experiences led to greater solidarity at local level. Second, organisation was extended across all industries involving road transport and the lorry drivers were consequently able to draw on the strength of this wider membership.

The control of delivery of supplies to industry is critical, especially in the case of processing industries. Drivers have the power to black, which can substitute for strike action and be employed as a weapon in and after a strike. The extent and degree to which blacking is successful is dependent upon drivers' links with workers in other industries. As a multi-industry union the T&G has many contact points and widespread presence. Thus, one finds, for example, that where a road-haulage firm refuses to pay the area rate, the T&G can readily arrange selective blacking of the firm through its widespread contact with shop stewards at major suppliers and customers. Workers in other industries are often also quite willing to co-operate, especially where they anticipate a need for future reciprocal support, i.e. when they strike drivers are expected to respect picket lines.

There is no doubt that lorry drivers learned a number of lessons from the conduct of the national strike. Primarily, the initial total withdrawal of labour was seen as a tactical mistake in so far as it caused difficulties for already completed individually negotiated agreements. It appeared that selective tactics could be used even more effectively and at less cost to manipulate the market to the disadvantage of recalcitrant employers. Certain drivers could be sent back to work to perform existing contracts, directly displacing the blacked operators. In one instance these methods caused a Hull-based haulier to settle within a week; this settlement, in turn, caused a severe break in the negotiating unity of employers nationally.

Notwithstanding the evolution of new tactics, blacklegging remained a problem. In some areas branch lists of members (of either the T&G or URTU) known to have crossed picket lines exist to this day. Since imposing fines was ineffective, the alternative of issuing telephone threats to employers that when the strike was over their firms would be blacked was adopted. Since these threats were also made known to the workers concerned, the threat of job loss by subsequent blacking also served as a means of disciplining drivers in the course of the strike action. With the current unemployment situation facing the industry this threat presumably still carries force. However, the extent to which threatened post-dispute blacking is effective depends on the response of employers, and their perceptions as to its lawfulness.

Road transport clearly has contemporary significance under the secondary action provisions of current government legislation, but it should be noted that the history of dispute tactics has often run more broadly than legislation has allowed. For instance, the bitter post-war confrontations over recognition led to the use of some very raw tactics. However, other legal remedies are available in such cases. A recent incident on the Liverpool docks where articulated vehicles were left on private property so as to obstruct the movement of containers off the terminal by out-of-town drivers brought a swift legal response under trespass law.

Whilst the period around the national strike was dominated by wage issues, concern by both sides of industry over the changed economic climate and the effects of increased competition for contracts has more recently shifted attention towards redundancy. This concern is expressed in various forms at local and national levels. In Hull, for instance, it resulted in a broad approach by port-worker shop stewards in 1980 to set up a Port Users' Joint Committee to discuss how to attract more business through the port. However, this level of awareness has not altered the strength of organisation that exists between different groups of workers wishing to take industrial action. What has changed is the context in which different tactics are discussed. For example, a dispute arose in 1981 when a local employer reduced the number of drivers on a contract which he had previously acquired from a competitor and which had been subject to union agreement on driver numbers. The union response was a token picket mounted at the employer's premises with the main emphasis placed on picketing delivery points and a call for all other vehicles subcontracted to the employer to be blacked. The tactic of a lockout by the firm collapsed after two days and all workers were reinstated.

There are a number of general points to be drawn from this particular industrial action which was not untypical of disputes in the Humberside area over the last two years. First, the position of the drivers as a small group of workers within a larger workforce meant that they required external support in order to bring pressure on a company whose production continued and which might sub-contract to independent hauliers. There was also need for blacking by other groups of workers, notably dockers. Dockers' blacking, for example, on one occasion threatened a contract on deliveries.

A second point concerns the lack of resort to law in this dispute. An infinite degree of speculation on this issue is available but it is most probable that the local culture and traditions of port-related industries held out too many fears for would-be plaintiffs. Added to this are two important considerations. First, with a serried rank of alternative tactics available to the workforce, resort to law might ultimately prove a sterile proposition. Second, the force of the recession and the existence of fierce competition probably rendered compliance more attractive than contention. The third general point to emerge from the analysis is that a dispute can cause severe damage to secondary firms, especially since employers often make reciprocal arrangements with other employers to cover a percentage of their work. Indeed they have traditionally topped up their own trade by seeking subcontracted business, which relies almost entirely on re-ciprocal agreements being made with road hauliers in other areas. If, therefore, out-of-town drivers were being turned away from the Hull docks then affected employers could be expected to take action against the Hull firm elsewhere. For example, Liverpool employers might refuse to load Hull vehicles for the home run. The irony then is that a single road-haulage operator can face pressure to settle quickly not only from the trade unions but from other employers as well.

We have noted that the general effect of economic recession at a national level has been to force road-haulage operators into being more competitive and chasing less and less work with the offer of lower haulage rates. One consequence is that drivers who regularly service container traffic are attempting to exclude other operators from seeking casual work on the docks. There has been particular hostility toward farmers and other operators of heavy goods vehicles subject to seasonal work who can afford to charge lower rates during their own off-peak periods. The major tactical response of drivers to such a challenge took the form of unofficial industrial action in 1981 over the container stamp issue.

1981 container stamp dispute

A national delegates conference of drivers in the container port sector resolved to co-ordinate a check on union cards to see if the appropriate 'container stamp', which different ports used to identify regular drivers, had been used. At the same time as penalising drivers of companies which do not regularly service the registered ports, it was hoped to bring pressure against shipping agents held to be responsible for placing return loads with out-of-town opera-tors. This activity met with different responses on docksides throughout the country but it was at Royal Seaforth, Liverpool that conflict emerged when the drivers were unable to carry out satisfac-tory card checks. The result was blanket picketing of the Seaforth terminal by drivers. This soon became an important occasion of employer resistance and retaliation by shipping agents who felt themselves to be on strong ground since the picketing did not get support from dockers for blacking return loads. The picketing then was an initiative by the Seaforth drivers acting alone rather than jointly with other docks drivers. This left them isolated and exposed to legal action by the docks main employers and the owners of the Seaforth terminal, the Merseyside Docks and Harbour Company (MDHC) and without the official support of their union the T&G.

The MDHC started legal action against four members of the *ad hoc* committee and a full-time T&G official, whom they believed also to be a member. *Ex parte* injunctions (i.e. made without hearing the defendants) restraining the defendants from engaging in or or-ganising picketing were obtained and served on the defendants. At the hearing before the High Court in Manchester a week later, the judge continued the injunction against the four, but discharged the injunction against the full-time official (*MDHC* v *Verrinder and others* [1982] I.R.L.R. 152). The plaintiffs alleged that they had lost some £200,000 in fees as a result of the picketing and that it amounted to a private nuisance in interfering with their enjoyment of their property. The defendants argued that since there was no allegation of violence, intimidation or obstruction their behaviour was consequently lawful: in fact, the judge found the pickets' per-sonal conduct 'exemplary' and no picketing he admitted could have been more practical. If such picketing was unlawful then no pick-eting could be lawful. However, the judge held that the pickets' purpose was not merely to communicate information; it was to force the MDHC to take action against the shipping companies employing the 'scalliwag' drivers. Therefore the conduct was capable of constituting a private nuisance. Nor was there protection under section 15 of TULRA as amended by the 1980 Act because of the pickets' purpose and the fact that Seaforth was not the pickets' place of work. The questions were serious enough for the injunctions to be continued until full trial. At the time of writing it is thought that this will take place in the late autumn of 1982. The injunction against the full-time official was discharged because it was not shown that he had taken part in the *ad hoc* committee.

Aside from the legal uncertainties generated by this case is the certainty that it took the *ad hoc* committee of drivers by surprise: they did not believe such action was likely to provoke legal attack. How far an injunction could have worked if the pickets had not already decided to call off their industrial action is also important. Had the picketing begun one week earlier when the drivers were in a much more determined mood, then the injunction might have had a very different reception.

The use of law in this dispute, therefore, had wide implications extending beyond the immediate picketing. The unofficial action was clearly designed to bring about a change in the union's policy and, together with further lobbying, resulted in the setting up of an internal union inquiry into the whole issue. Up to that point the unofficial action had been repudiated as unconstitutional, and the union endeavoured to dissociate itself from the legal actions arising out of the disputes. For instance, the union separately instructed counsel to represent their District Official who was one of the named individuals subject to the court order. This action is interesting because it raises questions about how unions might react to law. In this case the use of law seemed acceptable as long as it was aimed at unofficial action. For the employers the success of the injunction was the way in which it dampened the impetus behind the unofficial action.

Finally, in this case, legal action was applied selectively: it was applied at the only port during a national dispute which could not be guaranteed dockers' support. The threat of secondary blacking was also pursued by lorry drivers outside Merseyside but ineffectively since they were unable to muster the support of other drivers. Use of the law was successful then but for highly contingent reasons.

Viewed over the longer time period, disputes in the road-haulage industry at large illustrate how, in contrast to the capitalisation and concentration of ownership which has accompanied the container revolution, the bargaining structure remains unchanged. The bargaining strength of drivers in times of economic expansion is quickly transformed into individual weaknesses at a local level if drivers fail to co-ordinate their action successfully. There is no tradition of solidarity behind unofficial action taken by drivers, and so the effectiveness of tactics such as picketing and blacking that do not have official union support is limited particularly where other critical union solidarity is lacking. On the other hand, whenever official support is actually delivered or threatened, the propensity of employers to take legal action is low. Removal of support, especially by dockers at periods of low economic demand, exposes lorry drivers to the threat of undercutting in the market and blacklegging by other workers.

Merchant shipping

The merchant-shipping industry epitomises a number of the themes discussed so far. In addition it has also recently been the locus of major disputes of national proportions as well as local disputes all of which have involved careful consideration and revision of tactics.

In order to understand the framework of disputes it is necessary first to consider aspects of the history and organisation of the merchant marine. The growth of a merchant-shipping fleet in this country has resulted in an immense concentration of private capital within a single industry, and has been closely associated with the historical development of Great Britain as a maritime power. Merchant seamen have also been employed under a very special regimen. The ability of the industry to perform like a 'loose limb' of the state, especially in wartime, has traditionally meant militaristic discipline on board backed up by severe sanctions operating under the Merchant Shipping Act 1894 and its successors. This legislation had the objective of preserving the authority of the ship's master and protecting the interests and property of the shipowners. In important respects, it has the strictness of the criminal code and for certain offences the master can imprison the seaman on board or call a 'court martial' in any port. For other offences, particularly in disciplinary matters, there are standard penalties of fines and the forfeiture of wages, though in recent times the practical effect of these measures has been mollified by the impact of collectively bargained procedures.

Significantly, the Merchant Shipping Acts remove from seamen engaged in industrial action the legal immunities afforded to shore-based workers. This means that seamen do not escape liability, even criminal liability, for the consequences of withdrawing their labour except in closely defined circumstances. In effect, the only method of strike action legally open to seamen is to withold labour once signed off from a voyage when the vessel is securely berthed in a British port. Seamen may not legally walk off a ship in a foreign port or refuse to work while on the high seas.

Although the National Union of Seamen is a single industry union organised by means of a pre-entry agreement with the employers, participation in union affairs is necessarily limited since membership is dispersed into small work units constrained by the timetabling of voyages, although pressure for more participation in the union's affairs by the membership emerged with the unofficial strikes in 1960 (MacFarlane, 1970). The employers have in the past showed no hesitation in seeking legal redress under the Merchant Shipping Acts or the general provisions of British labour law.

The point at which industrial relations in the shipping industry becomes important for our purposes is 1965. The wages settlement of that year was the signal for the shipping employers to attempt to extend the working week. This heralded a new-found militancy which, along with the imposition of a statutory incomes policy by the Wilson government, gave rise to a particularly bitter and drawn-out strike the following year. The outcome was a defeat for the union which left many of the newer militant activists with a feeling of real bitterness and anger. The defeat, in consequence, stored up resentment which has had vital repercussions for industrial relations in the industry in recent times.

The causes of the 1981 dispute

Although the experience of the 1966 strike died hard in the minds of the activists it was nevertheless followed by a period of relative quiescence and acceptance of successive pay norms. The NUS was expelled from the TUC over the issue of union registration under the 1971 Industrial Relations Act and accepted the social contract without demur. However, there can be little doubt that the potential

for industrial conflict remained since each of the annual pay agreements had left unsettled the longstanding grievance that overtime
payments, at the rate of time and a quarter, were not in line with
the rest of industry.

In addition, the industry faced financial pressures and was
undergoing structural change, both of which issues produced difficulties over pay, job security and working practices. Eventually,
confronted with a recession, the shipping employers pursued a strategy to lower transport costs through a combined policy of wage
restraint and demanning, though the policy was applied unevenly
to different sections of the shipping fleet. For example, on deep-sea
vessels employers encouraged the development of smaller crews
working longer hours, while workers in the relatively prosperous
ferry services enjoyed better pay and conditions. Changes in the
ownership and structure of the industry were also having a dramatic
impact on employment. Tonnage, especially British, was declining
as was the total number of shipping lines while increasing diversification was also occurring. Furthermore, foreign competition
threatened jobs, and job insecurity was increased by the ease with
which vessels operated under foreign flags. Ownership had become
bewilderingly multinational with the result that employers were
increasingly mistrusted by the unions who also objected to the legal
immunities shipowners possess to withhold information about their
reserves and assets (Hodgins and Prescott, 1966). To complete the
background picture it needs to be said that within the union the
activists of the 1960s had won national positions and brought forward a different set of aspirations for the membership.

A number of these anxieties surfaced in the final quarter of 1980
in a dispute over the decision of the Cunard shipping line to sail
two of its prestigious cruise liners under a foreign flag with 'cut-
price' crews. On their own initiative the British crew took direct
action in Bridgetown Barbados and refused to leave the ship after
being served with notice of dismissal. The NUS leadership gave
backing to the unofficial action and instructed their members to
continue sitting in on board the ship. By giving this instruction they
openly counselled breaches of the civil and criminal law, and in the
event did so with impunity. They were, however, concerned that
police might board one of the ships and arrest the crew and so
pre-empted such a course of action by threatening to black the
remainder of the Cunard fleet. This proved, in industrial relations

terms, to be the *hors d'oeuvre* to the main course of the dispute over the annual wage settlement.

The 1981 dispute

Immediately following the Cunard conflict came the national dispute itself. The response of the union executive to the first rumblings of the campaign was to organise the indefinite stoppage of vessels in British ports and to give support to those vessels on total stoppage in foreign ports and encourage overtime bans and delays of sailing. After overcoming much hesitancy on the part of ferrymen, the union concentrated on building up unity so as to be able to threaten the employers with further escalation. In order to achieve this they used the new tactic of involving their members on a world-wide basis, and more deep-sea vessels became immobilised as part of a plan to hit selected companies hardest. Added impetus came from the ferrymen's action which could disrupt company operations at very short notice and with negligible loss of earnings to the members taking part. The ferry operators were limited in the counter-pressure which they could bring to bear since the seamen could rely on support from other key transport workers especially the dockers. The slow build-up of industrial action that affected the container carrying ships was, however, the key to the union's strategy.

Instead of a call for a complete withdrawal of labour, the union matched each stage in the negotiations with new tactics. The major tactical weapon declared at the outset was, of course, to take selective industrial action without prior warning. Unlike the 1966 strike this meant that owners could not retaliate simply and effectively by redirecting vessels to continental ports in order to avoid British industrial action.

Pressure was put on the General Council of British Shipping to agree to independent arbitration but no more than talks about talks were achieved via ACAS. Instead there was a new offer from the employers which did little to stem the rising tide of industrial action. At the same time, the employers' organisation was faced with a further complication when their pay talks with the Merchant Navy Officers Association broke down. This meant that the employers were faced with a uniquely united workforce.

The dispute had become a test of unity with the first blow being dealt to the employer's side by the breaking away of a member company to sign an independent agreement that satisfied the union demands on overtime. The remaining two weeks of the dispute saw other companies, including a ferry operator, settling independently with union negotiators.

Tactical considerations

The NUS lodged their annual pay claim at the time when employers and union negotiators in a variety of industries, including shipping, were facing the combined effects of an economic recession and government pressure to curb wage settlements. The union's pay claim, of just over 25 per cent, flew in the face of those pressures. Added to this the dispute occurred at a time of year when the volume of freight being transported was at its lowest, and the employers had the least to fear from customer pressure. Furthermore, the consequence of a strong pound had been to encourage stockpiling which would also reduce the economic impact of the strike. Of particular interest, therefore, is the way in which the dispute was confined almost exclusively to the two major parties involved.

The union strategy of not calling for a ballot on all-out strike action enabled the pursuit of guerrilla tactics to proceed almost unnoticed outside of the industry. The gradual and somewhat unpredictable escalation of the industrial action meant that pressure on the government to intervene, and its ability to do so, was diminished. The unnotified nature of the union action made a calculated and effective response by the employers and government difficult to say the least.

In the merchant-shipping industry, where there has not been major industrial action for fifteen years, it is conceivable that each side embarked on the conflict with considerable uncertainty about the others' organisational powers and solidarity. The NUS received strong backing for industrial action and was able to maintain the unity of its constituent groups and widely scattered membership. It had preceded the action by detailed discussion with the International Transport Federation and thereby secured international support. The employers' normal competitiveness, sharpened by a world-wide recession in shipping, made it difficult to co-ordinate an employers' campaign in response. This encouraged the union in its belief that break-away agreements with individual companies were possible. The employers also had the difficult task of estimating the strength of the new leadership over the columns of union members and they may well have miscalculated on this score. Certainly the union went to considerable lengths to hide its tactical plans from the employers. In addition to the objective tactical advantages which may accrue to either side in a dispute it is important therefore also to recognise the possibility of serious misjudgments. In this instance the union's tactics were clearly successful.

Use of law

Given the tactics used by the union, the employers could have used the criminal law under the Merchant Shipping Acts, the common law or the 1980 Employment Act but chose only to suspend seamen from duty and penalise them by making pay deductions. This raises two questions: whether the breaches of the civil and criminal law were sanctioned by the union leadership, and why the employers did not use the law. Curiously much of the industrial action, especially that taken by the ferrymen, was lawful under section 42 of the 1970 Merchant Shipping Act since it allows refusal to obey orders to set sail for 48 hours as notice of intention to go into official dispute. Originally drafted to protect shipowners from the effects of unofficial action, this could be turned to the advantage of the union when taking selective action. Taking legal action against seamen was considered by the employers on several occasions during the course of this dispute, both in the predispute controversy affecting the foreign registration of the Cunard vessels and in the extensive industrial action taken in foreign ports. The union leadership certainly realised the possibilities of legal action.

Why, then, was the law, which has been a major constraint in the past, not a determinant in this dispute? It may be simply that the law would have achieved little progress in quelling the militancy of the seamen in a highly charged industrial relations situation. Also the aloofness of the government from the dispute, although part of their general industrial strategy of non-intervention, in this instance played down the dispute's importance and so worked against legal action. More generally, however, the whole industry has been gradually moving towards treating seamen like shore-based workers. Most of the clearest situations where the law could have been used would have involved the Merchant Shipping Acts and been flatly contradictory to this trend. The longer-term restructuring of the industrial relations of the industry would have been severely damaged by such action during a national dispute. Within the overall tactics of the campaign those instances of secondary picketing, as defined by the 1980 Act, were of minor importance and using the Act against them would have caused more problems than it would have solved.

The use of law during a dispute between the NUS and the ship-owners, at any rate at national level, seems to have declined as industrial relations within the industry approaches those of other sectors. However, highly selective disputes, especially those not directly involving employment with British shipowners, may be treated differently. So, the law has been used successfully by ship-owners in response to the ITWF campaign to black flag-of-convenience vessels world wide. Here the scale of industrial action, in terms of the number of vessels affected at any particular time in British ports, is small. Furthermore, tactics aimed at a specific vessel are easier to make the target of legal action.

One illustration of legal action involved a claim by the foreign crew of the MV *Antama* while docked in Hull for backpay owing to them at ITWF agreed rates. On this claim being refused local and national ITWF officials decided to black the vessels and informed their affiliated unions. The owners of the *Antama* immediately sought an interim injunction relying on the secondary action provisions of section 17 of the 1980 Act to restrain the officials from calling on the Hull lockgatemen (NUR members employed by the port authority) to refuse the vessel passage through the gates. The injunction was granted, but suspended to allow an appeal, which was rejected by the Court of Appeal (*Marine Shipping Ltd* v. *Laughton* [1982] I.C.R. 215). Before 1 August 1980 the defendants would have been protected by section 13 of TULRA in inducing the lockgatemen to break their contracts of employment, but under the 1980 Act their secondary action was unjustified because there was no contract between the shipowners and the port authority; only between the shipping agents and the authority.

In strict terms the litigation succeeded in its objective in that the blacking was lifted in order to comply with the injunction. The crew, however, proceeded to take strike action and risked selective dismissal from the ship's master. The status of the striking crew remained unclear and was compounded by the fact that a foreign vessel, even though berthed in a British port, represents foreign territory. In effect the ship was under occupation with crew members relying on shoreworkers for information and essential supplies. The ship's master had orders to sail and endeavoured to muster a blackleg crew with which to take charge of the vessel. Initial attempts at removing the original crew failed. There was no physical confrontation and the actions of all parties (police, solicitors, company representatives, union officials, other port officials and workers) involved in this dispute were immersed in various different interpretations of regulations governing navigation out of the port, safety considerations, jurisdiction of the police, etc. Thus, the attempt at blacklegging was obstructed by the complexities of the local situation, and the owners took recourse to the courts once more. The request for a possession order was granted and with the crew paid off, the vessel sailed but perhaps is cruelly exposed to future blacking by the ITWF.

This is an area of shipping where the Employment Act has had some impact, because unlike the British seamen's national pay dispute, it involved sympathy action carried out on a selective rather than industry-wide basis. However, using the legislation is made problematic by the uncertainties of contract, ownership and chartering in shipping. The ITWF does not know in advance what contractual arrangements exist and therefore cannot clearly predict the legality of their actions. Furthermore, in such circumstances the law is most likely to be used by foreign companies who do not have any direct interest in dockside industrial relations.

Regulation and tactics

As we have seen, tactical choices can be closely related to the regulatory framework of an industry. Many disputes in the docks are almost unintelligible except within such a context, and the differences between registered and unregistered ports and dockwork lies at the centre of many of the strategic choices made as to tactics during disputes. The framework has in fact ossified as successive governments have shied away from the difficulties of modernisation in the industry. In the docks the regulatory framework itself will continue to be the centre for disputes as long as the dockers believe it is the only alternative to redundancy and decline. This will continue until government accepts the political implications of reform in the docks.

In shipping, on the other hand, the importance of the legal framework seems to have declined as economic pressures have forced shipowners to bring the terms and conditions of employment in the industry increasingly into line with shore-based work. Whether, however, this countervailing pressure would be enough to prevent the use of law as a dispute tactic in a situation where a conflict was threatening national economic policies and the owners were receiving government and perhaps public support remains to be seen.

In road haulage it is the organisational form of capital which is much more significant in influencing tactics than the regulatory framework, although that form has itself been partly influenced by earlier legal interventions. For this reason law is much more likely to be used by those outside the industry who are suffering the consequences of dispute. This was what occurred in 1979 during the national road strike when, amid massive publicity, United Biscuits took action against a picketing T&G shop steward and the judge applied the criteria that the picketing was a consequence of the dispute and not in 'furtherance' of it. During the first two years of the 1980 Employment Act, however, the impact of the recession has been so to reduce the extent of disputes in the industry as to make this form of legal intervention currently exceedingly unlikely.

PART 3

10
The impact of legal intervention

We have attempted to examine the effect of the 1980 Employment Act and in particular its provisions relating to picketing and secondary action. Without placing the Act in the larger social environment in which it was supposed to operate, we were bound to say nothing of consequence. As a result we have attempted to locate it within the industrial environment it was presumably intended for, within the framework of overall governmental industrial and economic policy, and within the historical traditions of British labour law. In order to understand this environment as a causal nexus, rather than simply as a 'context' for the law, we have examined industrial politics well beyond the period of the contemporary government. We are aware of only one considered attempt to assess the influence of a piece of modern labour law within an existing context (Weeks *et al.*, 1975) and, for all its merits, we believe that the attempt was ultimately unsuccessful. We are not aware of any similar work in the United States so we are conscious of having attempted something original and hope that we have, in some small way, charted new ground in the sociology of law; the discipline within which anyone examining the impact of legislation must work. We hope, however, to have achieved other things as well. We hope to have said something of value about the phenomenon of picketing which might not have been said before. In particular, we hope we have produced a structurally situated analysis of industrial tactics absent in the industrial relations literature until now.

We have attached great importance to the larger sphere of industrial politics and political economy. Short of outlawing trade unions and/or reproducing outright wage slavery, every modern industrial state is in the business of institutionalising conflict. The Employment Act is a minor contribution to that process. Similarly, all employers and managers save the very primitive are engaged in the exercise: thus, collective bargaining and the whole range of work-place procedures. Capital has its own interests which that process of institutionalisation is constructed to serve and these may or may not in their purest forms coincide with those of particular governments, let alone the larger concerns of the British state. Indeed, the interests of different capitals may conflict and in some circumstances the struggles between these interests will not produce a coherent state strategy. Government, however, more or less coherently follows an economic policy and will seek to advance its perceived interests through a process of institutionalisation which will include persuasion, bribery, direction and all manner of means more or less subtle.

The economy is the major concern of any modern government, and its industrial and labour policies lie at the heart of all it does. Governments will use the formal legal system to achieve their ends to the extent that such devices seem feasible, politic and convenient. No government, however, will use the legal-rational process to the exclusion of all else. Within the British state, as we have pointed out earlier, the formal legal system is amongst the least developed and most submerged in the Western world, as is witnessed by the nature of our public law in general. In a continental country it would be easier, even if ultimately unwise, to undertake to examine the effect of a new piece of industrial legislation by concentrating one's research on the legal system. In Britain such a course would amount to egregious incompetence.

What we have sought to do, therefore, is to attempt to understand the formal structures of different sectors of industry, to inquire after the 'domestic' forms of institutionalising conflict, to examine the range of tactics effectively available to capital and labour within those sectors, and to link those with the interventions of governments and, in particular, the present government. The Employment Act is but one such intervention and compared with all the rest relatively minor. We have tried to assess its impact and also to say something about the influence which labour law can expect to have within contemporary industry.

Rhetoric and law

We need to repeat here what we have only touched upon previously: that law is frequently a matter of rhetoric, that it often seeks to appeal to abstract expectations. As a matter of political necessity, then, certain laws will be introduced as an earnest of integrity, as a matter of mollifying the many largely intangible hopes and fears. Labour legislation in Britain has often had this quality, and the Employment Act is no exception, quite apart from any more tangible achievements it might have. Something of that flavour can be culled from the debate leading to its introduction, which we touched upon in Chapter 2, and the way in which 'law and order' and the 'trade union problem' were elided by the Conservative Party during their election campaign. It clearly did not need our research to confirm that labour law, like most other laws, will only operate at the margins. Such was clearly known to Mr Prior and the rest of the Cabinet at the time the Act was formulated. Nevertheless, it was essentially a popular piece of legislation, and to the extent that it met a felt need it had already worked at one level.

The Act also very clearly reassured a certain style of management. We detected time and again during our interviews with management a mild *frisson* over its introduction. Few of the managers we spoke to expected the law would have any very direct effect. Practically none said they would be prepared to use the provisions with which we were most directly concerned against their own workforce or even against third parties, which would normally be local trade-union officials with whom they expected to negotiate again in the near future. This says nothing, of course, about the Act as a potential deterrent or even what these same managements would actually do in a crisis. However, most of all we noted a psychological gratification on the part of managers that at last a government was 'on their side'. It was, many said, an encouragement to take control of the reins more vigorously. In a small way it was a reinforcement of the managers' right to manage. Such an effect should not be under-estimated, but is uncommonly difficult to measure. The Act must be seen in harness with many other things which have been happening in the economy as a whole over the last two or three years. There is no doubt that some sectors of industry have witnessed a very different style of management which is less consensus-minded and welfare-based than has been the norm in recent years. There is also little doubt that the government wishes to encourage management to stand on its own feet. The passing of new industrial legislation played its part in this process.

One other point needs to be made here. The Employment Act is only one piece of legislation that has touched upon the lives of workers in the last few years. The social-security legislation must be taken into account as well. Not only has the position in relation to strikers been amended to ensure that less and less state support is available to those who take industrial action, but the whole of the supplementary benefits scheme was amended in 1980 in such a way as to have indirect effects on strikers' families. One of the effects of the changes in the social-security system is that strike pay up to the value of £12 per week (now increased to £13 per week) is imputed to those on strike. Furthermore, the repayment of income tax is now delayed and is no longer an additional source of financial support during a strike. These measures were resented by nearly all the strikers we spoke to, and without doubt have had a considerable effect on the financial consequences of taking strike action. The tax measure was especially objected to since it was perceived as government holding on to money which rightfully belonged to the workers involved. This is not the place to analyse the detailed effect of these measures, but the social-security changes clearly represent some pressure for strikes not to be made official. Given the impact which we have said lack of official support can have upon workers, this cannot be regarded as a minor consequence. More particularly, we have no doubt that the legal measures as a whole have entered the thinking of many workers in deciding upon tactical considerations. Overtime bans, selective strikes and other action short of total withdrawal of labour become ever more attractive propositions.

The limits of law : tactical choices

The use and impact of law cannot be determined in a mathematical fashion. We have stressed continuously that the impact of law is highly contingent. The use of law depends on the convergence of a number of very different factors: in particular it depends upon the normal constraints on conflict having broken down, upon circumstances requiring that certain tactics be considered and upon the tactical sense of employers. However, before we spell this out in more detail let us attempt to relate some of the foregoing to the Employment Act itself.

When the Act was introduced it was accompanied by statements concerning the mischiefs it was intended to remedy. Thus, for example, we were informed that it was directed at protecting neutral employers, at ensuring that workers were not intimidated, and the like. Sections 16 and 17 were directed at blacking and secondary action. Little attempt was made at the time to explain that picketing was a highly differentiated phenomenon or that whether secondary action or blacking were employed depended upon the nature and structure of the industry concerned. As we have demonstrated, this is, in fact, the case. In some industries, as we have shown, a range of different tactics exist which may or may not include blacking and secondary action. In those industries or sectors, during the course of disputes, workers will choose which tactics to employ. Where tactical choices are relatively 'open', then there is every possibility that measures such as sections 16 and 17 will have an impact. In such cases, the costs of alternative tactics are often measured, and those which are potentially most costly are put to one side. In such circumstances the Employment Act could be successful in deterring certain tactics, though alternative tactics might well produce the same result. However, to make such an argument about informed choices, one has to show that those considering industrial action are properly informed of the legal 'costs' of certain tactics.

There is, as we have indicated, no automatic relationship between law being passed and law being understood. First, the law needs to be relatively straightforward for it to be fully understood. We have shown in Chapter 3 that it is almost impossible for a lay person to understand the language in which the conflict sections of the Act are drawn, depending as they do on the very singular and curious way in which our labour laws have developed out of common-law liabilities superimposed with immunities and qualified liabilities. None the less, some trade unions are more concerned about informing their membership about legal obligations than are others. For example, the FBU, the CCSU and ASLEF all issued picketing guidelines after the 1980 Act was passed on occasions of industrial action. However, the view of the law these guidelines presented varied considerably. On the other hand, some union officials made a deliberate decision not to inform their members, while still others themselves did not understand the law, or did not carefully consider a response.

Where, therefore, the law is as complex as the 1980 Act more often than not it will be improperly understood by those in dispute. In particular the neat lawyer's distinction between civil law and criminal law is not part of everyday consciousness. Law tends to be associated with wrongdoing, and with police, and with crime and criminal sanctions. Trade unionists as much failed to understand the civil-law nature of the picketing and secondary action provisions of the 1980 Act as they previously failed to grasp the civil nature of NIRC set up under the 1971 Act. Given the way government campaigning had linked the need for industrial legislation with 'law and order', and that the 'Pentonville Five' had firmly lodged in the Labour movement's folk memory that civil law tended to have criminal sanctions at the end of it, this is hardly surprising. However, these influences were set against the Secretary of State for Employment's assurances that the new law was not criminal and quite unlike the 1971 Act in its consequences. The result was to deepen further the confusion about the new Act and what exactly it meant. Out of this confusion only the simplest messages got across. There is no doubt at all from our fieldwork that the aspect of the new law most frequently in the minds of workers was the Code of Practice recommendation of a maximum of six pickets. As we have also made clear, that recommendation is in fact devoid of direct legal, though not necessarily practical, effect. In fact we can say without hesitation that this particular provision has had considerable influence over the last two years. The way in which the civil law is dependent upon employer initiative, on the other hand, has been very largely misunderstood.

In these circumstances workers can respond in one of two ways; either they limit their actions to the literal specifications of the Act or they ignore the legal requirements altogether. Our experience was that the latter was the more common response. Sometimes this was because whilst workers broadly understood the Act's provisions they saw them as politically partial and as a matter of principle did not acknowledge them in their decisions. On other occasions, workers in dispute were uncertain and/or confused about the Act's provisions and so simply relied upon past practice: if new rules are unfathomable then stick to the old ones. There was, however, a general fear of the legal system and what sanctions it might bring to bear. Confusion about the Act reinforced this fear, and seemed to create a widespread belief in the class partiality of law. This attitude is worth recording since in a different sense law, in the guise of justice, was never far from the lips of most strikers we spoke to. Given the risks involved in taking industrial action, especially in the contemporary economic climate, it is hardly surprising that such acts are invariably underscored by a strong claim to justice. People on picket lines usually have a profound belief that they have been treated unjustly, and when they seek secondary support will often do so on the basis of the justice of their case. We were frequently asked why the law couldn't stop an employer's actions or some other perceived injustice: surely, it was often said, the law must be able to stop the government keeping back income-tax repayments. Hydra-like, the law was feared as partial and terrible, and appealed to in order to correct an injustice. The deterrent or other effects of any particular legislation can only be understood within these conflicting responses to the law.

The categories upon which most workers' reactions to the 1980 Act are based are not those of the lawyer, the legislator or administrator. Nicely turned distinctions, between civil and criminal or between sections and subsections, will have little impact on workers' detailed tactical decisions if such distinctions derive from a contextually meaningless set of categories. Not only, for example, are the 1980 Act's sections on secondary action technically confusing but, as we have explained earlier, they distinguish secondary from primary action in ways which make little sense for many workers during a dispute. The 1980 Act then was frequently technically unclear, confusing in its provisions, unknown because of its complexity, and unrelated to the experience categories of those in dispute. Therefore, even in a case where tactical choices are at their most 'open', any possible effects of the Act are very difficult to predict. Whilst resort to law, any law, may well have an impact, a specific and conscious effect from the 1980 Act is most likely to occur where maximum tactical choice exists and where the worker's behaviour is orientated towards legal-rational decisions by, say, a union's legal department or advisers. As will be clear from what has gone earlier, such situations are not common.

Where tactical choices are less 'open', where the proscribed conduct was fundamental to the industrial action's success rather than simply one choice among several, then the possibility of legal influence is different. If the Act could impinge successfully upon these cases then it clearly would achieve a great deal. Whether or not the Act could have been used successfully in such an event is substantially a matter of judgment of the particulars of each case. We have shown, for instance, that in the case of the miners it did not have the desired effect and seems, if anything, to have increased their eagerness to undertake secondary action and picketing. In other unions, actions that might have had a critical impact were deterred.

If, therefore, the Act was to be successful in its declared aims, it would have been so in a highly differentiated manner. In some industries and sectors, including for example public services, it was unlikely to have a major impact on the primary workforce, since the tactics proscribed were largely irrelevant. In yet others, where the proscribed tactics were possibilities among a numbers of others, then it could be expected to have some (though variable) impact without necessarily securing against the mischief of the legislation. In a third set of circumstances the Act was directed at a vital artery, tactically speaking. It could hope to have an effect in such cases but it would have a great deal to overcome. If the workers concerned were sufficiently desperate or reckless it would in all likelihood be of little positive effect. Indeed, the political origins of the Act sometimes produced a negative reaction. Even in favourable circumstances, the organisational form and authority structure of a union can reduce the possible impact of the legislation. By underplaying the bureaucratic and formal, and stressing the spontaneous, responsive and charismatic, a union can immunise its decision-making to legal influence. As far as future law-givers are concerned then, always assuming legislation is intended to be more than mere rhetoric, the natural process would be to look across the various sectors of British industry examining structures and processes in order to target legislation at the optimum level. There is some evidence beginning to emerge that the current government has understood this at least in the public sector where it is beginning to use the administrative-bureaucratic 'Whitehall legal system' to achieve its ends. Innovations in the bargaining arrangements of both the civil service and water industry are designed to fragment formidable worker solidarity.

Law and dispute forms

Let us return to the issue of the tactics which are most appropriate for different industries and different sectors. Tactics adopted during the course of an industrial dispute are in no sense random, but as we have repeatedly stressed are the product of and determined by the nature of production and work, the organisation of capital, the representational patterns of workers and management, and the organisation of supply and distribution. Law unaided will find it extremely difficult to dislodge established patterns of behaviour and rationally chosen courses of action. Picketing and secondary action, for instance, are often eschewed simply as a matter of process and production.

Picketing itself is highly differentiated and may vary in its purposes. For example, where its primary purpose is informational, forms of behaviour other than picketing might equally well serve. In such an event, law directed at that form of picketing will have every chance of 'working' but have no effect whatsoever on outcomes. During the health-service dispute, quite apart from picketing, which was clearly unlawful under the Employment Act and against which no action has been taken at the time of writing, demonstrations and the like have been regular occurrences. This has often, of course, been the Continental pattern of behaviour, and law which successfully removes one tactical form is quite likely to create thereby an alternative which may in the end become just as politically problematic (see Crouch, 1982, pp. 87 ff.).

In the public sector workers have continued to develop the selective industrial tactics they used during the disputes of the 'winter of discontent'. In other words they have manipulated resources in a more differentiated way than is traditional with organised British labour. The available range of tactical choices has developed with each successive dispute. From the strike by the post-office workers in 1971 onward, public-service unions have tended to draw the lesson from defeats that their selection of tactics must be more hard-heartedly strategic. The price of relatively easy tactical victories by the contemporary government is likely to be a tactical toughening of public service unions and workers, and a very hard fight for some future government. This is not to say that law cannot or has not affected behaviour; we have shown that even in the public sector the 1980 Act has had some effect on tactics, but not in our experience in any crucial fashion as far as outcomes have been concerned. What this means then is that traditions, ethics and processes have combined to suggest their own set of tactics, and these in turn will be modified on the basis of the results of their use during disputes.

The organisation of labour

We have already alluded above to how the organisational and authority structures of trade unions can affect their responsiveness to legal forms of control. However, more generally, some characteristics of union organisation are vitally important in affecting the choice of tactics in the course of industrial disputes; thus density of unionisation, the nature of the unions, the extent of non-unionisation are all of great significance. What this indicates is that laws other than those which directly proscribe particular tactics have some chance of successfully affecting tactics and choices. The Employment Act itself of course was a first step towards encouraging non-unionisation through the provisions affecting the closed shop. At the time of writing the 1982 Employment Bill is taking this process a stage or two further. The weakening of unionism then is a less direct way but probably a more powerful attempt to influence industrial outcomes. Such attempts to use law to change, or erode, the representation of labour would attempt more dramatically to change the way in which dispute tactics are chosen than anything contained in the 1980 Act. We shall return to this theme at the end of the chapter.

The organisational capacity of trade unions and in particular their capacity to absorb change and therefore pursue effective tactics is vital to the waging of disputes. We have noted the failure of the ISTC to incorporate newly emerging local leadership in the 1980 campaign in contrast with the success of the NUM in doing just that after the 1969 – 72 unrest. Organisational capacity is clearly vital to unions if they wish to respond to economic and industrial change effectively.

Whatever else can be said of the first two or three years of Mrs Thatcher's government they have been a period of considerable change. The change has occurred in macro-economic terms, which in turn has often spurred new management styles. One of the major features of these years has been the fact that government policy has provoked numerous disputes in the public sector, broadly defined, and the terms of debate in the public sector have changed dramatically. We have seen national disputes relating to the civil service, the fire service, the health service and so on. Only in the health service has secondary action been an important factor. It has been important there because of the limits of action health workers observe and because of the need to make a strong impression upon government. In no instances, at the time of writing, have the 1980 Act's provisions been resorted to against public-sector workers themselves. It will be a day of great significance when the Minister concerned seeks an injunction against workers in the public sector. Such a day may not be far off, and we will reserve judgment on its likely repercussions. The injunction and subsequent contempt proceedings taken recently by the Newspaper Publishers Association against the action threatened by the Fleet Street electricians may have affected the public temper in this regard in such a way as to make such an event more likely. Be that as it may the tactics which are rational within much of the public sector would not seriously be touched by engaging the provisions of the 1980 Act.

What has occurred is that, partly as a result of recent disputes, militant public-sector unionism has developed and now appears to be a permanent feature of industrial relations life. Thus the CPSA has changed remarkably both in terms of personnel, and the civil-service unions as a whole now have local committees. Such a development has clearly been hastened by recent government policies and will not be greatly affected by laws of the sort which we have been examining. Other legal and administrative devices are of course available, and the government has threatened on a number of occasions to use the civil-service disciplinary procedures against sympathetic trade-union activity. There has also been the emergence of new proposals. The Social Democratic Party wishes to place key public-sector workers in a different legal position from others, and their voice is not alone in speaking the language of differential treatment for these groups. There is an irony to this since, as we have seen, the dispute with the fire service in 1981 occurred because the government refused to accept a wages deal which was the *quid pro quo* of a *de facto* no strike agreement created by the Callaghan government.

Trade unions which for so long have worked and developed their strategies within a tripartite relation with government are currently having to rethink those strategies. We have indicated how some unions are capable of such change and others not. More generally, however, the broader framework of the labour movement is similarly being forced to reconsider. For example, at the TUC conference in 1982 the membership of the General Council was changed: the dominance of the traditional industrial unions was broken by the addition of more white-collar unions. We have discussed how white-collar unions often have different tactical needs than those which have been traditional in the British labour movement, and the TUC is likely to be forced to re-examine its general tactical response to disputes as a result of these changes.

The organisation of capital

A word, too, should be said about the nature of capital in terms of its effect on disputes and tactics. We have seen that a condition for continued capital accumulation is the capacity to reorganise capital for use where it may provide maximum return. Movements of capital imply different forms of ownership and control so that a question of major importance becomes how far some arrangements for organising capital effectively are more vulnerable to industrial action than others.

The mobility of capital is clearly a major issue, and we have traced the implications of this in previous chapters, most notably in relation to transport of various forms. The containerisation revolution necessitated forms of secondary action if traditional jobs were to be protected as we have seen, but we have also seen that a further change has made capital infinitely more mobile and less vulnerable to fatal industrial action. It is too early to gauge whether organised labour is a match for this mobile capital on a large scale. The process itself has fascinating implications for the future of industrial tactics which would be bound to be extended beyond the primary workplace if workers were to secure their own interests and futures. We examined an engagement with some of this capital by the National Union of Seamen which deployed enormously subtle and effective tactics against the shipping companies less than two years ago, and has continued to be successful since. Although the Employment Act has been used at the fringes of the industry one of the most important features has been that the law has been almost entirely absent in the face of some of the most blatant 'lawlessness' imaginable. This in circumstances where not only the 1980 Act was treated with disdain but so also was the much more rigorous code of maritime labour law. This indicates that where employers are in some sense constrained, where conflict is deep-rooted, where organised labour is sufficiently aware and determined, then it is very difficult to see any form of labour law affecting the form of industrial action which is most likely to prosper. This, as we shall continue to underline, is not to argue that law will have no effect; rather it is to attempt to draw the limits of its effectiveness. We can emphasise this point by saying for example that we have every reason to believe that even in such circumstances as we have been describing, the law might represent one of several factors taken into account which dissuade unions from acting at a particular time. Law may then affect the timing of industrial action without ever resulting in its abandonment. If a union, such as the NUS, feels sufficiently aggrieved and if it feels that it has the upper hand tactically speaking, then the law will be unlikely to feature very strongly. If, however, matters are more finely balanced it may well be influential especially since morale is such a vital matter and can be undermined by timely legal intervention. Timing matters very greatly indeed as we have shown in Chapter 8. The circumstances we describe there, when employers went to law, were 'felt' to be right. In most cases though we were clearly informed by management that they deliberately avoided recourse to law when it might have the effect of, for instance, creating solidarity.

Picketing

Of all the tactics used during industrial disputes it was picketing which the 1980 Act was especially concerned with. It must be repeated that picketing as a phenomenon takes many forms and tries to achieve many different purposes. It is worth repeating because the popular image represents it as unruly behaviour, accompanied by bad temper and constant intimidation. Of course, such behaviour occasionally occurs though we have not borne witness to it in our regions over the last two years in spite of the number of picket lines we have observed. Our work would perhaps be justified in one respect if only for being able to point out that in the vast majority of cases picket lines are not even thought deserving of a police presence.

Some picketing may take place in a reassuring blaze of publicity, and some may even occur in summertime in balmy weather. We saw very few picket lines of this kind. In the two years of our research the normal picket line was located on a minor industrial road, and consisted of a few people, usually huddled in a makeshift shelter round a brazier to avoid the rain and cold or even snow, with crudely hand-drawn notices announcing their picket. There would be flurries of activity in the early morning, and again in the evening, when management and sometimes non-striking workers turned up for work. Otherwise there would be the occasional delivery lorry and an odd patrolling police car to wave at. Our visits were nearly always greeted warmly since they broke the boredom and provided a chance for the pickets to expound their case. The pickets were often disappointed when they discovered we were not from the press, and would not provide the much sought publicity for their case. Such picketing would often go on day and night and for long periods: we first visited a small picket line in South Yorkshire under a foot of winter snow, and by the time the pickets gave up in defeat it was late summer. The organisation of picket duty often mirrors the practice of the workplace with pickets working shifts, and relief pickets for breaks. The nearest pub, or better still working man's club, becomes the temporary strike headquarters where strikers endlessly discuss the justice of their case and attempt to fathom their management.

We give this description not to romanticise picketing, but simply to help the reader who may never have picketed understand what such activity normally consists of. The majority of strikers are ordinary workers who feel impelled to picket as a necessary tactic during a conflict in which they believe they have a just cause. There are occasional outside political agitators, usually rejected by the strikers unless their union is giving them no real support. To accept the financial consequences of striking, and what many of them see as the indignity of picketing, such workers obviously feel very strongly indeed. These are the men and women, in such a context, that the law seeks to influence. Regardless of what they might say about new employment laws in answer to opinion polls or questionnaires outside the context of an industrial dispute, their actual response to the law can only be known in this context.

We need to reiterate that picketing can have a variety of purposes: making appeals to workers who are maintaining production in spite of strike calls, preventing the removal of goods, and as a symbolic action or an attempt to publicise or to convey information which might positively be helpful to the public, as we saw when civil servants were able to instruct their 'clients' about alternative arrangements for payments during the course of the dispute. We have shown too that in much of the public-sector picketing is seen to be unnecessary and yet is occasionally used as a publicity device or even as a protest against the existence of the law which prohibits the behaviour. In such circumstances it is in no way central to the outcome and it is therefore hardly surprising that the public-sector employers who have considered legal action over the last year or so have desisted for fear of inflaming the situation.

The contingencies of tactics and law

There is, we have argued, a logical set of tactics available to both sides of industry depending upon context, experience, etc. That internal logic will normally be mutually understood and taken into account. There are usually, then, unspoken assumptions about how a dispute which results in industrial action will be conducted. This means that certain forms of conduct are 'normal' within one firm or industry and quite alien in another. Occasionally we have detected that one or the other party breaks the rules of the game and engages in behaviour which flouts understandings developed over a period of years: appealing over the head of union leaders to the workforce or issuing dismissal notices during a strike for example. It is unpredictable behaviour of this sort which can produce unpredictable counter-behaviour. Nevertheless, the extent of the choices available in deciding tactics, including picketing and secondary action, are a direct product of the context and form of each particular industrial dispute. Thus, it is perfectly possible to make generalisable statements about the likely incidence of disputes, the tactics which will be employed and the response which those tactics will receive, including the use of law, although at the end of the day such statements will still be contingent upon human agency. The extent of the support which one side or the other receives from a powerful external source, such as government for example, can critically affect the willingness or confidence of the actors involved to follow any particular course of action. Similarly, as many commentators have pointed out, British industrial conflict still has elements of a 'macho' fight and just as in a fight a serious misjudgment or miscalculation can disrupt and alter what otherwise would have been the predictable outcome.

We can illustrate this by returning to the seamen's dispute of 1981 as an example of the fact that serious tactical misjudgments can be made about both the likelihood and form of an industrial dispute. No major industrial action had taken place in the industry for some 15 years, at which time the union was badly battered. Many things, including the sheer passage of time, conspired to ensure that both sides embarked upon the dispute without any clear notion of the organisational capacity of the other. In fact the owners were the more disadvantaged in this respect. However, cunning though the union was, they could not be sure of the strength of their position. In such circumstances events can simply develop their own momentum and forecasting is dangerous. Much will depend upon leadership. That was manifestly the case with the NUS where the 1966 leadership had been replaced by a tougher breed of official weaned on the failures of the earlier action. Personalities can similarly be important influences in other industries too; mining and the docks immediately spring to mind.

Disputes and the 1980 Act

Let us say a final word about our experiences of the use of law. The criminal law aside, we have monitored four instances of action taken under the 1980 Act as well as four to five other instances of use of the civil law. The *Antama* case was unusual in a number of respects not least since it was an example of the 1980 Act paying off. The orders were observed and the ship's owners secured their objectives. Whether such legal action would have been effective in terms of national industrial action where much more may have been at stake is highly problematic. The orders were brought by a foreign ship-owner who no doubt felt he had little to lose in terms of British port industrial relations. Even then the assumption may ultimately prove to be mistaken if ITF blacking on an international scale is successful.

The Mersey Docks and Harbour Board case was yet another 'third party' action. Third party cases are always more likely to give rise to legal action than are simply employer/worker relations since in the latter case long-term relationships are at stake and in the former they are not, or are less importantly so. Even here, however, it is difficult to express any positive conclusions since the pickets had decided to call off their action independently of the court order. It is difficult to resist the speculation that had the picketing begun a week earlier, when the drivers were in a more resolute frame of mind, the impact of the legal action might have been very different indeed.

Our third experience of the Act related to a small two-site firm in Derbyshire shortly after the Act had been passed. Its reception was such a surprise that the case was settled out of court and the offending picketing lifted. It is difficult to draw any general conclusions from such an isolated event.

The final case involved one of those *causes célèbres* where a very individualist management took on the trade unions in cavalier style; fringe left political groups joined in, the publicity conscious local police chief made speeches, and the management flew equipment out of a picketed factory in a dawn helicopter operation. By the time of this incident the dispute was already months old, the local union leadership was in conflict with its NEC, and many of the original workers involved in the dispute had drifted away. The pickets then turned their attention to the company's other factory in South Yorkshire. As we explained lack of support and bad weather meant this secondary picketing was totally unsuccessful. Nevertheless the company successfully applied for injunctions against named pickets under the 1980 Act. The picketing stopped although the injunctions were clearly no more than the formal identification of a lost cause: indeed if some real support had still existed for the picketing, such as official union support, the injunctions would almost certainly have inflamed the situation and rallied further support.

We have explained the circumstances of the other cases in which some form of legal action was taken and need add no more here. What perhaps is important to say is that of all the disputes we have followed the law has been used in such a minuscule proportion of cases. Its infringement, on the other hand, has been a very common occurrence indeed.

Controlling industrial disputes

There is another way of examining the significance of the 1980 Act, and that is to see how far its aims and purposes could be, or have been, achieved by other means. There is no disputing that the recession, whose peculiarly British form has been much influenced by government policy, has done more to dampen down all forms of industrial action than the Employment Act could ever have been expected to do. The demoralised and fearful state of organised labour has itself reduced industrial action. Even there, however, there is more to say. First, the recession and financial stringency have forced many firms to rationalise and cut costs. Under such pressures, managerial objectives have become very much less blurred, and management has adopted harder and less flexible industrial relations attitudes. Such management has itself been both a deterrent against and a cause of industrial disputes with or without picketing and secondary action. It is a deterrent because once a management makes clear what it will stand for and what it will not, the effect can be to inject a sense of 'realism' or self-interest into the labour-force. Such management style may be a cause of disputes because a change in management styles can be misunderstood. Workers, on the basis of past, and perhaps no longer relevant experience, can underestimate management's resolve and circumstances.

The recession has also produced its own industrial turmoil. There have been numerous examples of industrial action directed against redundancies which have not been accepted by the workforce. As we showed, particularly in Chapter 8, these circumstances often give rise to different tactical necessities than might be the case within the industry in more prosperous times. Sometimes they involve secondary action and sometimes not. Usually they involve workers who are desperate enough not to care very greatly about the impact of law and management who, under altered circumstances, might for the first time ever consider its employment. The recession though is but part of the matter.

We have been at pains throughout this book to show that successive British governments affect industrial relations, create their own industrial politics, through devices very few of which fit into the rational-legal category. Over recent times these devices have been used for numerous purposes but those which we designate neo-corporatist have been the most common. The present administration has now largely abandoned these strategies but has adopted monetarist and neo-liberal policies in their stead which have produced different attitudes and the use of different mechanisms of control: cash limits, privatisation, nationalisation, deregulation and the like. They have thus far side-stepped confrontation with groups whose industrial muscle disturbs them; the miners, the dockers, the power and water workers for example. Yet in many other situations, mainly but not entirely within the public sector of the economy including the nationalised industries, their interventions have produced effects as contradictory and countervailing as has the recession itself. Although there is little doubt that taken overall these interventions have dampened down industrial action, there have been occasions when the interventions, not through the formal legal system, have been the cause of industrial unrest, primary and secondary picketing, demonstrations, vigils, *et al*. At the time of writing the hospital workers' dispute illustrates this point. It remains to be seen whether these strategies, some of them equivalent to undeclared incomes policies, can continue to hold down the lid as (relatively) successfully as heretofore or whether sooner or later it will blow off, as always in the past whenever strong government interventions have occurred either within or without the formal legal order. The strategies which the present government are employing are subtler, more purposeful, and above all more coherent than previous attempts, so that we are sailing uncharted seas.

Industrial conflict and the police

We must reassert that most industrial disputes do not involve the police at all. This is an important statement given public beliefs which, especially in this area, are often very wide of the mark indeed. We have seen, for instance, that the police attitude towards 'normal' and 'abnormal' picket lines is not well understood. We have also seen that much of the public, including members of parliament, do not appreciate the tension between enforcing the law and the maintenance of public order. The latter will of course be the primary consideration in circumstances where the former can simply operate as an impediment. The failure to appreciate this is part of the reason why the belief existed in 1980 in some quarters that the police needed to be given more extensive powers than they possessed. Although there was some division in police ranks over the matter it is clear that the police generally are and were perfectly satisfied with the powers which they possess. What ought to be more widely appreciated is that the police have enormous discretion in dealing with picket lines and it is the nature of the exercise of that discretion which is of the most vital importance.

Of course the 1980 Act did not directly alter the criminal law in any way. What it did seek to do was to delegitimise certain kinds of behaviour associated with picketing, and the Code of Practice conflated the civil and the criminal law in people's minds. We have explained too that some police behaviour which we have observed can only be accounted for by their conflating the two systems as well. We cannot say, however, that overall the Code has marked any very great change in police behaviour although there is little doubt that in many respects police behaviour has changed in recent years. Most of that change relates to organisational forms and technological developments having more to do with developing professionalism and combating terrorism and serious public disorder than anything else.

It is not possible at this juncture to be authoritative about police behaviour in general though some clear patterns can be discerned. Police conduct during industrial disputes varies considerably and one of the reasons is that different forces are at different stages of organisational change while the sheer geography of police regions means that different command structures currently exist. The geographical locations of different police forces also embeds them, and their operation, firmly within local cultures. Britain may be a small country but it has quite distinct local cultures which frequently closely mirror the traditional industries in the area. The actions of both management and workers on the Humberside docks, for example, would be almost incomprehensible, and certainly apparently irrational, to anyone who did not understand the culture of the docks: the Dock Labour Scheme, and its centrality in disputes, simply reflected this cultural uniqueness and isolation. Whilst the docks also have their own separate police force, – the British Transport Police – the Humberside Police also have to come to terms with this culture if called upon to control, say, secondary action during a dock strike. In a similar way steel and engineering historically underlie the culture of South Yorkshire. During the steel strike not only did many policemen have close relatives in the industry, or had even worked in it themselves, but many of their cultural beliefs and attitudes were closely related to steel and steel making. There was then a close culture resonance between South Yorkshire police officers and steel strikers, and an underlying sympathy towards the strikers' case. The policing of the disputes was influenced by this empathy, as was the operational difficulty of using police from other forces who did not understand these relationships. All police forces (with the possible exception of the Metropolitan police) will have such local cultural links. Although, as we have explained, local cultural links are threatened at senior level by a growing national professionalism, such links will continue to differentiate the policing of disputes through the impact junior officers have on senior officers' outlooks and perceptions. At the end of the day the way in which the policing especially of large-scale disputes is carried out will continue to depend upon what we have called 'a curious balancing of interests, powers and ideas' and which we explained in detail in Chapter 5.

We stress that ordinarily the police have views on what constitutes normal and abnormal picketing. We have said that at the heart of the police notion of a normal picket line is that it is an occurrence whose behaviour can be the subject of negotiation with the pickets concerned. The police control the normal picket line not by enforcing legal rules but by negotiating reasonable compromises, with rule enforcement held out as the alternative if negotiation breaks down. Low police/picket ratios reinforce the wish to negotiate outcomes. In the abnormal dispute the police will be more likely to be present in large numbers, and that very fact will often account for arrests being made. The police will quite simply be in a position to effect them; such action would not be possible on any large scale in the case of the 'normal' picket-line. Even here more often than not we will not be talking about a clear-cut decision in advance to make arrests but rather a decision to take firm action which, if resisted, can result in arrests. In the normal case where negotiation is successful it can even, as we have seen, take the form of self-policing by trade union 'marshals', with the police relatively inconspicuous.

Several concerns about the future policing of industrial conflict exist. The first is that the line between industrial disputes and threats to public order may become increasingly blurred, partly as a result of the new-found ability of the police to respond to public-order situations. With new organisational forms and new technology such a blurring of the line could have disastrous effects on the traditional tolerant set of relations between police and pickets. Indeed even the Code of Practice itself is capable of exacerbating those relations in so far as it demands the presence of union officials, with whom the police are normally unhappy. The police are also reluctant to demand compliance with certain organisational specifications of the Code, e.g. designation of picket organisers and wearing of armbands, for fear of upsetting effective established local understandings.

We would go further. If co-operation between government and

unions, neo-corporatism if you like, is replaced by overt conflict between them, policing industrial disputes will take on further political connotations. The form of neutrality and impartiality deployed by the British police has not been unconnected with co-operatively based economic policy. If new tactics are devised by trade unions as a result of the changing situation in which they find themselves there is also the chance that the police will be taken by surprise. In such a case there is the strong possibility that industrial action will be classified in advance as a potential public-order situation rather than a normal dispute and that the whole panoply of potential police response will be activated.

The police already regard some industrial dispute tactics, such as mass picketing, as more of a public order than an industrial policing problem. The long-awaited new Public Order Act could provide the means of legally making such a distinction. As we have explained some sections in the police welcome such legal distinctions as a basis for neutral policing based upon the rule of law. The danger is that 'public order' has become a code phrase for a particular type of policing response, and a legal change which defined some industrial tactics as 'public-order problems' could create an organisationally fixed response in the hands of an unsubtle commander. Such a response would be seen as partial policing by many strikers, and the search for 'neutrality' by the police seriously undermined.

Finally, not only is police behaviour and conduct in industrial disputes characterised by a high level of discretion, but the changing nature of the British police has occurred almost unnoticed by the general public. At the very time an attempt is being made to delegitimise certain forms of action by those involved in industrial disputes, our legal system has remained largely indifferent to policing itself. There is currently much debate about the need for new legislation relating to the police but little thought seems so far to have been given to notions of police accountability within the context of industrial disputes.

Towards the future

Government policy has been the major determinant of industrial action in the last few years. Quite apart from more or less direct interventions in the public sector its general economic policies, especially in so far as they have fostered rationalisation, have produced high social costs for labour and union organisation. Rationalisation has largely defined the nature of disputes in private industry while the structure of ownership and control and union organisation have determined the form which industrial disputes have taken. We have attempted to show how limited the role of law has been in this respect. In particular there has been a movement away from traditional patterns of industrial control to a more finance-oriented domination.

In the public sector and also in those sections of the economy subject to elaborate regulatory frameworks, described in Chapter 9, government policy has been and will continue to be crucial. Even within dockwork we have tried to show that initiatives belong less with employers, armed as they are by the 1980 Act, than with government in relation to its attitudes towards the future of the National Dock Labour Board. In the public-sector proper, the determination of the present government to implement its relatively simple but interlocking set of economic objectives are of the essence. The railway unions and the TUC have been waging industrial battles based upon strategies and understandings which are no longer operational. 'Butskellite' bipartisanship and consensus surrounding much of the socio-industrial endeavour would make sense of much that the NUR and the TUC have been doing and thinking. The current political and economic climate makes a mockery of it. In steel, industrial accord has been centrally constructed historically from Mond-Turner onwards around notions of consensus and the structure of unionisation, and its assumptions have been correspondingly influenced. This proved not only crucial to the lack of success of the steel unions in the 1980 strike but has continued to influence events ever since. There can currently be no doubt of the resolve of the British Steel management or of the government's determination to privatise as much of the industry as possible. Whether the historical nature of industrial relations and union organisation will continue to dog the ability of the ISTC to resist developments with which it is unhappy is infinitely more important than the impact of the 1980 Employment Act. However, were the events of 1980 to be repeated with greater subtlety, purpose and solidarity on the union side, it is unclear how they would respond to the almost inevitable resort to law.

There are, however, countervailing tendencies in the public sector at least. The growth of 'factory offices' and large computer centres in the civil service has increased solidarity within and between a number of key groups. The events of recent years have also 'socialised' many civil servants and others, previously extremely ambivalent about unionisation, into the adoption of stronger attitudes accompanied by a wide and subtle range of tactical choices. Workers in the health service have assumed far greater militancy in recent years than heretofore. This we could expect to continue and if law is to have an impact upon these developments, it must find a way of striking at the heart of unionisation itself. There are already signs that such moves may be on the political agenda.

There has been a tendency in recent years towards strikes becoming bigger and longer (see e.g. Crouch, 1982, pp. 100-1). This has been in no small measure due to increased government involvement at various levels from old-style incomes policies, to decisions on the financing of the nationalised industries, and so on. There is currently no doubting the government's resolve, but there is increasing evidence to show that such resolve can reinforce that of private employers, quite aside from any calculation of business or commercial advantage. This has also to be seen in terms of newer and more aggressive styles of management which government has been encouraging and is continuing to encourage. We have touched upon some features of the 1980 Employment Act other than the picketing and secondary action provisions which we think have made some sort of impact. Removing around 1 million workers from the protective ambit of the unfair dismissal provisions will have buttressed managerial powers, which will no doubt be reinforced by the provisions of the 1982 Employment Bill which affect an employer's ability to dismiss strikers selectively. We shall say a little about other aspects of that proposed legislation shortly, but it should not be forgotten that its impetus towards non-unionsation as a desirable state of affairs began with the 1980 Act which not only removed the recognition provisions of the 1975 Employment Protection Act but also removed Schedule 11 which guaranteed the generability of terms and conditions bargained by unions across the face of industry. Two issues seem here to emerge. One is that, whatever the level of industrial unrest in the near future, the trend to longer and larger disputes is likely to continue. In each dispute more is at stake than formerly. On the other hand, it has become clear that the combination of government economic policy, government determination to stick doggedly to such policy, and a range of legal interventions have greatly affected management attitudes in recent years. It would have been a simplistic error to argue that law has had practically no effect simply by counting the number of writs issued or the number of arrests on picket lines. If we take into account the *whole* of the 1980 Act along with other attendant legislation, the 1982 Bill which is already being used as psychological support by some management, and wider economic strategy, we are talking of an impact which is clearly substantial.

Attempts to gauge the success of any future legal reform must be made within the context of government's vision of industrial politics and the economic strategies which accompany it. The new proposals emerging under the stewardship of Mr Tebbit look to be significant in two major respects. The first is concerned with the proposals to make official union funds susceptible to legal action. This is a 'policing' measure in the most obvious sense and can be expected to have some effect in provoking divisions between the leadership and the grass roots unless some dramatic *cause célèbre* emerges to deny the legislation its way. That is closely related to the second matter which is a half-way house to the deunionisation of British industry. The rest of the Bill is littered with allusions to that state of affairs. It is completely in accord with government philosophy currently which argues that the market works better without the intervention of trade unions. That is a clear position to adopt. It is not only a gamble, but would make it, if possible, extremely difficult to revert to 'normal' British traditions of incorporation for the purposes of economic planning and/or crisis avoidance.

What exactly the present government believes will replace traditional British unionism is unclear. Sometimes its spokesmen seem to suggest that industrial life can operate without any representational forms: at any rate that would seem to be the logic of the purest versions of the market philosophy. It is doubtful, however, whether many ministers and certainly not Mr Tebbit believe this solution is possible. What seems much closer to their ideas is that representatives of workers should not have a political role: that workplace representation should not be a basis for class politics. This would depend on breaking any connection between the terms and conditions of employment and state or government action. Whether the first connection is in fact necessary is itself a question of political philosophy: neo-liberalism believes it is not necessary. As to the second, we have demonstrated repeatedly that in contemporary Britain government actions nearly always have repercussions, direct or indirect, for workplace disputes. One solution would be to foster the growth of parallel industrial unions federated into different political groups as exist in some European countries. Such unions are still political organisations but there is a union counterweight available against attempts to use workplace conflict to build a class politics. Some of the problems of traditional British unionism would then go away but, as a glance across the Channel will confirm, new problems could take their place.

The alternative is to encourage the setting up of representational structures within each company, That, ultimately, leads to the questions of workers' representation on company boards, or other decision-making bodies. Such a move hardly seems to fit the present government's philosophy.

The Social Democratic Party combines hostility to organised labour and strong union leadership – evident in its support of the new Employment Bill, its opposition to the pre-entry closed shop, its advocacy of works councils that bypass union structures, its plans for enforceable procedure agreements and its desire for strike ballots even if not automatic – with a hankering after corporatist arrangements, including incomes policy. Such a combination is somewhat reminiscent of Labour policies of the late 1960s, and later Tory policies, which failed to secure lasting trade-union reform or long-term commitment to wage restraint. Whether altered economic conditions would allow such apparently contradictory policies to work is unclear, but their success remains unlikely. The Social Democratic Party, of course, has advocated 'contracting in' to pay the political levy. Such a measure could have the effect of seriously weakening the political side of organised labour. They have also suggested using the law to enforce periodic ballots for union leaders with the stated intent of counselling moderation, although ironically the union which comes nearest to this pattern is the NUM. Such policies would clearly work most powerfully if combined with an attempt to recast the form of workplace representation and this is also part of the SDP proposals.

What will not emerge in the near future, we believe, is a general code of labour law, although the SDP appears to be more attracted to a set of general principles as a way of ordering the conduct of parties to industrial disputes. Something of this nature was hinted at in the government's Green Paper on Trade Union Immunities produced early in 1981. Its reference to the possibility of a code of rights has not been found attractive in many quarters. In early 1982 the Lord Chancellor was heard to express the following views to the House of Commons Select Committee on employment:

> Although theoretically the need for comprehensive legislation still exists and must one day be met, I do not think the state of public opinion at the moment justifies a maximalist or comprehensive approach either to trade union or industrial relations law.

We are sure that that view represents official government thinking at the time of writing. Much remains to be done before such an attempt is made to rekindle the notion of a British labour Rechtstaat. If it is one day attempted it will be within the framework of a new constitutional settlement which will either re-establish the conventional practices of neo-corporatism or herald the official establishment of neo-liberalism.

The response of organised labour to current developments is the most fascinating of all the problems to be posed in the field of labour relations and labour law. We have written at length about new developments in relation to management and more generally in relation to capital. Capital has always been able to change its form, to relocate, to move into other sectors or other countries. Labour does not have those choices available to it so that if it is to meet the challenge of the increasingly supple nature of modern capital, it must prove equally supple in all tactical senses. The party which enjoys the most alternatives in the exchanges involved in the contract of labour will have the greater power to dictate its terms. Will organised labour in Britain be equal to these new challenges? We have seen evidence in recent years that British trade unions have not understood the nature of the changes taking place. This has been most marked in the traditional industries and especially in the public sector where the fact that consensus politics is no longer being pursued has not been properly registered. If labour tactics are employed which are intended merely to disrupt a non-existent consensus, they will stand little chance of working. Where the 'wrong' tactics are employed then the existence of law scarcely matters one way or another: it is surplus to the requirements of control. A policy of 'marketisation' in particular is not susceptible to many of the old tactics employed by the British labour movement.

If British trade unionism does begin to recognise that at least, though not necessarily, temporarily the strategy of incorporation has ceased, it may be forced into taking much more vigorous action than we have seen for a very long time. In such a case the whole of the legal system might be on trial. As we noted earlier it might also cause the use of police tactics of a most formidable kind given the organisational and technological response of which it has recently become capable. If, on the other hand, the attempts to deunionise British industrial life are successful then we shall have to refashion almost all former thinking about the place of law in British labour relations.

Bibliography

Anderman, S. and Davies, P. (1973), 'Injunction procedure in labour disputes', *Industrial Law Journal*, vol. 2. pp. 213-28.

Barker, A. (1982), 'Governmental bodies and the networks of mutual accountability', in A. Barker (ed.), *Quangos in Britain*, London, Macmillan.

Berridge, J. (1976), *A Suitable Case for Treatment: A case study of industrial relations in the National Health Service*, Milton Keynes, Open University.

Blackaby, F.T. (1978), *British Economic Policy 1960-1974*, Cambridge University Press.

Blake, J. (1979), 'Civil disorder in Britain 1910-39: The role of civil government and military authority', unpublished D. Phil. thesis, University of Sussex.

Bosanquet, N. (ed.) (1979), *Industrial Relations in the National Health Service: the search for a system*, London, King Edwards Hospital Fund.

Congdon, T. (1978), *Monetarism*, London, Centre for Policy Studies.

Crouch, C. (1982), *Trade Unions: the logic of collective action*, London, Fontana.

Daintith, T. (1974), 'Public law and economic policy', *Journal of Business Law*, pp. 9-22.

Daintith, T. (1979), 'Regulations by contract: the new prerogative', *Current Legal Problems*, 32, pp. 41-59.

Davies, P. and Freedland, M. (1979), *Labour Law*, London, Weidenfeld.

Department of Employment (1982), *Employment Gazette*, vol. 90, no. 7.

Department of Health and Social Security (1968), *Hospital, scientific and technical services: report of the Committee 1967-8;* chairman Sir S. Zucketnan, London, HMSO.

Dyson, K. (1980), *The State Tradition in Western Europe*, Oxford, Martin Robertson.

Eltis, W. and Bacon, R. (1976), *Britain's Economic Problem: Too Few Producers*, London, Macmillan.

Flanders, A. and Clegg, H.A. (1954), *The System of Industrial Relations in Great Britain*, Oxford, Blackwell.

Ganz, G. (1977), *Government and Industry*, Abingdon, Professional Books.

Grant, W. (1982), *The Political Economy of Industrial Policy*, London, Butterworths.

Hayek, F.A. (1976), *The Road to Serfdom*, London, Routledge & Kegan Paul.

Hayek, F.A. (1979), *Law, Legislation and Liberty, Vol. 3: The Political Order of a Free People*, London, Routledge & Kegan Paul.

Hodgins, C. and Prescott, J. (1966), *Not Wanted on Voyage – The Seaman's Reply*, National Union of Seamen Hull Dispute Committee.

Hood, C. (1982), 'Governmental bodies and government growth', in A. Barker (ed.), *Quangos in Britain*, London, Macmillan.

Jessop, B. (1979), 'Corporatism, Parliamentarism, and Social Democracy', in P. Schmitter and G. Lehmbruch, *Trends towards Corporalist Intermediation*, London, Beverly Hills.

Joseph, K. (1978), *Conditions for Fuller Employment*, London, Centre for Policy Studies.

Kahn-Freund, O. (1977), *Labour and the Law*, London, Stevens, 2nd ed.

Kamenka, E. and Tay, A. (1975), 'Beyond bourgeois individualism', in E. Kamenka and A. Tay (eds), *Feudalism, Capitalism and Beyond*, London, Edward Arnold.

Lewis, N. (1976), 'The solar plexus', in J.R. Carby-Hall (ed.), *Studies in Labour Law*, Bradford, MCB Books.

Lewis, R. (1976), 'The historical development of labour law', *British Journal of Industrial Relations*,, vol. 14, no. 1, pp. 1-17.

MacFarlane, J. 'Our seamen: A study of labour relations in the British Merchant Navy', in K. Coates, T. Topham and M.B. Brown (1970), *Trade Union Register*, London, Merlin Press.

Middlemas, K. (1979), *Politics in Industrial Society*, London, Deutsch.

Ministry of Health (1966), *Report of the Committee on Senior Nursing Staff Structure;* Chairman: B. Salmon, London, HMSO.

Morris, G.S. (1977), 'A study of the protection of public and essential services in labour disputes 1920-1976', unpublished PhD thesis, University of Cambridge.

Poggi, G. (1978), *The Development of the Modern State*, London, Hutchinson.

Police (1979), editorial comment, vol. xii (4).

Powell, J.E. (1969), *Freedom and Reality*, Tadworth, Surrey, Elliot Right Way Books.

Turner, T. (1980), *Diary of the Docks' Dispute 1972-73*, Industrial Studies Unit, Department of Adult Education, University of Hull.

Weeks, B., O. Mellish, O. Dickens and O. Lloyd (1975), *Industrial Relations and the Limits of the Law*, Oxford, Blackwells.

Index